Jason McKeown

Jason McKeown is a Marketing Copywriter by trade, having previously gained experience working in Corporate Communications and studying Journalism at Sunderland University. A keen writer, he combines his passion for following Bradford City by contributing articles and match reports for the City fan's site, 'boyfrombrazil.co.uk', and a regular column for the 'City Gent' fanzine. He has also produced articles for 'When Saturday Comes' and 'TwoHundredPercent.net'. Originally from Wales, Jason lives in the North Yorkshire town of Skipton with his wife Rachel.

Dedication

To Rachel for all your love and support, and to our families.

To Steve and Michael for all the friendship and good times.

Dedication

PAYING ON THE GATE

A Bantam's journey into the heart of lower league Football

JASON McKEOWN

peakpublish

Peakpublish
An imprint of Peak Platform
New Bridge, Calver
Hope Valley
Derbyshire S32 3XT, U.K.
First published by Peakpublish 2011

A CIP catalogue record for this book is available from the
British Library

ISBN: 978-1-907219-25-2
www.peakplatform.com

Contents

Chapter 1	Below the ignorance	1
Chapter 2	BC (Before City)	6
Chapter 3	1997/98 - Finding Valley Parade	15
Chapter 4	1998/99 - Gloriously inexpensive	38
Chapter 5	1999/00 – Dining at the top table	65
Chapter 6	2000/01 – Failing to get comfortable	92
Chapter 7	2001/02 – "What else is on?"	11!
Chapter 8	2002/03 – Living as paupers	14
Chapter 9	2003/04 – Utter misery	16
Chapter 10	2004/05 – Priced out	19
Chapter 11	2005/06 – A cycle of false hope	22
Chapter 12	2006/07 – Journey to rock bottom	24
Chapter 13	2011 – Lower leagues, the best place in the world to be	26

Chapter One

Below the ignorance

A few years ago, I spent a wintry Sunday afternoon in a Doncaster pub with my friend Simon, watching the live Premier League Sky games. During a lull in conversation, I glanced around the half-full room and realised, with great excitement that a then-player of my football team, Bradford City, was sitting on the next table. His name was Ben Muirhead (he hailed from the town), and he was out with what seemed to be his family and a bald, chubby-looking friend. I turned to Simon, a Manchester United supporter, and quietly explained my startling discovery. He gave a sly look around to see for himself, seemed impressed that a professional footballer lived just around the corner from where he lived, and we went back to watching the TV game.

I was in two-minds about whether to go over and speak to Muirhead. He'd hardly expect someone in a Doncaster pub to recognise him, and was clearly relaxing with family. But still, what a great chance to get his autograph, and to tell him how well I thought he played on his recent return from injury. Perhaps he'd welcome the attention and regale me with behind the scenes tales which I could then proudly share with others. Yes, what's the harm in saying hello? I concluded to myself. One more pint first though, just to get some more courage.

As I returned from the bar with a round of drinks, Simon informed Muirhead had got up and left. I was gutted and somehow refused to believe him, so turned to the corner where he'd been sat to check anyway. Sure enough Muirhead was still there, holding a baby. "Good one" I said to Si, assuming he'd been attempting a poor joke. "No he has gone!" he argued back, "He got up and left when you went to toilet." "No he's sat in the corner holding a baby" I uttered back, somewhat bored of the conversation. Si looked back at Muirhead and then spoke in a tone of someone who'd just had a dawning realisation. "Ahh right, so that's the Bradford player. I thought you'd meant that bald fat guy played for you, he's the one who left."

There was something deeply offensive about his assumption which sums up the ignorant views of the lower leagues that many football fans hold. I said a player was sat near us; he had visions of some pie-munching never-has-been who runs around a little stadium in front of 50 fans for £20 a week, struggling to see the ball at his feet below his sizeable beer belly. It didn't occur to him that Bradford City players might be and are just as slim-line and athletic-looking as his precious Manchester United stars. And while his assumption may be very extreme, it is still prevalent of a culture of football support in England that is focused on the elite few and oblivious to the rest.

Football has never been more popular than it is right now. And if you're passionate about the sport, its status and social acceptance is largely a good thing. The Premier League is fantastic to watch, with excitement and drama. There are so many outstanding players to admire, and numerous talking points to dominate conversations at work or in the pub.

But it also brings lots of problems, and chiefly in this country people are too focused on the Premier League. The media donates so much coverage to tedious managerial mind-games, fuels manufactured rivalries by blowing the most trivial of occurrences way out of proportion, and hypes up annual fixtures like Manchester United v Liverpool as the biggest event in the world, ever.

Millions of people lap it all up; get a Sky dish stuck onto their roof or spend 'Super Sunday' down the pub. They passionately cheer on their team, through watching them on a TV screen. Those who go to live Premier League games have to face eye-wateringly expensive ticket prices which surpass almost every other type of entertainment in this country, and all that resultant revenue seems to go on is making dodgy-looking owners richer and for paying players ridiculous sums of money.

And the Premier League is not even that competitive, only four teams start the season having a realistic chance of winning the title. For at least 12 of the 20 participants, the sole target is to retain their membership and maybe snatch a place in the Europa-chuffing league. This annual fight for survival consumes everything, meaning the distraction of cup glory is sacrificed in the shape of managers playing reserve teams, because they're under such intense pressure to keep their job.

But beyond this soap opera is another world which is not especially different. It's played out in more modest surroundings and it hasn't got the X factor appeal, but in the lower leagues there is drama, excitement and passion and the occasional slice of unadulterated glory. In the lower leagues there are clubs who survive on gates of barely 1,000 and with players on wages comparable to the supporters watching them. In the lower leagues ticket prices are more affordable and demand rarely outstrips supply. In the lower leagues there is great character and a down to earth attitude that somehow puts the whole thing into perspective. Of course it's not "only a game" down here either, but we are more inclined to have a drink with opposition fans than consider them scum. (Local rivalries exempted.)

Although to merely laud the lower leagues for not featuring the negative aspects of the over-hyped Premier League is to do it a great disservice. We lower league supporters are not a smug bunch of tossers, believing we're morally superior to those who happily supplement Rupert Murdoch's empire. We just enjoy watching our team.

The quality on the pitch might be lacking, but there is no shortage of drama and excitement to the football we enjoy. It's hugely competitive, with few teams giving you an easy ride. The mixed blessing which is the play offs gives everyone realistic hopes of glory. Even in March you can hear fans of a team hopelessly stuck in mid-table wistfully talk of a "late play off surge". In the lower leagues over the years I've seen some hugely talented up-and-coming players who have gone onto great things at the top end of English football and even abroad, not to mention viewed a number of has-beens whose career is on the downturn.

We have the delights of terracing and a huge range of quirky, run-down or beautiful stadiums. I've found there is little which can beat standing in a shabby away end, with your team having just scored a vital goal inches in front of you. You and your team are the centre of your own world and nothing else is important. Down in the Football League your support matters, there's not exactly an abundance of other people willing to take your place and, if you don't come and watch them, who else will? The bond between supporters and club is much more relevant and meaningful, the respective fortunes intrinsically linked. I matter to my club, they may not be in my name but I feel with justification that I own a part of them. Can you get the same feeling on a Super Sunday?

Talking to a typical TV-viewing Premier League supporter, the reaction upon hearing you follow a lower league club is often one of bemusement and sometimes snootiness. There is a sense of uncomfortable admiration from them towards you, like when someone tells you they do charity work or are about to run a marathon. "I don't know how you do it" is a phrase I've heard more than once before too, as though we're not even talking about following the same sport anymore. Football without the big stars and famous managers? Sounds crazy.

This is the story of my time supporting Bradford City, which has involved all four of English football's professional divisions – including a short stay among the Premier League. It's about the lessons I've learned and the ups – and quite considerably large number of downs – I've experienced along the way. It's about the simple joys of winning at Rochdale, and the dismal despair of getting thrashed at home to Oldham. It's about being part of a tiny away following at Notts Forest, where a friend in the home end will tell you after the game he couldn't hear the cheers when we scored.

It's about relegation. And then another relegation. And then, incredibly, another one. It's about coping with failure, it's about foolish optimism.

If you support a lower league club, I hope you can relate to some of the experiences. If you follow a Premier League club, I hope it helps you to discover whether there's something missing about the way you follow them, and that football can still be enjoyed without Alan Hansen telling you it was bad defending.

Although if you're worried about the lack of big names and that the standard of this story might not be as high as you're used to, I'll understand if you want to part ways now and instead turn on the TV for the "big one" between Everton and Man City.

Just please at least take one thing away from having got this far – lower league footballers rarely ever have the appearance of overweight baldies, okay?

Chapter Two

BC (Before City)

Okay before I go any further I have a shocking omission to make. It will most likely lead to you judging me, and you'll almost definitely take a negative viewpoint. I could keep it quiet from you I suppose, after all how would you find out? But I feel it is important to disclose it, as I hope you'll agree it gives me a slightly different perspective to support my comparing the Premier League unfavourably to the lower leagues. I also hope that, by the end of my story, you'll have changed your negative view of me.

So here goes…Pause for deep breath…I used to support Manchester United. There, I've said it. Even typing those words caused me to shudder. No matter if you haven't missed a game for 20 years or take a small interest in how your team performs; everyone knows that a football fan is never supposed to change their team. You can change your career, wife etc – but football team? You stick with who you picked – or had picked for you – and you like it or lump it.

I can only hold my hands up and plead guilty to the charge of breaking the golden rule. I used to passionately cheer on Manchester United, now I passionately cheer on Bradford City. I no longer have any feelings for my "first love" – when they lose I join in others in laughing at their failure, when they win I feel indifferent. I'll go onto explain just what happened in a moment, but like I said I hope you can see this gives me a different perspective to usual. I can't be accused of ignorantly not understanding the viewpoint of the armchair supporter, because I've been there and sat on that side of the fence. My actions are of course wrong in principle, but does the end justify the means? Well again, that's for you to judge – but first please give me a chance.

As a kid at Primary School in my village of Glusburn, North Yorkshire, I hated football. Of course I played it with everyone else in my class during lunchtimes and I do remember times when it was enjoyable. Generally however, I was a disinterested participant usually nowhere near the action. I wasn't even sure why I joined in, but it seemed the thing all of us boys in the class had to do.

I largely put my youthful dislike of football down to my parents, not that I'm particularly bitter about it. My dad was especially not keen on football; something I know was a disappointment to his own dad, a passionate Manchester United fan. My dad was born and bred in Middleton, just a few miles outside of Manchester. My mum's dad was a Manchester City fan who was a regular at Maine Road for many years. He even developed a liking for Man United after the Second World War, when the bombing of Old Trafford had meant United became City's tenants at Maine Road for a few seasons. My Grandpa would go every week, with United and City at home alternate weekends. He told me that when United played City he was torn over who to support.

A few years after getting married, my parents decided to move to Caernarfon in North Wales; a part of the country they really liked. It wasn't a fully positive experience; Caernarfon during the 70s and 80s could be a very ignorant place with locals conversing almost exclusively in Welsh to exclude 'outsiders'. But while living there they had me and younger brothers, Justin and Kevin, and Dad, a bus driver, still nostalgically harps on about what a beautiful area it was to work. With the local primary school determined to teach me in Welsh, my parents decided that a move back to England would be better for our education.

Looking for another bus driving job, it was then my dad saw an advert for vacancies in Keighley, West Yorkshire. Initially he worked there while we stayed back in Wales, until suitable accommodation could be found. It was hardly ideal, especially as Justin was taken seriously ill. He was diagnosed with Leukaemia and a battle lasting two years would follow. Tragically, it was a fight Justin was unable to win. When he was six and I was eight, he passed away. While he was in

7

hospital me and Kevin would spend periods living with our Grandparents in Manchester, with school work from my new Primary School in Glusburn, five miles from Keighley, sent over for me to complete.

These days when we visit the crematorium in Skipton, we will often ask the unanswerable question of what Justin would be like now and what would he be doing with his life. I sometimes wonder which football team he would have supported and if he would have contributed to the world wars that ensued between Kevin (a Leeds fan) and me – I just hope it wouldn't have been Burnley! Then again, he may have carried on like I might have in disliking football.

It would be wrong to fully blame my childhood indifference to football on my upbringing. My mum, in fact, was an occasional Oldham Athletic supporter as a teenager while the football bug hit Kevin at a young age. He played football for the primary school football team and was a useful goalkeeper. He began supporting Leeds, though I can't remember why. Not surprisingly, there were a lot of kids on our local estate who supported the Whites, so it's likely their influence helped. Another factor was probably the fact the Leeds team at the time were arguably the best in country. In 1992, they won the last ever First Division title, before England's top division clubs broke away to form the Premier League. As Kevin got older through primary school, his passion for football grew. It meant that even I began to take an interest. If nothing else, knowing Leeds had lost meant I was able to wind him up. Slowly but surely, my awareness of football grew; especially as I began to realise that pretty much every lad in my form at secondary school followed a team. But this was 1994, still three and a half years before my first visit to Valley Parade.

French collars and Megastores

What makes you support your football team? It's a question not everyone can easily answer. Some of us will have supported our team since we can remember; either because we had been taken to live matches as a toddler, or because our parents had bought baby replica shirts before we had even learnt to speak. Maybe you choose your team on the school playground, either to follow your friend or the latest trend. Some even chose to go against who everyone else supported as a way of carving out an identity.

In football, there lives this ideal that you should always support your local team. It's largely through this type of loyalty that lower league clubs continue to exist. But increasingly these days, the pull of the Premiership is much stronger. If you're an impressionable child living in Scunthorpe and you see Wayne Rooney bang in a wonder goal on TV, you're are probably more likely to pledge allegiance to Manchester United than take a trip to Glanford Park. This is a problem lower league clubs face and, pretty much wherever you live, there will always be more exposure to the big clubs of the Premiership than your local club around the corner.

And that's the other route into football many people take, the glory route. Unfortunately I can already be accused of being a glory supporter and my defence is weak. In 1994, when my interest in football began, Manchester United had just lifted the Premier League and FA Cup double. What I will say though it that I first became aware of United in 1990 when they were due to play Crystal Palace in the FA Cup final. It was the talk of the class and someone went round asking every boy who they would be rooting for. I plumped for Manchester United, not because I thought Mark Hughes was a great player or that Palace were a struggling team fortunate to be there (I didn't know these factors, but others did); with my childhood imagination, I assumed Palace must literally play inside a crystal palace. This sounded strange, so I went for the more normal Manchester United name. It meant I was able to join in with the others gloating after United won, as I had backed the right team.

Sound feeble? Well okay, I can't really get away from the fact Man United being the Champions was a big pull back in 1994. But equally I became more aware that laughing at Leeds losing was a good way to wind up Kevin. Am I trying to claim I started supported Man United to annoy him? Was I that immature? You will have to ask my parents what I was like at 11, but I think they will agree a factor in my choice of team was that it wound up Kevin even more…

I can't really pin the moment when football began to take over my life, but I'm pretty sure it was during the World Cup of 1994. Along with my brother, I followed the progress of the Republic of Ireland with interest (no England this year while Wales, who I still consider as my team and support, never make it). I don't think I watched every game, but I certainly remember feeling very excited about the final, between Italy and Brazil. It was a dull game to many but, for someone learning the game, I found it interesting to watch. Brazil eventually triumphed 3-2 on penalties after a goalless 120 minutes. Roberto Baggio, Italy's star player and easily identifiable because of his ponytail, famously blasted the final penalty over. As he stood still and stared at the ground in despair, I sat at home enthralled and there was no way back.

After an impatient wait through the rest of the summer, the new season (1994-95) kicked off with the Champions, Manchester United, having a new supporter on board. It's fair to say the first season was a learning curve for me as I began to develop an understanding of the rules of football and the players of Manchester United. I also learned how to consume the game with the discovery of Match of the Day and Radio 5 Live. The first Man United game I watched was the opening Champions League group match against IFK Gothenburg of Sweden, live on ITV, with my Manchester United-supporting Granddad. It felt a weird moment, almost embarrassing for me, being in the presence of an experienced United fan for my first match. We talked a bit while the game played out and he told me about some of the previous European football nights at Old Trafford, as well as his thoughts on the current players. Man United came from behind to win 4-2, it was a memorable experience.

The 1994-95 season was famously the year United lost the title to Blackburn Rovers, something which spawned a few glory hunters pledging allegiance to Blue and White around our way. It was also the season that my first football hero, Eric Cantona, attacked a Crystal Palace fan and was banned for the rest of the season. Ultimately, this was to cost United. The title race was exciting and went right to the wire and I remember listening to the final match, where United could only draw with West Ham. It meant Blackburn, despite losing to Liverpool, were the Champions. I spent that evening in A&E having fallen on my ankle jumping up and down in desperation during the commentary. At the time it hadn't felt too bad, but after the match the pain began to grow and I asked my parents to take me down. Part of the hurt, no doubt, was from the events at Upton Park.

Despite a few calls of glory supporter from fellow kids in my form, my interest in football did begin to win me more friends as I found I had more in common with classmates. There were only a couple of other Man United fans in the form, but they were both people who I didn't get on with. Instead I would be chatting to Leeds, Liverpool and Arsenal fans. There were also a few Burnley fans who were regulars at Turf Moor - just over the Lancashire border - and this was my first appreciation of supporting your local team, despite them not playing in the Premier League.

If my first season as a football fan ended in disappointment, the second was incredible. Alex Ferguson famously ditched top players – Paul Ince, Andrei Kanchelskis and Mark Hughes – and went with the emerging kids. It also the year Newcastle sprinted ahead but blew it. As a title race, it was a real thriller and I followed every kick from the radio in my bedroom; cursing the days 5 Live didn't put Man United as the commentary game. There was no chance my parents would ever get Sky, especially if it led to us hogging the TV at weekends to watch football, although my friend would kindly tape live games for me to watch later during the week. The season was not without its ups and downs, but after United beat Middlesbrough 3-0 on the last day of the season I was able to celebrate my first success as a football fan by jumping around my bedroom. A week later, I watched Cantona's spectacular winner defeat Liverpool in the FA Cup final on the BBC. Just wait until I get into school on Monday morning…

Three tickets for the Chelsea game please···

With a succession of trophies, great players and glamour; why would any supporter give up following Manchester United? My journey from Old Trafford to Valley Parade truly began during the 1996-97 season, where the downside of supporting a team with such a huge fanbase began to be realised. As a person, I tend to get passionate about the things I am interested in and that included a strong desire to attend live games. Here I am now at 14 years old, a keen follower of the sport who would spend hours of his free time watching or listening to matches – not to mention spend every other waking minute thinking about it – yet I had never attended a live game.

For Man United matches, I would typically sit in my room tuned into Radio 5 Live hoping that they would select Man U for the commentary game. Living in Yorkshire, local radio commentary was not an option, although I was always guaranteed to be able to listen to the Man United-Leeds fixtures by tuning into Radio Leeds. If Man United were in Champions League action, I would be able to watch their games on ITV.

I had visited the outside of Old Trafford on a few occasions. My Granddad first took me to view the stadium from the outside one evening. I remember thinking the stadium didn't look very big, especially compared to what you see on TV. For a 14th birthday treat, I was taken on a stadium tour of Old Trafford so got to glimpse the stadium from the inside. We also went to the open top bus parade around Manchester after the double win of 1995-96. On other occasions we visited the two Megastores at Old Trafford, one at each end of the ground. We would often eat lunch in the United café.

By my 15th birthday, I decided to pluck up the courage to ask to attend a game as my present. I was worried about the expense, but felt it was worth at least posing the question. My parents agreed and were ready to buy tickets for myself, Kevin and my Granddad – who would take us. It was left to me to choose a game and, with Arsenal and Chelsea due at Old Trafford soon, I decided I would rather go to the Chelsea game (probably because it was the first fixture of the two and I couldn't wait to go).

Over the years the ticket office staff at Old Trafford must have got used to clueless requests from people thinking attending a game is as simple as booking a ticket for a film at the cinema; still I don't think any of us were prepared for the response when my dad went up to the window and said, "Can we get three tickets for the Chelsea game please?" The member of staff patiently explained that not only are there no tickets available for this game and the Arsenal one, but that every match is sold out. To get tickets, you need to become members. There was a three-year waiting list to become a member and even then there were no promises you will get a ticket.

Talk about slamming the door. It was at this moment that the decline in my affections for Man United started. I was a passionate fan; I followed every game (usually from my radio), knew every player and had read up on the club's history. I had several replica tops, numerous videos and a Cantona flag. My bedroom at home was decorated with posters of players and I bought the club magazine every month. But could I go to a game? No chance.

Such is the problem of supporting a huge club, of the glory-supporting culture and following a team 40 miles down the road. To Manchester United, I didn't exist. The merchandise I purchased made little difference to their vast profits and my tuning into games on the radio had no influence on their performances. I once wrote a letter to the club magazine, but they didn't print it. The problem was there were millions of people like me dotted around the world. Each had their posters of Cantona, they all owned the replica shirts and the videos and they could all claim to be just as passionate as I felt I was. At the end of the 1996-97 season, Manchester United were again crowned Champions. Their fate sealed on a night they weren't even playing as rivals Newcastle and Liverpool, both in action, failed to win. As the final whistles sounded I jumped up and down in my room and sprayed a can of coke which I had shaken up. But I was alone, and felt very alone. I watched the scenes at Old Trafford, where fans gathered outside to celebrate, on TV the following day. No one was outside dancing in the streets of Glusburn.

Given the millions of fans around the world, I was not the only supporter not celebrating outside Old Trafford that evening; yet when comparing to the glory moments I have experienced following Bradford City, there was a major difference. When City beat Wolves 3-2 at Molineux to gain promotion to the Premiership I was there to see it, dancing around in the away end hugging strangers. Even for the darker moments, such as subsequent relegations, I was able to experience it first hand. Which was why the information the Old Trafford ticket office staff gave us that day was so devastating; it meant I had hit a brick wall. How can you continue the passion with something in which you have such limited involvement? I didn't have any first hand knowledge of how good the players were; you rely on media coverage and other fans opinions to shape your own views. You might see Jordi Cruyff score a brilliant goal on TV, but you hear from other sources that he is a poor player not good enough to play for the club.

I did eventually get to attend a Man United game. The following pre-season (1997-98) United played Inter Milan in a pre-season friendly and tickets were on sale to anyone. I joined thousands of others in experiencing the rare treat of seeing our heroes live in the flesh. Every corner or moment a player like Ryan Giggs ran in front of supporters, flashes from cameras could be seen around the stadium. I had my own camera as well of course, and captured the moment Giggs gathered the ball to take a corner which led to the equaliser in a 1-1 draw. The experience of seeing a live game was fantastic, but it also left me frustrated and longing for more. It didn't look as though I would get to see much more action at Old Trafford though. It may have only been 40 miles away, but it might as well be 4,000.

Chapter Three

1997 - 98
Finding Valley Parade

15 miles down the road from where I lived, a football revolution of sorts was taking place. Bradford City, a perennial lower league outfit, had seen attendances triple from 5,000 to 15,000 in the space of two years, danced around Wembley having won the Division Two play off final and was now talking realistically of reaching the Premier League.

I was partly aware that it was exciting times for my nearest professional football club, but its sudden rise up the football pecking order had begun with my attention firmly elsewhere. With unknown players, unglamorous opposition and little to no profile, I remained largely ignorant of its existence. Central midfielder Lee Duxbury was a player I had heard of. He had attended the same secondary school, South Craven, in Crosshills, as me and some teachers would occasionally talk about what he was like. There were other players I would have heard of, such as Ian Ormondroyd and David Brightwell, but I knew little about the club and never looked at its results.

What was taking place though was quite remarkable. In January 1994, a Leeds-born-businessman-made-good successfully completed a deal to take over City. Acquiring the mid-table Division Two side for one he had triumphantly led into the Football League a few years earlier, Scarborough. He was now in charge of a club that he felt had the potential to become one of the biggest in England. That man was Geoffrey Richmond and he was to have a major impact on Bradford City, the surrounding area and myself.

Shortly after taking over, he told a fans forum that, in five years, City would be in the Premiership. For a club that were last in the top flight 72 years ago and who's only major honour was an FA Cup win in 1911, it was only to be expected that his prediction was greeted by sniggers. Yet five years later Richmond was able to bask in the glory of that very achievement as City reached the top flight. It took a couple of seasons for Richmond to even lead City out of Division Two but, in May 1996, the club enjoyed that day out at Wembley with a 2-0 play off final victory over Notts County. 40,000 Bradfordians had travelled to London to cheer on the team, vastly outnumbering their Nottinghamshire rivals. It was further evidence to Richmond's belief that the City of Bradford was capable of housing something greater than a lower league outfit with average gates of fewer than 6,000. Both on pitch and off the pitch, Richmond was busying himself with a master plan that, for a time at least, would see all those beliefs come to reality.

Back in my bedroom with my transistor radio tuned into Five Live, I was blissfully unaware of what was happening so close by. I knew that, as United lifted the 'double double' in 1995-96, Bradford City fans were also celebrating that Wembley triumph. In the years to come though, as I read about moments such as the dramatic semi final play off win, where City came back from a 2-0 first leg home defeat to Sam Alladyce's Blackpool to win 3-0 at Bloomfield Road, I could only curse myself that I hadn't 'discovered' the club earlier and avoided missing out on experiencing such special moments along the journey. In reality though, growing up not liking football and with no parental influence over who to support, it was unlikely the road could ever have led directly to Valley Parade.

As City were now in Division One and up against more glamorous opposition, I became slightly more interested in their fortunes. Man City had been relegated from the Premiership the season before, so I thought about attending when they visited Valley Parade to cheer Bradford on against United's rivals. I guess my interest still wasn't strong enough though, as I never bothered to check when they were due at Bradford. Every so often, I would check where Bradford's league position and hoped they would win the relegation battle they were embroiled in.

Ultimately, City survived after winning the final two matches, and I was becoming more and more interested in going to a game. The fact that Middlesbrough had now been relegated from the Premiership and so would be rolling up to Valley Parade only strengthened my intentions. Some of my friends were equally up for the idea but then disappointment – the weekend of the Middlesbrough fixture, mid September, was the same weekend my parents had booked for us to go away to Wales.

My friends, Stephen and Alan, went to the game – a 2-2 draw which was part of a promising start to the season that saw the club briefly top the league. Hearing afterwards how much they enjoyed the match only made me more determined to go sometime, yet Stephen and Alan showed no intention of going again and I did fear that going to a game against less glamorous opposition might not prove exciting.

At the same time, I was growing more disinterested in Manchester United. I was back on radio duty, which I was fed up of. Where is the fun in supporting a team who wins the league every season, but who you only follow from a distance? I had the inferiority complex of not going to games, was I a proper supporter? When I cheer a goal, who hears? If I listen to the game on the radio tonight, what difference will it make? If I never visit the Megastore again, what impact will it have on United's vast wealth? I knew I still loved football, but the easiness success came along left me unsatisfied. I began to wish I had chosen someone else to support. I had reached a football cross roads.

Luckily the answer was only 15 miles down the road...

West Brom (home) – who's our number 6?

Just like me, Stephen and Alan (both brothers) had a morning paper round. We each had our own patch and worked six days a week, with Sunday our only day for a lie-in. On Saturday 1 November 1997, I walked down to the shop to pick up my bag to discover the papers had not yet been delivered to the shop.

There was nothing unusual about this on a Saturday so, after reading the magazines of interest on the shelf while we waited, I joined Stephen and Alan, who were sitting on the window ledge outside the shop enjoying the morning air.

We fell into conversation about what each of us were doing that day, when Alan told me they were going to watch Bradford City play West Bromwich Albion with their older brother David (who had been several City games before). I instantly felt envious of them, especially considering my Saturday afternoon was going to be spent by the radio listening to Man United score updates. An afternoon out at a live game sounded infinitely more appealing but, with no invitation to join them forthcoming, I resigned myself to not going along and was soon on my way to do my round, the papers having arrived.

Throughout the morning I couldn't stop thinking about their plans. Should I ring them and invite myself? After all, it's not as though they would mind me going; or is it a family thing with David taking his two young brothers? I decided to tell my mum about what they were doing and my sadness must have come across as she straight away began encouraging me to join them. I expressed my concerns that it might be a family thing, but she was more confident and even rang up their mum on my behalf to see if they had set off yet. They had started walking to David's house, which was just down the road from me, and she was sure I would be welcome and urged me to get down to David's while she called him to explain. So within 10 minutes of talking to mum, I was out the door with my paper round wage in my pocket rushing to join them in time for the bus. I'm sure neither my mum or myself had any idea of the implications of my trip to the game as I left the house – I think she either felt I needed an interest or was just keen to get me out from under her feet! Whatever her reasons, her pushiness was how I ended up going.

I got over to David's before they set off and, sure enough, they were happy for me to go along with them. We then began the route that would shortly become very familiar to us; catch the bus at the end of David's street, go along three miles to Steeton, five minute walk to the train station before making the 37 minute journey through Keighley, Bingley, Saltaire and Shipley, arriving at Bradford Forster Square station. I can't say

I especially felt excited as we got on board the train, I remember not even having any intention of supporting Bradford City.

I have two favourite walks in life, both relating to the excitement of the destination we were reaching. My second, which would emerge later in life at University with friends, was the one from the Newcastle City Centre Metro station to our favourite nightclub, Shindig. The walk would always give me a buzz as I knew I was close to the start of a great night. We walked through the shopping centre, with all the shutters up for the night; past a couple of cheesy bars, which we considered ourselves too cool to ever set foot near.

My favourite walk was one I was experiencing for the first time on this November day – from the train station to Valley Parade along Manningham Lane. It's hardly the prettiest route you will ever take, with plenty of traffic passing through and assorted sex and junk shops along the way, but it always signifies the excitement of getting to the ground for the game, the hope of three points and the expectation of being part of a good atmosphere. You never have any idea of what you are going to see, but after a week waiting for the match and the often-tedious bus and train journey, you are just glad it's almost the moment to set foot inside Valley Parade.

On my first ever walk that way I had not even seen the stadium before. I had no idea how close or far we were from the ground, only that it was 2.40pm and we needed to get a move on to make kick off. The first glimpse of the top of the floodlights could be seen as we walked by a large music shop. As we passed a row of houses I could see the top of a stand. Then finally, we turned right after a car showroom and there was part of Valley Parade at the bottom of the road. We queued up at the nearby ticket office to book seats, only to be told it was cheaper to stand. So instead we walked around to the terrace I would quickly learn was called the Kop and paid £5 on the gate. I found a programme seller at the top of the stand and paid £1.80 for a copy. I then got took in my first look at the stadium, pitch and surroundings – a moment I will never forget.

At the time I had never heard of Nick Hornby's Fever Pitch, yet when watching the film version a few years later I excitedly realised the moment the main character – up to that moment a disinterested kid forced to go to the football by his father – first sets eyes on Highbury produced exactly the same reaction that I'd had at viewing Valley Parade's interior. I scanned the ground from the back of the Kop and was stunned by how large it was, by how many people were inside the stadium, by the greenness of the pitch, by the fact each stand looked different in size and layout and, most crucially, that this wonderful football club was right on my doorstop. Just like the kid in Fever Pitch, I also instantly wanted to know when the next fixture would be and hurriedly looked it up in my programme; Tranmere Rovers in two weeks, then Norwich City two weeks later. I already wanted to go to both of those matches and was anxiously telling Stephen and Alan about them. It truly was love at first sight. I took a lingering look around the stadium and felt instantly at home.

David led us to the front to find a good place to stand a few rows back. We were at pitch level and, as the teams were read out over the PA system, I realised I knew quite a few players such as former Man United goalkeeper Gary Walsh, recently signed from Middlesbrough. There was also a Man United youngster on loan, full back John O'Kane. Former Ipswich centre back Eddie Youds was in the centre of defence with ex-Everton and Man City winger Peter Beagrie on the left. Up front was Edinho, the Brazilian striker who had been earning a good reputation both locally and nationally. The fact Bradford City had a Brazilian only heightened the sudden rush of glamour I was experiencing.

The game with West Brom was to finish 0-0, although I don't think I've seen as entertaining a goalless draw before or since. Of course it helped that, during the quieter moments, I was gawping around at the stadium and soaking up the sights and smells within it. At the time, both clubs were in the top six and both produced some excellent football. West Brom, attacking towards the Kop in the first half, started well. It allowed us to see the capabilities of a new hero. Every ball in the box seemed to be headed out by our number 6. After a while we looked at each other to ask who this brilliant player was. Tall, imposing and a Frank Bruno lookalike; I looked him up in the programme to discover he was called Darren Moore. Goodness knows what some of the regulars made of us excitedly yelling out "who is this guy?!" A few looked round and seemed unimpressed, but didn't utter a word of complaint about the obvious cluelessness of this group of people stood with them.

As the half wore on, City got more into the game and hit the post. The second half was more of the same and City pressed well as they attacked towards us. I had no goal to cheer on my first game, but I was certainly in no doubt which team I wanted to score. I was amazed by how close to the action we were and it felt as though we could reach out and touch the players. It was certainly a contrast to listening to your team on the radio, where you had to attempt to picture the action. The match may have involved the 22 players and referee, but I felt as though I was a part of it too.

One of the main memories of the game, and indeed my early games at Valley Parade, was the atmosphere. There was a drummer in the Midland Road stand to the left of us, which helped everyone keep chanting. It was easy to pick up a lot of the chants and I had no fears about singing along. This was my first taste of joining in with a large crowd making noise. This quickly became one of the things I looked forward to the most.

The final whistle was blown all too quickly and it was time to walk back to the train station. I took one last look at the stadium as we left and knew I simply had to be back in two weeks for the Tranmere game. I spent a good part of the journey home trying to persuade Alan, and Stephen the same thing, but they didn't seem as keen. Just like me, they each supported a Premiership team. Alan Blackburn Rovers, while David and Stephen followed a certain team not too far away, who happened to play in white and were considered City's biggest rivals!

As for me and Man United, it might sound strange to say, I woke up that day as a United fan and finished it not caring about them, but as the new-found feelings of love for Bradford City took over, those I had for United were very quickly pushed out. After a few months of feeling confused and questioning why I supported a club who couldn't care less if I even existed, I appeared to have found the answer. When I got home I found out United had won 6-1 against Sheffield Wednesday, yet I can honestly say I didn't feel happy or sad about it, just indifference.

A couple of days later I watched Man United's Champions League tie away at Feyenoord on ITV, my feelings still confused. As Andy Cole helped himself to a hat trick in a 3-1 win, I couldn't be bothered to cheer. I just didn't care, they could have lost the game and I would have felt the same. It was at this moment I knew for sure that it was over. I may have only been to one match, I didn't know the names of most of the City players and I felt a large degree of trepidation in telling friends and family that my allegiance had changed; but I knew that the team 15 miles down the road was the one for me. I spent two weeks excited about going to the next game. Stephen, Alan and David were eventually up for going too, and it was soon time to walk down to David's house in preparation for catching the bus, still grateful that the papers had been delivered late two weeks ago.

Swindon (away) – the dilemma

The Saturday afternoon after the West Brom game, I was again listening to football on the radio, only it wasn't the usual radio station and it wasn't the usual football team. Rather than Five Live and Manchester United, I had Radio Leeds on and was listening to Bradford City's match at Swindon.

There's only one major rule that binds together football fans – you never change your football team. Yet here I was on the brink of doing just that. I didn't sit there and think of the pros and cons of dropping Man United for Bradford City – had I thought clearly about it, the cons would surely have been far greater anyway. Man United were the English Champions, playing in Europe with a squad packed full of talent. Bradford City were in Division One and, while they might be good enough for a play off spot this season, would be facing opposition like Crewe, Oxford and Port Vale. But even allowing for the step down there will be people who tell me I'm stupid and not a proper fan for ditching my team for another. The easiest thing in the world for me to do would be to carry on as I was, never go near Valley Parade again and retain self respect by supporting the Red Devils. But where was the benefit for me? If I'm going to spend the rest of my life watching football, can't I at least be happy with the team I follow?

When I thought of my afternoon at Valley Parade I felt happy. It might not be a place I feel 100% comfortable at – couldn't everyone else tell I was phoney who'd never been before? –but I knew I'd be able to grow into the role of a City fan and, eventually, be respected for it. After all I can turn up ten minutes before the game kicks off and pay on the gate to go in, so they clearly needed my support – could the same be said at Old Trafford?

I had three friends in the same position of conflict – Alan with Blackburn Rovers and Stephen and David with Leeds. The fact we might all start going to watch City regularly meant we could break that one football supporter rule together and not feel as guilty about it. It was more than just going to watch live football, but a social thing we could enjoy together. Something to fill a big gap in our lives that we knew was there but didn't quite know how to fix.

Life hadn't been the kindest to David, Stephen or Alan. Their mum and dad had split up when they were kids and Stephen, who was the same age as me, had suffered a horrendous accident watching a fireworks display on bonfire night, where a faulty rocket had accidentally flown into the hood of his jacket, setting it on fire and causing him brain damage. I'd not known Stephen before this happened but we'd slowly become friends as he was in my class at primary school. He was a nice lad with bags of enthusiasm, but quite slow and gullible which other people cruelly attempted to take advantage of.

David was older than us by almost 10 years. I'd known him for a number of years because of Stephen, but his sometimes aggressive nature meant I wasn't too comfortable around him. After school David had joined the army, only to be kicked out quickly as he struggled with the fitness and discipline. He'd moved back home before quickly leaving as he didn't get on with his mum's boyfriend,.

David was much slimmer and in better shape than his two brothers, who were both overweight, and had a stronger self-confidence which meant he had little trouble speaking to anyone. He worked in a bank in Bradford but was too much of a dreamer, wishing his way to the top while neglecting to do the admin role he was supposed to do competently. The sack wouldn't be far away.

Alan was my brother Kevin's age and the two had been best friends at primary school, before drifting apart at secondary. He and Stephen were particularly close and having an older brother like him meant Alan had to quickly grow up and be more than the youngest child. Stephen looked up to David and would follow him around, always wanting to sit next to and act like his older brother; but Alan especially was always there for him.

They didn't have many friends between them, but I certainly wanted to and needed them to be mine now. Changing football teams and going on my own would not have been as rewarding and would have left me with a complexion of feeling stupid. I was seemingly otherwise destined to spend the rest of my life locked in my room with a fuzzy radio on Saturdays, hoping for the day I could afford Sky, so in some ways going to watch City on my own wouldn't have been a step down. But still I wanted friends to enjoy it with and I wanted us all to break that rule and abandon our teams collectively, so that none of us were any better or worse than each other.

Those early games

A close look at the attendances Bradford City attracted during the years from 1995 to 2000 suggests I was not the only supporter to 'discover' the Bantams around this time. In the space of a couple of seasons, gates at Valley Parade tripled, backing up Geoffrey Richmond's foresight in developing the ground. One of the main reasons for this success was the ticketing strategy he adopted, which made attending games affordable for so many. I was paying £5 a game to stand on the Kop and sitting down was only £9. True I was under 16, but even David only had to pay £9 for his adult Kop entry.

While it's hard for me to judge seeing as I wasn't going to games before, I would suggest there were lots of other teenage groups suddenly going to City. It was a common sight, on train journeys or inside the ground, to see large groups of school friends. Within the group there would inevitably be two or three really fanatical about City; they may even include one kid who was going to games before the rest anyway. There would be other lads who looked las if they were there because

24

it was the fashionable thing to do. They would generally not have any hesitation nipping off to get food and drink during the game and be more inclined to chat rather than pay full attention to matters on the pitch. There would also be a few girls in the group, usually sat together and often even less interested in the game. How long these groups kept coming to matches was questionable, but there's little doubt that a handful of males and females from this group would still be going years later. There were also a lot of kids going with their dads, with that old tradition of the father standing a few rows back while the kid stands at the front by the advertising boards with other people their age.

Could you imagine this happening in the Premier League now? The idea of groups of teenage friends going to top flight matches is something which belongs in the history books. Yet it remains a heart-warming sight in the lower divisions, a great way of bonding and growing up.

Tranmere was my second City match, although it was one we almost missed. Me, Stephen and Alan had arrived at David's house in good time for the bus, but he was running late after sleeping in. Considering all the time we would go on to spend together watching City in the years ahead, it's fair to say we grew to know each other's habits pretty well. On this day I was to learn that David will never leave the house until he is meticulously ready. His shirt must be well ironed, he needs to have had a proper shave, breakfast must be finished and, if he is taking his walkman, his music choices have to be ready. We left the house late, due to what seemed to me like unnecessary preparation on David's part, and had to run to the bus stop, quickly discovering we had missed our bus. We caught the next one 10 minutes later, but it was going to be cutting it fine to get off at Steeton top and make it to the train station at the bottom of the hill in time for our connection. We had to run, not something that Stephen and Alan could manage well. Me and David ran ahead and made it to the platform as the train pulled up. We asked the guard if he could wait a minute for our friends, but there wasn't even any sign of them crossing the bridge towards the platform. The guard refused and the train pulled out of the station long before Stephen and Alan arrived. We had to wait another half hour for the next train, which was due at 2.40pm and wouldn't arrive at

Bradford Forster Square station until 3.07pm. Then there was the 10-15 minute walk to the ground.

At this point it might have been best to turn around and give up, as there was no way of knowing if we would be allowed into the ground 20 minutes after the game had kicked off. But we vowed to go on and caught the next train, with David, who had left the army six months ago, lecturing his two younger brothers on fitness. After what seemed an uncomfortably long time, the train arrived in Bradford and we set off walking with a growing expectation we'd have negotiate with a steward to be let in. Frustrated and desperate, I decided to run and leave them behind. It might not have been fair, but I couldn't bear the thought of going all this way and not seeing the game.

My heart sank as I arrived at the turnstiles, they were closed. Out of breath, I knelt down before deciding to try the one around the corner – it was open! I paid my £5 and dashed down to our spot on the Kop. It was 15 minutes into the game and there was no score. I was chuffed to be there and, 10 minutes later, Stephen, Alan and David had arrived and we all got to enjoy the rest of the game together.

Not that it was a one to savour. Tranmere Rovers striker John Aldridge's second half header was the first goal I was to witness at Valley Parade and led to my first defeat. Since the West Brom draw, City had played two games on the road – a draw and a loss. This result meant City were fast dropping out of the play off picture. On the train journey home we sat with a larger group of friends of David, who'd been at the game. They were all his age and keen supporters, going both home and away. The journey was spent debating City's failings and prospects for the season. This was only my second game and I was a long way off having the confidence to express an opinion, so listened intently instead.

City's dip in form continued with a midweek draw at home to Sheffield United (I was not allowed to go through, it was a school night, so missed new signing John McGinlay's first goal for City) and a defeat at Man City the following Saturday. It was then time for the Norwich home game, although I was still struggling to get Stephen and Alan suitably enthused to go. Despite my best efforts, they decided they wouldn't attend.

I was still determined to go on my own, although worried my parents wouldn't let me travel to Bradford on my own. Luckily they bowed down to my desperate begging, although I was told to take the bus instead of train. It meant an extremely long bus journey from Keighley to Bradford, stopping every two minutes to pick up passengers. I was less sure of where Valley Parade was travelling on the road from Shipley. I kept my face pushed against the glass and finally the bus went past the ground. I pressed the bell and got off a few yards further on Manningham Lane.

The advantage of going on my own was being able to plan the time I set off, and I arrived deliberately early so I could pay my first visit to the club shop. I entered the ground just after 2pm, keen to get my first glimpse of the stadium empty. The empty environment made me feel slightly uneasy, as though I was in someone's house when they were out. I felt wary of where I was stood and, while there was no objects to touch, I worried someone might suddenly appear and question what I was doing there. A ridiculous question popped in my head, "are you sure we're playing today?" I went to our spot on the Kop for the last two home games and waited for the ground to fill up.

As the game was about to kick off, I noticed David had turned up and was stood close by. At this stage I didn't know him well enough to see about going to the game with him and assumed he would be joining his regular mates instead. I pretended not to notice him, feeling slightly shy. I think he also pretended not to notice me for similar reasons and we almost comically stood by each other engrossed in the game, waiting to see if the other would make the first move of acknowledging the other. Norwich, who was on the attack, fired a shot wide in front of us. One of their players appealed for a corner and fans around began shouting abuse at him. It was then that Dave turned round to agree with the vocal fan and we both caught each other's eye. "Jason! I didn't realise you were coming!" I said similar things and we spent the rest of the half chatting while watching the game. It was an afternoon when our friendship, independent of his two younger brothers for the first time, was sealed. It was also an afternoon memorable for other reasons.

In my two previous City matches I had not even had the pleasure of cheering a goal. 13 minutes in, that was to change. Rob Steiner picked up the ball just inside the Norwich half and embarked on a mazy dribble that saw him end up in their penalty area. After holding off an opponent, he fired low into the net and City was in front. Everyone around cheered and I went crazy jumping up and down. After a few seconds I had to rein myself back, conscious I was probably celebrating more wildly than anyone else. Still, it was a great moment and a wonderful feeling.

Three minutes into the second half, the lightweight winger Shaun Murray played Steiner through on goal and he fired the ball past the on rushing keeper for 2-0. Just behind the goal the ball was rolling into, I had the perfect view as it eventually crossed the line. I hadn't dared celebrate until it had, even though it was obvious it was going in. Everyone around me had already started cheering and I again felt slightly conscious. This time, I wasn't celebrating enough, but was soon up to everyone else's level. With 13 minutes to go, Norwich's Craig Bellamy ran through and slotted home for 2-1. That caused a nervy final few moments, but fortunately we held out. At last, I had seen City score, had seen us win and had made better friends with David. All in all, it was a memorable afternoon.

Whether Stephen and Alan had really been too ill to go to the Norwich game, or just weren't getting hooked, I don't know; but both were very keen to attend the following home game against Bury. Again I was to witness another City win and another goal in front of us in the Kop. 23 minutes in, a corner was half cleared and McGinlay reacted quickest to fire home a brilliant first time volley with his back to goal. Against a limited, struggling team, one goal was enough to win; although there was a spectacular brawl at the end, involving almost every player on the field, to add to the entertainment.

Just after Christmas, I got my first taste of a West Yorkshire derby against Huddersfield and a feeling of disappointment I was to get used to from this fixture. Huddersfield were battling relegation while City, whose mini revival had stalled due to a couple of away defeats, were now sinking to mid-table. Being Christmas there was a bigger crowd than usual, and most of us were celebrating when Robbie Blake gave us the lead. But Town equalised and were then the better side. We trooped out disappointed with a draw, though as I reflected on things that New Years Eve I felt a mixture of nerves and enthusiasm about what was in store for 1998.

It was my GCSE year and in a few months I had all those exams to sit through, a daunting prospect for anyone; but I felt excitement at my recent discovery of Bradford City and the fun I was going to have pursuing it. I had swapped red for claret and amber, the comfort of a team that always wins to one that regularly loses; the warmness of a bedroom listening to the radio to the coldness of a terrace, witnessing events first-hand. Life seemed very exciting and, as I tore down my Man United posters and hid my replica red shirts, I was already excitedly thinking about my next City game.

Man City (away) and Swindon Town (home) - Kamara goes, friends try the magic of Valley Parade

My new found love of Bradford City had meant I was desperate to attend every City match possible, so I was eagerly looking forward to the 3rd Round Draw of the FA Cup where I hoped we might be drawn to play Premiership opposition at home. Instead we got Man City away, from the same division. I was disappointed as I had mentally sounded out the FA Cup weekend as one where I might be seeing a game. But as I thought about the predicament a solution popped into my head that made me even more excited, "why not go to the game anyway?"

At this point, attending an away game was not something I had even contemplated, but this was a great opportunity. My grandparents lived in Manchester, so my parents would probably be happy to take me over there and visit them while I went to the game. Better still, my Grandpa was a Man City fan who used to go all the time. I wonder if he would like to attend the game? I raised the idea with my parents, who were beginning to realise that Bradford City was going to take over my life. After discussing it with my Grandpa they agreed – I could go to the game and me, Kevin and Grandpa would sit in the away end.

We picked Grandpa up on the way and arrived at Maine Road quite early and got to our seats in good time. It was fair to say the ground had been transformed since my Grandpa had last been so was a sight for us all to behold. 4,000 other City fans had made the short trip over and by kick off the atmosphere in the away end was electric.

Unbeknown until a few days later, I had started watching City just as manager Chris Kamara's reign was coming to its end. I don't have the same great memories other City fans have of the man who led City to Division One and kept us up. This game did provide my favourite Kamara memory though; with the teams on the pitch about to kick off, he ran onto the pitch towards us away fans and began applauding us for the great backing we were providing. It was a touching moment that showed the bond he had with the fans. It seemed to be his way of saying, "thanks for coming and thanks for your great support." Everyone responded with a chant of "There's only one Chris Kamara".

Right from kick off we took the game to Man City, a poor side struggling near the bottom of Division One. Unfortunately we couldn't score and were punished when Man City took a shock lead through Uwe Rosler. Two minutes later, our man Peter Beagrie shot from the edge of the area, at the end where we were sat, and the ball beat the keeper but hit the post, before agonisingly rolling along the goal line and hitting the other post. It felt as though it wasn't our day, and this was confirmed a minute later when a slip at the back allowed Man City's Michael Brown in to score a second. It was hard to take and all of us in the away end sat with heads in our hands disbelieving the turn of events.

It was then I remembered Grandpa would not be feeling so despondent, and looked over to check. His face was something I will never forget. He was laughing to himself and looking proud as punch. Sadly, he passed away in February 2010 and so this game proved to be his last. I'm so thankful to have shared this afternoon with him. With my dad not caring for football and my original liking for a team that were inaccessible, this day almost symbolically marked the passing down of the football baton between generations. I'm sure he would prefer me to be a blue supporter but, compared to my first football team, I bet he was relieved!

Two days later, Chris Kamara was sacked. I discovered his fate after loading up teletext in the evening. It came as shock, as there seemed to have been no indication he was close to receiving his P45. The official line from Geoffrey Richmond was that he felt Chris had taken the club as far as he could; with three wins from the last 21 matches backing up his argument. At this time, I didn't really know where to find other fans' opinions and was left perplexed by the whole thing. I had quickly grown to love Kamara and, with the club lying in 11th position and showing reasonable form just before Christmas, it was a decision I didn't agree with. Yet being so new to City, I felt unjustified in feeling outraged.

In the meantime, Paul Jewell was promoted from assistant manager to caretaker. In his first game in charge, City earned a surprise win at Stockport. Two weeks later Jewell was given the job until the end of the season at least.

Meanwhile the four of us were becoming increasingly fanatical. We all travelled to the away match at Sheffield United (a 2-1 defeat) at the end of February, after the other three had heard how much fun Man City away had been. We took a supporters coach from Valley Parade which was easy and enjoyable, each of us bringing walkmans to pass the time. It would be our transport of choice to away games for the next few years.

There was no longer a need to ask if we were going to the next game, no need to ring the night before and beg each other to go – we were going to every home match, we were hooked and I, at least, was wondering how on earth I'd previously lived without this fantastic lifestyle on my doorstop. While I was the only one of us to instantly stop supporting the club I loved upon going to City, Stephen and David were wilting and soon followed in abandoning their support of Leeds United. The first confirmation they'd truly swapped sides was when they both joined in the anti-Leeds chants for the first time, both grinning as though they'd finally been able to come clean about feelings they no longer held. Alan stuck with Blackburn as his 'other' club, something that would prove significant a few years later.

~~Tranmere (away)~~, ~~Man City (home)~~, Norwich City (away), ~~Notts Forest (home)~~ – changing priorities

The problem with suddenly discovering a pastime that takes over your life is adapting the rest of your life to suit. My spiritual home on a Saturday afternoon was now Valley Parade, but for friends and family alike, accepting this change in behaviour took time. Over the next couple of months there were several attractive matches that I was forced to miss for a variety of reasons; all beyond my and other people's control, but that didn't stop my teenage whining.

The first of which was self inflicted, or rather a nasty injury picked up when playing football in PE at school. I fell awkwardly on my ankle when attempting to tackle someone. I spent the rest of the day struggling to walk and my parents had to take me to A&E after school. I had damaged ligaments in my ankle and would have to use crutches for a month or so. At first this seemed quite exciting and a novelty, although the first couple of occasions at school of someone stealing your crutches and passing them around the classroom to others while you hobbled about after in vain attempt to reclaim them showed there was a downside. I also realised, with horror, that my parents were unlikely to let me stand on the Kop in this state. Sure enough, they said no to going to the next home game, Birmingham. I managed to persuade them in the end though, by saying we would sit in seats. It meant at first experience of watching a game from a different angle as we all sat in the Main Stand to witness a strong Birmingham side batter us incessantly for 90 minutes, though we held out for a 0-0 draw.

The following week was away at Tranmere, a match I had earmarked as one we could go to. Unfortunately, Stephen and Alan couldn't afford it while David, who had missed the Birmingham match, had recently started a Saturday job. It was a role he managed to stick for around a month, which saw him miss several matches. He returned 'to action' triumphantly declaring that "Saturday's are for football, not working."

Still this left me with a problem, as I had no one to go to Tranmere with. I was prepared to go on my own but, still on crutches, my parents said I had to find someone to go with. I spent the Friday before asking every friend at school if they wanted to go – even ones who didn't like football, let alone Bradford City. My efforts failed dismally and I was forced to miss the trip. Although after City feebly lost 3-1, prompting Jewell to apologise to those fans who made the trip, it was probably a good thing that I had to stay at home.

The following week was another biggie, but one I was also going to miss. Man City was in town and it was a fixture I was desperate to attend. However, Saturday 28 March 1998 was also the day my Grandma and Grandpa were holding a 50th Wedding Anniversary bash. I knew there was no way I could even ask if I could miss that one, but that didn't stop me complaining about my rotten luck. I can only feel embarrassed, looking back, at the way I must have sulked that day. Fortunately, it was just my parents who had to bare the brunt of it and, while my grandparents were aware of my huge 'sacrifice', I didn't make a big deal of it in front of them. Still, there was someone who had it worse. My uncle Peter, a distant relative I rarely see, had travelled up from his home in Long Eaton and missed his beloved Notts County's match. It may have been March, but County had run away with the 3rd Division and their win this afternoon sealed promotion! I can almost imagine he was, for once, hoping County would lose, so he didn't miss the party. It was another 13 years before County achieved another promotion, I wonder if at times he cursed this double-booking!

When I heard that City had come from behind to beat Man City 2-1, I felt mixed emotions. A great result, but I had missed what sounded like a rousing second half fight back and goals from Edinho and Nigel Pepper. Still, missing my grandparents' celebrations would have been unthinkable. And while I was immature about the situation then, I would still be cringing now if I had made the wrong choice that afternoon.

But still worse was to come. The next home game was against Nottingham Forest, runaway leaders and another of the 'glamour' fixtures. I was forced to listen to the game – a 3-0 home loss – on Talksport Radio, 100 or so miles away on holiday in Wales. My parents had decided to book us a weekend break to Llandudno, but it was fair to say my mind was elsewhere. I had at least been fortunate enough to attend the away game at Norwich City sandwiched in between the Man City and Forest games. Geoffrey Richmond had laid on free coach travel for those who bought match tickets - something he seemed to do from time to time for no real reason - and we had taken advantage, being rewarded with our first City away win, with three goals scored quickly either side of half time. Norwich, looking over its shoulders at the relegation zone, pulled two goals back but we held on.

As for my parents, they were learning the hard way that my new found love was not some passing fad. Three days of me complaining and looking glum in Llandudno was enough to tell them that future weekends away would have to be planned after consulting the fixture list.

It's also good that they were married in June as there won't be any issues celebrating their 50th wedding anniversary in a few years time.

Crewe (away) and Portsmouth (home) – my short-lived radio career and an impatient summer

In my first season watching Bradford City and live football I was learning many new things. I had learned that food on sale at grounds is ridiculously overpriced and poor quality, to yell "woooooooah...you fat bastard!" when the opposition goalkeeper takes a goal kick in front of the Kop and to buy the Yorkshire Sports (pink paper) and brilliant fanzine 'The City Gent' for in-depth news and views. At the end of April I would also learn that, despite the efforts we supporters will go to in following our team, players will not always fully appreciate it by matching with effort.

Once my GCSEs were over I had a long summer before I planned to enrol in sixth form at the same school. My parents had encouraged me to get a summer job and my dad, who is a train enthusiast, had seen an advert for summer staff to work on the Keighley and Worth Valley Railway. Although the railway is run by volunteers, they had to take on some paid staff during the summer to guarantee the railway could be open every day. I applied for a job and quickly heard I'd got an interview; this is where the problems started, it was on the morning of Saturday 28 April – the same day we were due to play Crewe away.

I had already spoken a lot, to those who have to listen to my ramblings, about going to Crewe; it was the last away match of the season and I was still feeling sore from the number of games I had recently had to miss. My dad, sensing another few weeks of me complaining, took pity and arranged to take a day's holiday so that he could drive me straight to Crewe after the interview, in time for the game. I arranged to meet Stephen, Alan and David there, as they took the coach. My mum and Kevin also came along and they would all find something to do in Crewe while I went to the game. For my dad – a train enthusiast, remember – a trip to Crewe was probably a bonus as it is a famous place in railway circles. So we got up early that morning, I went to the interview (which went okay and I later found out I had got the job) after which we went straight to Gresty Road as fast as we could; arriving around 2pm and meeting up with the others.

So that was all the lengths that I – and the rest of my family – had gone in enabling me to attend this fixture; you would think the least we could expect in return was for the players to put in the required effort. How we and all the other City fans present were badly let down, 20 minutes – 1-0 Crewe, 25 minutes – 2-0 Crewe, 30 minutes 3-0 Crewe and a desperate Jewell makes an early substitution in an effort to shake things up, 40 minutes – 4-0 Crewe. It was depressing viewing, City were awful and didn't seem to care. Crewe, just like us comfortably in mid table, ran us ragged. At half time, an upset Jewell ordered his players out of the dressing room to spend the interval sitting on the pitch in the centre circle. It was a bizarre sight, which had the Crewe fans laughing. In the away end, meanwhile, we simply booed them.

There was at least a slight improvement after half time, but Crewe quickly made it 5-0. A few fights broke out in the away end as City supporters clashed about something; some players were subject to terrible abuse. All in all it was a depressing afternoon which left me wondering why we had made such an effort to see it. I was pleased to have been there, in a way, as it meant I had now seen my first disgraceful moment – Jewell yet again apologised to us fans – and could claim to have followed City through some bad times. True, it hardly compared to the years of lower league football that longer-suffering supporters had endured, but it was a start. "Glory supporter? You should have seen the Crewe game."

In fact, I had no idea at the time, but the players' half time centre circle sit down was to prove a key moment in City's history. Geoffrey Richmond, watching and despairing from the Crewe director's box, was so impressed by the stance that Jewell had taken in forcing the team back on to the pitch so early, it convinced him to give the about-to-be-out-of-contract manager a new two-year deal.

The final game of the season also saw a defeat – but one which was relatively painless. Opponents Portsmouth needed to win to avoid relegation. Man City was their main rivals and the idea of the Maine Road club getting relegated had us laughing. We wanted City to win of course, but if defeat condemned Man City to the drop we would hardly be too devastated.

Soon 3-0 down, we all stopped caring about City's own failings and applauded the opposition. Portsmouth is a club I have a huge amount of respect for as their fans are simply amazing. For this game, around 6,000 Pompey fans had made the long trip North. They made an amazing racket all afternoon and their side responded superbly. News came through that Man City were winning 5-2, but the final score at Valley Parade (1-3) meant they were relegated.

At the final whistle both sets of fans ran onto the pitch. There was no trouble; it was all friendly although stewards kept both sides apart. The four of us felt nervous watching the fans run on, but as so many charged over the advertising boards and the stewards did little to stop them, we became brave enough to go on ourselves. The feeling of actually standing on the Valley Parade turf, with the four stands around you, was very special. Walking down Midland Road to get the train after, there was a sea of fans from both clubs and the atmosphere was great.

The four of us caught the train home and got off, as usual, in Keighley to catch the bus. As it was a Sunday, we had to wait for an hour until the next bus was due, so we sat in the sun and David listened to the Arsenal game on his walkman – a 4-0 win over Everton confirming them as champions, much to David's glee. Me, I sat there feeling a little depressed. The season was now over and there were three long months ahead before we would be going to Valley Parade again. I reflected on the last few months, where I had discovered Valley Parade. In an instant my life had been transformed, I'd made the ultimate football fan 'don't do' of switching allegiances. I had learned all about a new squad of players, acquired new heroes. I had travelled to watch City play at Man City, Sheffield United, Norwich City and Crewe. I had seen City thrill and excite, I had seen City disappoint and frustrate. The season had ended with four defeats and a draw from the final five games, meaning most fans were glad to see the back of it. But for me, only 'joining' in November, I didn't feel ready for my summer break.

The sensible side of me knew it was a good thing; in less than two weeks I would be sitting my first GCSE and being distracted by the ups and downs of the football season wasn't exactly the best way to prepare. My parents were also moving house, just down the road in Sutton, meaning I would be living closer to David. I knew we would be back in a few months, as we had all purchased season tickets on the Kop for the 1998-99 campaign. Added to the fact it was World Cup year, meaning football to watch on TV for a month or so, I tried not to be despondent at the reality of a summer absent of Saturday journeys to Valley Parade, though it was almost impossible not to feel empty.

Chapter Four

1998 - 99
Gloriously inexpensive

There's nothing like the satisfaction of a bargain. And if we think hard about it, all of us can probably find something we have purchased in the past and view it to be one of the best things we ever bought. It might be due to the amount of joy it subsequently provided, how long we were able to use it for or how little we had to pay for it. Purchases I will always be grateful I made include the pair of DJ record decks when I was 21; my copy of Oasis' Definitely Maybe album; the entry fee into a nightclub where I would get together with my future wife; my concert ticket to see New Order in 2002 – though that was a freebie. Top of the list and ticking all of those boxes above, however, would be the Bradford City season ticket I purchased on the Kop for the 1998-99 season.

As I was enrolling in Sixth Form at South Craven School, I qualified for a student season ticket. This concession meant that it cost a mere £66. With entry to the 23 home games, it worked out at under £3 per game. Alan, who was still under 16, was able to buy a junior season ticket for just £19 (£1.21 per game)! This was to be an unforgettable season on the pitch, ending with promotion to the top flight for the first time in 77 years and featuring some of the best football to have ever been seen ay Valley Parade. To pay a mere £66 for the privilege represented astonishing value. Have you ever bought something for that price and had as much pleasure, providing a collection of memories that still keep you warm over a decade later?

But that's what lower league football should always be, affordable. The product is not as enticing as the Premier League, but understanding this and being realistic means the Football League can position itself as a fantastic alternative. Even allowing for subsequent inflation since 1998, £66 is a truly remarkable figure. And when you compare it to season ticket and match day prices for the 2009/10 Premier League season it shows how out of reach live football at this level is for adults, juniors and students (indeed student season tickets are largely a thing of the past, even City no longer do them). At Chelsea for example, a match-day ticket can cost as much as £65 – just £1 cheaper than my 23-game season ticket of 1998/99. The top end of Arsenal's season ticket prices are £1,825, the cheapest season ticket price at newly-promoted Wolves was £522. To have a season ticket at Manchester United could have cost me as much as £931. However it's not all bad, with Bolton Wanderers offering £49 season tickets for juniors. Helping to ensure at least youngsters in one part of the country can grow up watching some of the world's best players.

Bradford City has not always offered the cheapest prices, and at times I've struggled to afford to attend. However in 2007 it launched an innovative season ticket offer which saw adult season tickets priced just £138. At time where gates had fallen drastically, it helped to increase attendances just as City began life in League Two.

And that should be the point. Of course lower league clubs, more than their Premier League counterparts, rely on ticket income; but is it better to have high prices and lots of empty seats, or to charge less and make the club more accessible to the community? While City took the latter route, our neighbours Leeds kept ticket prices very high when they slumped. Ken Bates argued they generate more money from fewer fans paying the high prices, and it can certainly be argued City's on-going slump in League Two might have ended sooner by bringing in more revenue from higher ticket prices to give the manager a larger budget.

But that is effectively taking advantage of the most loyal fans, who'll pay anything, while excluding those who they should be trying to entice. And lower league clubs need to be wary of going too far the way of Bates. Premier League clubs are able to get away with charging obscene prices, because there is the cushion of huge amounts of TV revenue to allow for a few empty seats, and the loyalty of their fan base to pay whatever they ask, even if they grumble about it loudly.

So this is where lower league clubs can entice these people, especially youngsters. Easily affordable ticket prices, a great atmosphere and decent standard of football right on the doorstep. If subsequent failure on the pitch can be put down to not charging supporters enough through tickets, I think it's a failure worth having because eventually the club will get it right. And, just like me and my £66 season ticket, those who'll be there to witness it are unlikely to ever forget it.

A Richmond kid

As I handed over the cash for this golden season ticket towards the end of the 1997-98 season, I truly became a Richmond kid. The Bradford City chairman is able to claim partial credit for enticing me to Valley Parade in the first place, as under his stewardship City had risen to Division One and games with higher profile opposition. I do believe that, had I discovered Valley Parade and City had been a struggling Division Two side, I would still have been captivated. The quality of the football certainly helped me turn to City, but it was the live atmosphere, brilliant stadium and goals that really got me hooked. They would all have existed regardless of whether Richmond had been in charge and City were still a lower league club.

However Richmond certainly deserves to take a huge slice of credit for winning me over. The fact that entry was so affordable was down to him. As I read a leaflet advertising season tickets, it was astonishing to learn the club had not raised prices for five years. In 1994, City were a mid-table Division Two side, yet here they now were in Division One with ambitions to get promoted to the Premiership. The policy of low prices meant growing crowds and a great atmosphere. When the entertainment was so high, what excuse was there not to go when it was so affordable? Given the fact crowds had tripled from 1994 its fair to say I was not the only Richmond kid. Long term beliefs that the City of Bradford and local district generally cared little about having a football team were being dispelled. People were coming to Valley Parade in their droves and getting remarkable value for money.

Not that is always looked like that. The poor end to the 1997/98 season had meant there was some discontent among supporters and many eyebrows were raised when Richmond gave Paul Jewell the full time manager position. Given how badly City had finished, it had been widely assumed that Jewell had not done enough to warrant an extension, and awarding him a two-year contract was seen by some as a cheap appointment that lacked ambition. Although that view would quickly be proved wrong by the events over the summer.

Largely unbeknown to most City fans, changes were taking place at boardroom that saw Professor David Rhodes, a local businessman who had built a huge fortune with his electronics company Filtronic, and his son Julian, join the club and immediately invest £3 million for team strengthening. So began a busy summer with seven new faces joining the squad.

The first new signing was arguably the most significant. After beginning at City in the 80s, Stuart McCall had gone onto enjoy a glittering career with Everton and Glasgow Rangers, winning a haul of medals at Rangers and earning 40 caps for Scotland. Now 34 and coming towards the end of his career, Stuart had decided to leave Rangers and move back to England. He was a hugely popular person with supporters and rumours of him rejoining City had been floating around almost since the day he left in 1988. Stuart's return would prove to be hugely successful, and it meant that one of City's most popular players would also become a legend to a new generation of supporters.

Stuart was quickly followed by former Rangers teammate Stephen Wright; from Crewe, we signed former Man United defender Ashley Westwood and academy product Gareth Whalley; from Southampton left back Lee Todd. All of these players had either come in on frees or for modest transfer fees, offering no indication of the huge sums of money about to be spent. Just before the season kicked off, that changed as Lee Mills was signed from Port Vale – becoming City's transfer record signing. He was the first £1 million City player and the second, Arsenal rookie Isaiah Rankin, followed just a few days later for another new record of £1.3 million. Whether you were a seasoned supporter of many years or about to begin your first full season supporting the club, these events came as a major shock.

After such a torturous wait for the season to start; me, Stephen and Alan decided to go to the first friendly, away at local non-league side Farsley Celtic. It involved catching two buses to Keighley and then Rodley. The journey was around an hour and then involved a walk up a big hill to the ground. After the game we were faced with the same long journey. We got back home very late but, after watching City win 3-1, I went to bed feeling relieved. A significant point in the build up to the new season had been reached and the wait for the proper games felt that bit nearer. We also went to home friendlies against Preston and Derby.

Unfortunately for me though, my season was to hit another stall. My parents had booked the usual two weeks for us to go away on holiday, which was always the first two weeks of August. This meant I would miss the opening few games and the first opportunity to use my season ticket. We were down in Cornwall and I was left to buy the paper each day for scraps of information about City. Unfortunately for my poor parents, this combination of missing the games and struggle to keep in touch meant I spent most of the holiday in a bad mood.

In truth I didn't miss much, the season began with a surprise 2-1 home defeat to Stockport, underwhelming League Cup home draw with Lincoln and 1-0 loss at Watford – leaving us near the bottom. It was early days, but hardly encouraging. Still as we eventually made our way home from holiday I was feeling slightly better and more excited. I would be attending next weekend's home game with Bolton and nine months of football lied in front of me. For me, the season was finally kicking off...

Birmingham (home) – beating the blues

It's the August bank holiday and we're walking the usual path from Forster Square railway station to Valley Parade for a home game with Birmingham City. While I usually do this walk in excitement and anticipation, today I was feeling miserable and full of dread. Three days earlier we had disappointingly lost at Crewe as the miserable start to the season continued. That came after the home game with Bolton, an encouraging 2-2 draw where we had twice come from behind with first league goals from our new strikers Isaiah Rankin and Lee Mills. The Crewe result felt like a massive set back which left me feeling really concerned about the team's prospects, as the early league table showed us near the bottom. We wanted to exit this division, but not that way.

Things weren't looking good and the pressure was growing on manager Paul Jewell. I met Alan, Stephen and David at the bus stop as usual as we headed for the Birmingham game and their first words were the excitement that Kenny Dalglish had just been sacked by Newcastle and that we should replace Jewell with the dour Scot. Apart from how ludicrous it sounded to think Dalglish would come and manage City, I thought the idea was terrible given how he had turned the Magpies into a dull and miserable side. I also didn't want us to sack Jewell, especially after just four games.

With Birmingham heavily fancied for promotion and the memory of their impressive display at Valley Parade last season still fresh, I expected them to continue their excellent start and consign City to another defeat. It was hard to see how we could win and it was the last fixture needed at this stage. It hardly left me feeling in confident mood and I was bracing myself for another defeat which I knew would be hard to take.

Fifty-five minutes into the game, those fears were being realised. After an even first half, Peter Nndlovu put Birmingham into the lead and they looked set for three points. Then, remarkably, City turned it round. First Lee Mills headed home from a corner on the hour mark and then, with 15 minutes on the clock, Darren Moore headed the ball powerfully into the net from another set piece. Despite late pressure, we held on for a win that just might get our season going. It clearly meant a lot to everyone, including the players. At the final whistle, Gary Walsh come over to us behind the Kop and threw his gloves into the crowd.

It was fair to say the journey home was happier than that to the game. It wasn't a great performance, but the fact we had beaten a very good side gave us all a huge lift. It didn't prove to be the end of our poor start – a 3-0 defeat away at Ipswich followed – but even this defeat didn't feel as bad as the Crewe one had done. I was more confident the team was capable of playing better football and winning matches. The word relegation had been uttered before kick off against Birmingham; it wouldn't be heard again all season.

Away from Valley Parade, things were changing for me as I began life in the Sixth form. It was quite a change from my previous experience of attending school. We no longer had to wear uniform, and we now had a common room (called the Sixth Form Lounge) which featured comfy chairs, stereo, tuck shop and vending machines. Instead of the wide range of subjects we were taught for GCSEs, we got to choose two or three to concentrate on. We all had the novelty of free periods and leaving school early if the last lesson of the day was a free period. Most satisfyingly, a lot of the idiots that blighted school life didn't stay on. None of the bullies or troublemakers enrolled, nor some of the biggest mickey takers and, at the same time, most of the swots and people who got picked on by others also never came back.

What was left was the middle range of people and a more relaxed atmosphere followed. We each had our groups which 'owned' parts of the Lounge. Without the previous separations (half of the year did French and classes were never mixed with the other half, who were taught German) there were friendships to make with the new students. The teachers also began to treat us differently, and were much more relaxed and prepared to have a laugh. I enrolled to do GNVQ Media Studies and an A Level in English Language. Only six of us took the Media Studies course, which meant we built a really nice close-knit group where we all became good friends.

In view of how happy we were during these next two years, what was happening with Bradford City only added to how brilliant life felt. Hints at what special times were coming emerged during my first few weeks in Sixth Form as the expensively assembled team began to gel and play better. The next home game was against Sheffield United and, after conceding a really poor opening goal, we played some excellent football to lead 2-1 with goals from Robbie Blake and Mills. Sheffield United did equalise in the second half to leave City still with just one win, but I walked out of Valley Parade feeling even more confident about our chances.

The following week we were away at West Brom and, despite the game being live on Sky, the four of us made our first away trip of the season. There were barely 200 other fans who did the same, but how we were rewarded. West Brom was another team well-fancied, but 15 minutes into the game Mills had struck twice to give us a 2-0 lead. No more goals followed, and our first away win of the season was earned after a very professional display. I had asked my mate to tape the Sky coverage and when I watched it back the pundits in the studio agreed we had played like Play Off candidates.

The Barnsley home game, the Saturday after, was one of those once-in-a-lifetime moments and easily my best City game so far. During midweek we had completed a two-leg Worthington Cup win over Halifax Town and the draw for the third round took place while we were making our way to the game, excitedly chatting about who we hoped City would get in the third round; the first choice unanimous – Leeds United. We met David outside the ground, as he was already in Bradford as part of a friend's stag do, and he told us the first piece of great news of the day, we HAD drawn Leeds away! We arrived on the Kop to a noticeable buzz and anti-Leeds chants going around – clearly we weren't the only excited fans. We instantly agreed we were going to the game, no doubt about it.

Having just come down from the Premier League, Barnsley were still a good team and took the lead early in the second half through Ashley Ward (more of him later). Despite the setback we kept attacking and began to really get on top. Barnsley were reduced to ten men after a horrible challenge on Peter Beagrie, who was looking especially threatening. With a man down Barnsley left the attacking line empty, save for Ward, and so Paul Jewell moved Stuart McCall back to right back allowing him to dictate play from his own half nearly unchallenged. Despite laying siege in the closing stages, it appeared as though they were going to hold out. By now we were playing with four strikers as Blake was pushed forward and Rankin and Gordon Watson came on. Watson had broken his leg 18 months earlier and was slowly making his return to fitness with a few sub appearances. Right in front of us in the Kop, he was able to release some of that frustration by firing in a late equaliser.

Wild celebrations followed, we'd saved a point.

45

Incredibly there was more to come as the players continued to pour forward. Blake went on a jinxing run, cut inside and shot from distance. The keeper could only parry the shot into the path of Watson, who gleefully rammed the ball into the net. In my short time supporting City, I had celebrated some great goals and gone crazy, but none had carried as much drama and significance as this one. I can't really remember the celebrations too much, all I know is I completely lost it along with everyone around me. We all went all jumping on each other, hugging strangers and screaming for joy at the top of our voices. In one moment I lost any sense of what was around me, what was going on and probably even where I was.

To go from staring defeat in the face to unbridled joy in the space of two minutes is something I will never forget. I've experienced bigger victories and celebrated wilder since, but this game is one that will always make my top five all time City games. Two goals at the end, celebrations more manic than I had ever being part of before, a City win AND we were going to play Leeds in the Cup. It took a long time to come down from the clouds.

Many supporters looking back on this season point to this game as the turning point. They are probably right, although the win and performance against West Brom was probably the moment were it turned for the players. Still just a couple of hundred of us had been there to witness it. The incredible fightback against Barnsley was seen by all and meant that we supporters could realistically start to believe that a play off spot was a realistic objective. Now bring on the Leeds...

Huddersfield Town (away) – the ugly side of football support

Sometimes it just isn't your day. A series of events seem to conspire against you, leaving you wishing you had never got out of bed that morning. We all experience days like this when it seems no matter what you try to do you fail in some way.

When this sort of day happens while going to the football, you know you're in for some trying times. That sort of luck befell the four of us on Saturday 18 November 1998 as we attended the West Yorkshire derby away at Huddersfield. Part of the bad day was due to my poor planning and there was a degree of naivety with lessons to be learned. It was events during the 90 minutes which ultimately shaped our mood and perspective, although give our experiences before and after it was easy to feel some form of responsibility for City suffering a painful defeat.

Living where we did in relation to Huddersfield and Bradford; I felt it made no sense for us to travel to Bradford to get the supporters' coach to get to the game. It was out of our way and would have cost a lot more. We would have had to set off earlier and be home later. Throughout all of our time following City, it has fallen on me to organise our journeys to and from away matches. I decided it was best to catch a bus to Keighley and then change to one which goes straight to Huddersfield. We set off in good time, so there were no worries about being late for kick off. But none of us were quite prepared for how long and how boring the journey between Keighley and Huddersfield would be. As buses do, it stopped off at lots of places and didn't take the quickest route. What would be a 30-45 minute car journey took an hour and a half. We all normally took our walkmans' on City away trips, but given how short the trip apparently was going to be, there seemed no need to do so for this game.

The long journey hardly put us in the most excitable moods, but we eventually pulled into Huddersfield bus station. The second mistake we made was wearing our City shirts with little thought of where we were going. This wasn't really an issue on the way, although we were certainly attracting some funny looks as we wandered through the town centre in the direction of the stadium, which could be seen clearly from a distance. We arrived in good time, found our seats with the players warming up and joined in with the chanting in what was a great atmosphere of a sell out away following, with kick off approaching.

City dominated the first half, creating chance after chance. Crucially, we only scored once. Robbie Blake latched onto a Peter Beagrie pass to finish coolly. City should have scored a hatful as they continued to dominate; the Huddersfield keeper Nico Vasen made some great stops while others, notably Isaiah Rankin, missed some sitters. As the second half progressed we were still well on top, but with just a one goal lead we were always susceptible.

Then, with 15 minutes to go, Huddersfield equalised. Major disappointment for us. Worse was to come as, horror upon horrors, two minutes later they scored again. It was incredible to have dominated a match and suddenly be behind. In the final stages we once again laid siege to Vasen's goal and he made an incredible save in injury time to deny Darren Moore. The home side were undeserved victors and we walked out of the ground disgusted, with disappointment etched on our faces. We headed towards the bus station, while other City fans went to the train station or supporters' coaches. As we moaned about our team's lack of killer instinct, I suddenly became aware that a group of people were following us closely, with menacing grins on their faces.

We got to the bus station and had 10 minutes to wait for our bus. There were a lot of people around luckily, with the group that were following us having seemingly disappeared. Before the bus came though, they reappeared. There were over 10 of them and we suddenly found ourselves subjected to a barrage of coins. There was no where to run and no where to hide. We could only stand there and try to dodge coins, hopelessly outnumbered and without any help. Fortunately, some police appeared eventually and scared the group off. We were mightily relieved when the bus showed up and felt embarrassed that there hadn't been anything we could do to retaliate. None of us were the type to fight and I was thankful that they could have done worse to us and we would have suffered badly. Wearing your club's colours in your local rivals' town centre is clearly asking for trouble, a lesson that none of us would quickly forget was taken on board.

On the bus ride home a young attractive woman got on and sat near us. In an attempt to brighten our moods, me and Dave got the confidence to start talking to her. When she asked what we had been up to that day, we said we had been to the football not thinking she would be interested. She then saw the City shirts and began pointing and laughing that we had lost and singing "Huddersfield". Chance of pulling for either of us quickly gone, thank goodness it was her stop soon after. We pretended not to look, but I think we all saw her laughing and giving us the V sign as the bus drove off.

A horrible match, an awful journey to and from. We sat there feeling fed up and cursing that the bus ride would still be at least another hour. What else can go wrong? At the next stop, a female got on and walked over to sit near us. I don't think any of us thought much but then we quickly did a double take. There was a knee length black dress, boots and a crop top; make up and ear rings too. But it was no female - it was a transvestite. 'She' decided to sit near us, no doubt to grab our attention. After such a weird and horrible day, this began to feel surreal. Still at least here was some light relief! We all began to laugh quite loudly, at the sight of him (sorry her), at our luck today and at what else could possibly happen this day.

The bus eventually arrived in Keighley, though naturally we narrowly missed our connecting bus. And while all of us were desperate to get home and end this horrible day, we at least had a smile on our faces as we reflected on everything we'd experienced that day. Lessons in transport, lessons in looking inconspicuous, lessons that in football you don't always get what you deserve and lessons that a tranny on a bus can lighten up even the most depressing of days!

Despite that misery, the autumn/winter of 1998 was one where we were all immensely happy. Stephen was one of the people to leave South Craven School and had enrolled at Shipley College, where lessons were much slower and there were people more like him to make friends with. Alan was enjoying life rising up the years at South Craven School, taking on three paper rounds at once to earn lots of money. David was in a decent job at a bank where he was happy, with a good set of friends.

And right there in the middle of our lives was going to watch City every weekend. After the amazing Barnsley win, City's form really took off and they won their next two home games 4-0 and 3-0 against Port Vale and Bury respectively. In between was a creditable 0-0 draw at leaders and eventual champions Sunderland. We went up to the game, of course, during the first half of the season we were going to away games regularly. We also went to Grimsby, a disappointing 2-0 loss, the only defeat in a run of 12 league games up to losing at Huddersfield. Some of the football we produced was really exciting to watch and with each passing week hopes of the play offs began to rise. At the end of October we demolished a poor Bristol City side 5-0 at Valley Parade. There were some great goals that day which helped propel us into the top six for the first time.

There was also that big League Cup tie at Elland Road. We went to the game and were part of 5,500 away following which made an incredible atmosphere. Sat in another stand nearby were my dad and Kevin. It was Kevin's first Leeds United match; putting up with an excitable big brother bragging he was going to the big game must have made him jealous. My dad, who was reluctantly learning to tolerate football with me and Kevin's passion showing no signs of dying, took him to the game as he was too young to go by himself. Kevin later told me Dad didn't enjoy the game and was the only 'home supporter' not to stand up and cheer when Leeds scored the game's only goal. It hurt to lose, but it was still a night where you could be proud of the players and chuffed to have been part of a special atmosphere.

The players kept up the league form with some impressive wins, particularly at home. In an effort to boost crowds, Richmond had decided to run the quid-a-kid scheme for the games with Bristol City and Swindon. Almost exactly a year after I was first enticed to Valley Parade, it was nice to know that there were others who were probably experiencing their first taste of Bradford City. It helped me to feel less the new boy and more established – something I was desperate to be.

I had some friends come along for these matches too, a few Leeds fans who were interested in coming with Leeds playing away whenever City were at home. For a very temporary time, going to Valley Parade became one of our sixth form social activities. The fact that the two quid-a-kid offerings saw City score eight without reply (they beat Swindon 3-0 after those five against Bristol), helped the floaters enjoy their day. It peaked with the QPR home game the week after that awful Huddersfield defeat. This game was also the last occasion the full Kop would be open with work due to commence on turning it into an all-seater stand (for the rest of the season only half of it would be open as building work took place behind). It proved an unfitting end, as City struggled to get going against a team battling relegation, missed some sitters and then conceded three second half goals. With over 10 minutes still on the clock, the Kop rapidly emptied. We stayed to the end but it wasn't the happy occasion we all hoped it would be. No final goals were scored in front of the Kop.

Hot on the heels of the Huddersfield defeat, there were predictions from some that the emphatic home defeat to Rangers had meant City's bubble had burst; instead these defeats would trigger a fantastic run of form and help Jewell put together the final piece of the jigsaw that could lead us to the Premiership. In both the Huddersfield and QPR defeats, Rankin had been guilty of missing sitters. Jewell now took action and dropped our record signing. In place, he moved Blake from out wide to up front with Lee Mills – and the best strike partnership I have ever seen at City was up and running. Between them, the pair would score 15 of City's next 17 goals.

The great football story

Whenever I reflect back on the 1998-99 season – which I still do quite regularly – I think about what a great football story it was; the kind that all football fans can appreciate. Promotions always make for good stories, but City's was littered with heroes and interesting angles.

A small club not expected to be capable of challenging for a place in the Premiership, a popular chairman with the vision and leadership to plot the challenge, a loyal club servant given the opportunity to manage and prove to be a huge success. The hero-worshipped former captain and legend returns to the club which launched his career to lead them beyond what was achieved in his first spell. Money is stumped for signings and spent well, a close knit squad with great spirit, terrific ability and hardworking attitude. Things didn't start well, prompting some supporters to criticise the manager, chairman and players. But then it's turned around and the club climb the division playing some wonderful attacking football. The majority of signings work out while others step up and prove their ability. Crowds go up and the volume of support remains loud as the fans get behind their heroes.

If the autumn of 1998 was about City clawing back from their bad start to threaten a play off push, the winter saw them take it further with some dazzling football climbing the Bantams to the automatic promotion places. Suddenly a place in the play offs, which everyone was hoping for at the start of the season, would be considered a disappointment as automatic promotion was achievable. It was a team effort, which naturally fits in with the great football story, although during the winter months it was City's two forwards who really come to the fore.

After the QPR defeat, City came back from away trips to Oxford and Swindon with 1-0 and 4-1 wins respectively – all goals coming from strikers Lee Mills and Robbie Blake. The week after, we faced Wolves at home and Blake had his finest game I had seen to date; his dribbling skills came to the fore and the ball seemed to be tied to string on the end of his boot. He wasn't the quickest, but his clever feet meant he was a handful. After scoring the opening goal he burst through on goal just after half time only to see his shot well saved and the ball roll towards the corner flag. Instead of standing there with head in hands, however, Robbie was off chasing the ball. He picked it up, cut inside and beat another player before pulling the ball back to Mills who blasted it home. Wolves pulled a goal back through Robbie Keane, but City held on to move up to third.

A 0-0 draw at Bolton followed on a cold Boxing Day afternoon, with Mills suspended; City then beat Tranmere 2-0, Grimsby in the FA Cup 2-1. Going to games was such a pleasure and between the four of us we were desperate to get to every match. This became a game of one-up-man-ship and I was left very disappointed at missing going to Oxford and Bolton away due to finances. By now I had a lowly paid job working for an after school club, which looked after children for a couple of hours in the evening until their parents finished work. I worked one night a week which meant I received very low pay. I also still had my paper round, but the cost of going to football meant I never really had any money. We had gone to a flurry of away games at the start of the season, but I was now struggling to keep pace.

Oxford away was £15 coach travel alone, something well beyond someone who was making barely £40 a month. So it was with great reluctance that when we made the trip to the ticket office before the QPR game, I was the only one not to purchase tickets for the following weekend's game. With the one-up-man-ship mentality displayed by Alan in particular, I was to be reminded about it quite a bit. This may be a male thing as, among the group of us, a slightly competitive element about who was the most committed supporter was growing. This was judged by how often we went and the fact I had missed quite a couple more games than the rest over the last year meant I was lagging behind.

So it was doubly hard listening to the Oxford game on the radio, knowing that behind the goal where Mills scored were Alan, Stephen and David going crazy. I also missed going with them to Bolton, but at least went to the next away game at Stockport. The short journey made travel affordable and we had a great afternoon stood on the away terrace cheering on City to a 2-1 win they probably didn't deserve. We scored two crackers from Blake and Peter Beagrie, with Stockport equalising in between and bombarding us in the second half. Although it was sunny, it was a bitterly cold afternoon and we were all grateful for Beagrie's winner which kept us warmer through celebrating. After that win came the Crewe 4-1 thrashing, when Mills scored a hat trick and Blake scored one of my favourite ever City goals. Picking up the ball deep, he dribbled past a couple of players before unleashing a magnificent curling effort into the top corner.

The level of organisation in the City team wasn't like anything I'd seen before or since. Every player went onto the field knowing exactly what their job was, and they attacked and defended as a team. Mills might be getting all the goals for example, but he was also a key player in defending corners. Playing 4-4-2 with two out-and-out wingers guaranteed excitement every week. When Beagrie picked up the ball out wide you could sense the ripple of excitement across the stadium. Stuart McCall's vision and non-stop work-rate pulled the strings. It was an exceptional team to watch, producing eye-catching passing football throughout.

Incredibly, that win lifted us to second. On the Tuesday after we faced Crystal Palace at home, a game in hand which meant we could go four points clear. Palace was struggling so it looked a home banker; yet 10 minutes into the second half, they scored in front of the Kop – now the nerves were jangling. If our rise from a low league position in September to 2nd had been hugely enjoyable, this evening was to be the first taste of the anxiety we would experience during the battles ahead. We now had automatic promotion hopes and this was a crucial game. We battled on, but didn't create much and the tension grew as Palace went 1-0 up.

With 15 minutes to go, we equalised. A corner was swung in and Ashley Westwood got on the end for his first City goal. At least a point had been saved we thought, but it still felt disappointing. City began to get on top and force some pressure; Rankin came on as sub and proved difficult for Palace to deal with. The pitch was a mess from the heavy rain and players were slipping over. Deep in stoppage time, the ball was pinged about in the Palace area. Rankin picked up the ball, tried to find space for a shot and was pulled down. "Penalty!!!" we screamed, and the referee answered us by pointing to the spot. Now the tension was at boiling point. We all took a deep breath, some probably not daring to look. Beagrie ran up, fired the ball into the left-hand corner and the keeper went the wrong way. Cue wild celebrations with an overriding sense of relief. As we filed out of the Kop and walked to the train station I knew I had just experienced a taste of the emotional roller-coaster that was ahead in the next few months.

We were now four points clear in second place, a position beyond our wildest dreams. It suddenly felt serious and that every game between now and May was going to test the nerves.

Huddersfield Town (home) – the run in, and how not to impress a woman

I didn't need much of an excuse to think about football, but as the season entered its closing stages it dominated my thoughts more than ever. I knew the rest of our fixture list off by heart; I also had a good idea of who our promotion rivals – Ipswich, Bolton and Birmingham – were playing each week. In my head I tried to predict our final few results and the other three. Of course we would ultimately triumph in my biased view, just as supporters of those three teams would have managed to calculate their team celebrating come May. The enjoyment factor of going to games was naturally suffering with the result so important. For players that too was probably the case, and suddenly it became a matter of grinding out results rather than playing sparkling football. Every goal scored and conceded suddenly mattered that little bit more. The stakes were high and the thought of disappointment at the end was too much to contemplate.

New signings arrived to bolster the squad's strength – striker Dean Windass from Oxford for just under £1 million and winger Lee Sharpe on loan from Leeds although the player had been cooling his heels on loan at Sampdoria before coming to Valley Parade. Over the Easter weekend they both proved their worth, Sharpe scored on his home debut in a 3-0 Easter Saturday win over Grimsby. Despite the scoreline, it was a very nervy display from City which left us all in no doubt that we were now entering the home straight. Two days later Windass netted his first two goals for us at Bury. There was a crowd of 8,000 at Gigg Lane that day, over half of which were us City fans. We packed both stands behind each goal and enjoyed a comfortable win against a team who would be relegated.

Next came another nervy home win, 2-1 against Portsmouth. In the part of the Kop where we stood, around three rows from the front behind the goal, we had made friends with quite a few others. It was typical of the terrace culture and the banter was hugely enjoyable. The four of us were quiet compared to others, but enjoyed being part of it all. For this Portsmouth game, our group were all in agreement that this was a poor performance and agreed not to applaud the players at the end. Looking back, it's embarrassing to think we acted like that. City did at least win the game, even if it was unconvincing, and they needed our support more than ever. Just like us fans, the nerves were clearly getting to them too.

In fact it was impossible for it not to affect your life. I went into school the day after a disappointing 1-1 draw at Port Vale game feeling moody and not wanting to chat to anyone. I lay awake thinking over the final few games and recent performances. It was hard to think of anything else or concentrate on anything. I also wouldn't recommend it as a time for dating.

Back at school, I had become interested in a girl named Louise. She had only joined South Craven School for the 6th Form and was in my form. She was a football fan, although alas, a Leeds supporter. We swapped plenty of banter at school about each other's football team and got on quite well. There seemed to be a spark there, although I wasn't sure. She did however volunteer to come along to a City match with me one weekend. Unfortunately the game she picked was Huddersfield at home.

I decided to travel earlier than Steve, Dave and Alan to the game; so me and Louise could spend time together. We had an enjoyable trip into Bradford and walked around the shops. Everything was going fine. We arrived on the Kop, met the other three after a while and got ready for the kick off. 11 minutes in, this crucial derby match was all going to plan – Robbie Blake got on the end of a huge clearance from Gary Walsh and fired us into the lead. Wild celebrations and relief, the day was going to turn out as I'd hoped. Maybe I'd even get a snog before the day was out.

Then it all went wrong. Huddersfield equalised on 19 minutes through a bizarre Stephen Wright own goal right in front of us. Two minutes later, Wayne Allison got free of Darren Moore and headed home a cross. From 1-0 up, we were 2-1 down and panic set in. A shell shocked City tried to get back in the game, but just before half time Ben Thornley broke clear and headed home a third in front of our disbelieving faces. At least Huddersfield then went down to ten men after Steve Jenkins was sent off, but as the half time whistle our worst nightmares were being realised.

Were we going to blow it? And worst of all were we going to blow it against Huddersfield? I tried to chat to Louise at half time, but I was no longer in a sociable mood. City attacked towards us in the second and, with 15 minutes to go, Sharpe suddenly came to life and began beating the opposition full back with his dribbles. From one of his charges, Windass was able to head home and we were back in it. 13 minutes to go, come on City!

The celebrations were short and quickly turned to anger. As the ball landed in the net, Windass did what all players who have scored to get their team back into the game attempt – run over to retrieve the ball to get the game going again. The Huddersfield keeper, Nico Vassen, who was lying on the floor, tried to stop him getting near it. Rising to his feet and trying to fend off Windass, Vassen suddenly swung his elbow into Deano's face. Deano fell to the ground and those of us behind

56

the goal, with a perfect view, began yelling to the referee to send off Vassen. Incredibly no action was taken and we were livid.

The game restarted and City were soon on the attack. Lee Sharpe swung over another cross and a hand shot up in the area. "Penalty!" we all screamed. The referee pointed to the spot. Now City had the chance to at least salvage a point. Deano stepped up and hit the ball towards the corner, but Vassen dived the right way and pushed it behind for a corner. Devastation quickly turned to anger. I can't say I recall my words or those of people around me, but I'm pretty sure they included the phrase "cheating bastard". With that save came the end of our hopes, there were still 10 minutes to go but players and supporters all seemed to realise that was it. We had lost a crucial game and dropped to third behind Ipswich, with just three games to go.

Once the red mist cleared and gave way to despair, I suddenly remembered Louise was with me and realised she had just witnessed me turn into a lunatic swearing loudly and waving my fist at the pitch – hardly a good way to impress and get the girl. We got off at Keighley Station after the game and Louise stayed on the train to Skipton, despite me asking if she wanted to do something that night. I had lost the girl and City the game. Bloody Huddersfield.

That defeat seemed to have cost us automatic promotion and we were all devastated. Yet the following week came an incredible twist. City travelled to QPR, a match I listened to on the radio at home. Peter Beagrie put us in front midway through the first half, and seven minutes after the break Ashley Westwood scrambled in a second. It was then that my attentions switched more to Ipswich, with their game still 0–0. They were playing Crewe at home, a team firmly rooted to the bottom and on the brink of having relegation sealed. It was a home banker, so how come Ipswich haven't scored yet?

Suddenly some unbelievable news came through, Crewe had taken the lead! There was still half an hour to go but there was real hope we could lift ourselves back to second. 10 minutes later Ipswich equalised and Crewe were reduced to 10 men. The best we could now hope for was for Crewe to hold out and at least Ipswich would have dropped two points. But then more astonishing news came through, Crewe had re-taken the lead! I was now jumping up and down on my bed in disbelief. City ended up winning their game 3-1, and news of the final whistle at Portman Road caused bigger celebration. City were back up to second with only two games to go. Ipswich's run-in looked harder than ours. Automatic promotion was back on.

The following weekend it could have been sealed. We played Oxford United at home, a team who were also on the verge of relegation. Ipswich played on Sunday away at Birmingham, who were in fourth place and looking to seal a play off spot. If we won and Ipswich lost, we were going to the Premiership. The game was also the final occasion where we could stand on the Kop and as I had only done so for barely a year, I couldn't pretend the day carried the emotion it did for others. Nevertheless I was sad to be giving up standing and knew that I was unlikely to see some of the regulars we stood next to ever again.

The game was a nerve-wracking affair. We tried to be patient and wait for City to take the lead, but the goal didn't seem to be coming. I remember constantly looking at the clock on the scoreboard in the second half and worrying how quickly time was passing. City struggled to break down a resolute Oxford, and the visitors looked more likely to score. A draw seemed as useless to Oxford as it did to City; nevertheless they seemed determined to leave Valley Parade with a point and nothing more. Deep into stoppage time, with the game looking over, City finally broke clear on the wing and a cross was swung in towards McCall.

Right in front of us, it looked like the most perfect script had been written.

Incredibly, he headed the ball over the bar; and then dropped to the floor in despair at missing such an easy chance. I think we all felt like joining him. The final whistle blew and a 0-0 draw. Two points dropped, have we blown it this time? We travelled home feeling gloomier than after the Town defeat. 24 hours later though, we would again be high as a kite. The four of us went to the White Bear in Eastburn to watch Ipswich lose 1-0 at Birmingham on Sky, leaving us one point clear with one game to go. It was still in our hands.

Wolves (away) – being part of history

The previous 18 months had seen the friendship between the four of us grow. Spending so many hours going to and from games home and away, standing or sitting alongside each other during matches and sharing the highs and lows; we had learned to celebrate victories and handle defeats together. It was a friendship where nothing major happened in our real lives, but the roller-coaster of watching Bradford City meant we had shared almost every emotion and built up a bond.

Despite this, we didn't especially see a lot of each other away from going to matches. I certainly only ever saw David on match days and might see Alan around school from a distance. Stephen was in my year at school, but had joined Shipley College instead of sixth form. Other than going to the football, most of my leisure time was spent hanging around with other friends. The one time we would see each other more was during the school holidays when we would try to arrange kick-a-bouts in the park.

It was fair to say that Alan and Stephen didn't enjoy playing football as much. I would spend quite a while on the phone trying to persuade them to come along and play. They would reluctantly turn up, but look miserable and struggle to perform well. Alan in particular began to grow wary of the phone ringing if it was a sunny afternoon during the holidays.

One one such day during the Easter holidays, he would really regret not picking up the phone when I called. While getting my hair cut in the morning, my ears pricked up when an older bloke in the shop begin talking about Bradford City. He told the other hairdresser that he had just returned from Valley Parade to pick up his Wolves away ticket. This was the final game of the season, a game which may determine promotion. He said the queue was really large and tickets looked set to sell out very soon. I returned home feeling anxious, we had planned to get tickets for this game but were waiting until before the Portsmouth home game on the Saturday. I spoke about it to my parents and decided that, with no other plans for the rest of the day; I needed to get to Valley Parade straightaway.

This was in the days before mobile phones were widespread, and neither I nor Alan, Stephen or David owned one. I called Alan at home but the phone just rang. I tried again and again, but no answer. I knew they were unlikely to be out, I suspected Alan could hear the phone but that he knew it was me and thought I was trying to persuade him to play football in the park. I had to stop trying and ran to catch the bus.

I arrived at Forster Square station and went to the nearby payphone to try Alan again. Again there was no answer. With tickets only on sale to season ticket holders, I couldn't get their tickets as I did not have their booklets. I walked to Valley Parade, found there was no queue and was able to purchase my Wolves ticket. Before getting back on the train I tried again from the payphone but it continued to just ring. Returning home an hour later, I tried again. It was now after 4pm and, sensing he was safe from being pressured into a kick-around, Alan finally answered the phone and smugly told me he knew I had been trying to call him all day, but he was ignoring it because he didn't want to play football. I told him about what I had heard in the hairdressers and where I had just been. I could now hear the panic in his voice.

It was too late for him to get to Valley Parade before the ticket office closed, so he went first thing the next day with Stephen and David. Their worst fears were realised, the game was sold out. They didn't have a ticket for the Wolves game, only I did. I felt guilty and tried to think of how I could have got a message to them. Should I have gone to his house before? There was no time and I didn't know if he was in, he wasn't answering the phone! He would probably also have pretended to ignore the door, thinking I was very persistent in trying to get him out to play football. I did feel bad, but I was also excited that I at least had a ticket to go. In the one-up-man-ship game that Alan had started – with the constant bragging about what a great day out they all had at Oxford without me which he was still going on about months later – the roles had been reserved. I had stolen in and taken the ultimate prize.

Unsurprisingly, he was very depressed when we travelled to the Portsmouth game, realising that he only had himself to blame. Stephen and David seemed less upset and I tried to steer the topic away from Wolves. For one thing, it wasn't clear if the game would even matter. The promotion race may be settled one way or another before the last game. Alan's mood got worse as we arrived on the Kop just before kick off when one of David's friends came up to him and offered a spare ticket for Wolves. A friend had bought a ticket but couldn't go. David snapped it up and suddenly two of us were going to Wolverhampton.

The Wolves game kicked off on Sunday lunchtime and was live on Sky; with Ipswich at home to Sheffield United having to better our result. We had to get up early and got a lift to Bradford through David's friend Rob's dad. We travelled on the supporters' coach as usual, which was noticeably quiet and nervy. Meanwhile Alan and Stephen trooped off to the White Bear to watch the game on TV. My mum and brother Kevin, plus Stephen and Alan's mum, joined them. It was the sort of occasion that carried interest beyond us normal City fans.

I was sat separate from David and Rob so we said our byes on the concourse at Molineux and went to our seats. Even saying 'see you later' felt significant. The nerves were jangling in us and I knew the next time I saw David we would either be feeling happier than we have ever felt in our lives or in the depths of gloom. Us City fans were housed in the bottom tier of the stand that ran alongside the pitch; I was at the far corner, level with one of the goals. We had only just arrived in time for kick off and the teams soon came out.

The atmosphere was incredible and Wolves, roared on by their passionate fans, settled better. After 12 minutes the worst thing possible happened, they scored. A scramble in the box, at the end opposite to where I was at, resulted in the ball being headed home despite a suspicion of a push on Walsh. The roar around us was huge but devastating. Wolves, desperate to win themselves to make the play offs, were in front. It was an uphill battle. All of us around me tried to stay calm and not panic. I tried not to think about the consequences but that was impossible. "Come on Sheffield United" I thought. But the man with a radio in the row in front turned round to tell us more bad news. Ipswich were winning. We had to win our game now, but we are losing. The day was going awful.

Then Beagrie picked up the ball on the opposite side of the pitch and darted towards the area. He sold the defender a dummy and cut back before firing a low shot past the Wolves keeper Mike Stowell. It rolled into the corner of the net nearest to us and we all leapt up in celebration. We're back in with a chance! News quickly followed that Ipswich were 2-0 up and it was becoming clear we had to win this game in order to be promoted. With four minutes to go until half time, Blake picked up possession and rolled an exquisite through ball which went past two defenders and into the path of the charging Mills. Stowell came out, but Mills fired the ball low past his right hand side and the ball was in the net. "YEEESSSSSSSS!!!!!!!!!!" There was pandemonium in the away end.

The half time whistle blew and the first 45 minutes had flown by. News that Ipswich were now 3-0 up didn't seem as bad as when we first heard they were winning – we were 45 minutes away from the Premier League. I walked along the concourse at half time where the scene was bedlam. There were fans jumping up and down and hugging while others shouted to calm down as we weren't there yet. I didn't see David and Rob, but as I went back to my seat I thought about Alan and Stephen and wished they were with us.

If the first half went quickly the second half felt anything but. City were certainly in control now, although a couple of long range efforts from Wolves players caused some skipped heartbeats. Wolves fans knew that their promotion rivals for the plays offs were all winning and that a home win probably wouldn't be enough anyway. It looked over for them, and very good for us, just past the hour mark as Blake picked up the ball on the edge of the area following a weak headed clearance, dribbled round a defender and found the space to fire home out third. 3-1! Now we were celebrating. There was a lot of time left, but we were now in amazing position.

It looked like 4-1 when, with 13 minutes to go, Jamie Lawrence charged into the box and was upended by former City defender Dean Richards. The referee blew for a penalty and Beagrie stepped up ready to seal promotion. We all stood up, but had our heads in our hands seconds later as Stowell pushed Beagrie's effort behind. Me and the fans around would not sit back in our seats for the rest of the afternoon.

Seconds after that miss, Paul Simpson fired the ball past Walsh at our end of the pitch. 3-2 and the Wolves fans were roaring. Now it was on a knife edge, should Wolves equalise then Ipswich, now 4-1 up on Sheffield United, would go into the Premiership and we were in the play offs. The last 10 minutes felt like the longest of my life.

Bradford, are you shitting yourselves?!" was the chant from the Wolves fans. I don't think any of us could answer, because we were! I stood there with my heart beating so loudly I felt I could hear it over the crowd. I was biting my nails, nervously checking my watch every 30 seconds and willing for time to go quicker. It was pure agony.

With five minutes left, Wolves won a free kick on the edge of the box and I could barely look. Simpson stepped up and hit a thunderous shot. From my position, directly level with the goal, the ball flew past the wall and past Walsh. It looked a goal to me, but incredibly the ball rebounded backwards – it had smacked the post and there was John Dreyer to whack the ball away. What a let off, although I'd almost suffered a heart attack.

On such a thin margin promotion was decided. We screamed for the referee to blow up and when he finally did we all went crazy. I struggle to recall my immediate reactions, all I know is I lost myself in a sea of happy Bradford City fans. When I came to I was hugging strangers, dancing up and down the gangway and singing 'We are Premier League' as best I could (I was losing my voice). Being part of that moment, with three thousand City fans reacting the same, is something that will stay with me until I die. I've had some amazing spine tingling moments in my life, but this was up there with anything.

On the pitch the players hugged each other, ran up to us away fans and danced around. It was a special moment. McCall ran up and threw his shorts into the crowd and embraced Jewell. He had brought his kids onto the pitch and was lapping up the chants from us. It was fairytale stuff and there was a watching football world equally disbelieving. Bradford City was in the Premiership, the first time in the top flight for 77 years.

Considering I had only been supporting Bradford City for 18 months, I couldn't pretend to fully appreciate what promotion to the Premiership meant to the club. I hadn't even been there for the start of the sudden rise which had begun in. I was very aware, at Molineux, that there were people surrounding me who had followed City for years longer than I had, who had been there for some of City's darker days and been there when barely another 1,000 souls were also present at games. I also know that there were supporters more worthy than me who had missed out on going to the game.

But still, it was an achievement that I was proud to be part of. During the weeks after the game I thought back to my time supporting Man United and how unfulfilling I had found it. I remembered watching them win the FA Cup against Liverpool in 1996 on TV, celebrating win the title in 1997 on my own in my bedroom. They were soon achievements consigned to the history books; I read about them in the paper the day after and enjoyed a little snippet about it on the news.

Yet with City's big achievement, promotion to the Premiership, I was actually there to witness it happen with my own eyes. I was making the noise, biting my nails and pleading for the final whistle to be blown at the end. I've seen the goals from that day a hundred times since, but I can still clearly picture them in my mind from the position I was sat. I was lucky enough to have experienced a first hand account of the moment – and I became a part of the history.

Two weeks after the Wolves win, Man United beat Bayern Munich 2-1 to win the European Cup and the treble – the equivalent of City earning promotion to the Premiership. I was naturally pleased for United, but more than that I felt a sense of relief that they had achieved something greater than when I had supported them. No one could ever accuse me of dropping United when they got rubbish now! I didn't need City to win promotion to stay supporting them, but being part of their most wonderful of moments helped strengthen the bond between myself and City.

Thank goodness the papers had been delayed that November morning eighteen months ago, so that I got the opportunity to join Stephen and Alan in trying out Valley Parade.

Chapter Five

1999 - 00
Dining at the top table

It may have its ills, but the Premier League is undoubtedly
where everyone wants to be. The huge revenues guaranteed
from TV money appeals to owners looking for a return on
their investment; for managers and players it's an opportunity
to test themselves against the best, and for fans it's a chance to
watch them do so in some of the finest stadiums in the world.
There is a circus-like feel about it at times, but my two-year
experience of Bradford City in the Premier League certainly
showed me the merits of being part of it.

The first most striking aspect is the difference in quality
which, although I'd watched plenty of Premier League football
on TV prior to, can only be appreciated by being live at a
game. The pace of the game is much faster, the players more
athletic and showing more guile. Mistakes are clinically
punished, possession not easily given up, the speed of attack
breathtaking. Then there were the top players, who seeing live
in the flesh was a real pleasure. Thierry Henry stood out as the
best player I saw, though David Beckham, Gianfranco Zola,
Paulo Di Canio, David Ginola and Roy Keane weren't bad
either. To see this calibre of player playing in your stadium
was both thrilling and daunting. The objective of supporting
your team was still the same; you desperately wanted them to
win.

The entertainment value is undoubtedly higher. There was
barely any occasions over City's first Premier League season
where I felt I'd watched a boring game. Even if the media
would later report on a dour match, it wouldn't have seemed it

from my seat. The tougher level of opposition also meant each point gained and each win achieved was celebrated that keener. For City, there was certainly no such thing as a home banker and, while expectation levels were high, we supporters never took that attitude either.

The downsides of the Premier League? Well the media coverage certainly wasn't as enjoyable as we'd thought it would be. It was fantastic to see City on Match of the Day and for every national newspaper to carry match reports of each game, but while other recent unlikely-to-be-promoted clubs Barnsley and Charlton had received positive coverage, City were sneered and laughed at. The club was completely written off as no hopers before a ball was kicked, even earning the nickname "Dad's Army" due to the number of over 30s we had. And as fellow newly promoted club Watford enjoyed early season wins over Liverpool and Chelsea, it was the Vicarage Road outfit who took on the role of media darlings while City were endlessly slagged off as no hopers. Once it became clear Watford were heading down and the Premier League title race was as good as over, City, who still had a great chance of saying up, suddenly found favour and became the focus of national attention in a positive way. But still it was hard to trust the media after the way they'd ridiculed the club and even supporters, and the novelty of being in the public spotlight quickly wore off.

And there were the ticket prices. Undoubtedly it was an expensive year following City on the road, and the need to take advantage of what could be our only opportunity to visit the country's best stadiums meant we were prepared to pay the price. Whether after a few seasons of supporting at this level, where trips to Old Trafford become routine, we'd have been willing to pay for tickets that were getting more expensive year-on-year is another matter. To be a Premier League supporter who goes to games is not a cheap pastime, and paying over-inflated prices is difficult to do on a regular basis.

City did survive relegation in the first season, only to go crashing back down the season after. And although that was ultimately very sad, there was a sense of relief too. Winning was such a rarity and losing such a regularity that a return to a level where we might find supporting our team more enjoyable again was welcomed. But still the experience of watching

Bradford City in the Premier League is one I'll always be thankful for. It was like a once-in-a-lifetime exotic holiday that even years later you want to look back over the photos of again and again. And while that may make you wistfully dream of going back to relive it again, deep down you know it's probably best to not let anything spoil those halcyon memories.

A summer of anticipation

So this was it – Bradford City was in the Premiership. As the euphoria of promotion died down, the challenges of the year ahead firmly came into focus. It was undoubtedly an exciting time to be a City fan and, like the summer before, June and July seemed to pass by agonisingly slowly. Never before had the publication of the fixture list carried so much excitement, and when it became available it was met with hours of study. The Leeds games, which we were all the most excited about, would be in November and March. We go to Old Trafford on Boxing Day, Anfield in November and Highbury August. Liverpool at home the last game, Middlesbrough away the opening match. Each fixture looked exciting and the next nine months were something to relish.

Like most other fans the realisation of City playing in the Premiership was a dream come true. I hoped that we would be able to compete of course, although my initial feeling was that we would go straight back down and to make the most of the year in the top flight. It wasn't until I read the editorial of the first City Gent of the season, written by David Pendleton, that I adopted the siege mentality that would stand me in good stead for the campaign ahead. David wrote, "Survival? Why not...At Valley Parade stout foundations are being built, there'll be no 'enjoying the experience' rubbish; we're in the serious business of survival." Such views helped persuade me that staying up was not a forlorn hope and that we supporters had a part to play in ensuring this season of Premiership football would not be our only one.

Of course the four of us had renewed season tickets for the season ahead, although the impact of the opening of the all-seater Kop would affect us as much as anyone. When season ticket prices were announced midway through the previous season, it included a pricing structure for the Kop where seats towards the middle would be more expensive. With Alan, Stephen and David able to call upon more financial support from their mum, they bought season ticket seats in a higher pricing tier than I could afford. They were to be in Block B, which was just behind the goal to the right in the bottom tier, almost exactly where we had been stood on the Kop. Meanwhile I had to buy a seat, on my own, in a cheaper area. I saved up and bought a seat in Block E, right in the corner of the bottom tier next to the Midland Road stand, but near the back. It meant that, for the season ahead, my immediate match day experience would be enjoyed separately from them. We still travelled to and from the ground together and I would always walk over at half time for a chat about the game so far, but I would experience the immediate highs and lows while sat next to other people.

Unfortunately, the club's preparation for the season was not without its difficulties. Things seemed to start off well enough with new signings; Lee Sharpe was signed up permanently and joined by Leeds full back Gunnar Halle. Paul Jewell then broke our transfer record by bringing in another player from Elland Road – £1.4 million was spent on David Wetherall. In also came Matt Clarke, Sheffield Wednesday's third choice goal keeper. The squad was shaping up well.

Pre season friendlies began, but results were not encouraging. City lost home games to Notts Forest and Barnsley and 1-0 at lower-league neighbours Halifax. Meanwhile some of City's promotion heroes were in contract disputes with the club. With the whiff of agents stirring problems, the larger deals they all thought they now deserved were not forthcoming. In a matter of days came the shock news that Darren Moore, Wayne Jacobs and Robbie Blake had been put on the transfer list as deals couldn't be agreed. Then Gordon Watson, out of contract and someone who hadn't been a regular the previous season, decided to quit in order to find first team football elsewhere. Darren Moore would be the only one of the three contract rebels to ultimately leave, but the dispute would have a bad effect on Blake's form during the season ahead.

Still despite the gloom, August was finally here and the season could begin. Well it could for players, management, officials and supporters – it was a delayed start for me. Yet again my parents had booked the usual two weeks for our family holiday – the first two weeks of August. It meant that I would miss the opening fortnight of the season as I would be in the Isle of Man. There was no way Alan, Steve and David would miss the big kick off, away at Middlesbrough. I was reduced to listening to Radio 5Live on my walkman, with reception not always guaranteed. I kept frantically trying to get tuned in and, with some luck, managed to catch the moment that news came through Dean Saunders had struck a late winner for City. Cue wild celebrations, in my head at least. Still I got to see the highlights on Match of the Day that night, watching City on the famous BBC highlights show was a memorable moment in itself.

I also missed the first home game, against Sheffield Wednesday. City struck late again, through a Peter Beagrie penalty, to level the scores at 1-1 and maintain an unbeaten start. At least the holiday was over then and the agony of missing out on such a significant part of City's history could be put to bed. I was also able to write an article about this experience in the City Gent. It was published in the next edition of the magazine which gave me a thrill; although I would not follow it up with any City writing for a few years.

Naturally the three of them had had an amazing day out at the Riverside, as Alan gleefully kept telling me when I saw him. Still I wouldn't have swapped it for Wolves, as I told him back! The next two games were unfortunately away, both ending in defeats at Watford (0-1) and Arsenal (0-2) respectively. On the Tuesday night of the Arsenal game I went to my local pub with a group of friends and had no idea how we had got on until we watched Match of the Day on the backroom TV later. I was very nervous and one of my non City-supporting friends decided to quietly ask someone else in the pub, who knew the score. He laughed when he heard; I was now desperate to hear and very worried. He told me it was 7-0 to Arsenal, before quickly adding he was joking. My heart skipped a few beats, I had actually believed him!

In the end City lost 2-0, but the highlights reflected that we had not been in it and, but for Gary Walsh, it probably would have been seven. Still, four games in, City had won one, drawn one and lost two. Crucially for me, I had yet to witness any of it.

West Ham United (home) – early Premiership impressions

Minutes into the second half of my first Premiership game, against West Ham, the visitors casually knocked the ball about in their own half before launching a long ball up towards Paulo Wanchope. The Costa Rican striker was up against John Dreyer, but easily beat him for strength. Now able to run at goal, he finished coolly past Gary Walsh. Bradford City 0 West Ham 3.

If the scoreline felt depressing, it was made even harder to take by the fact City had started the game very well, taking the game to the Hammers and forcing strong pressure. Yet the visitors, full of talented players but hardly the best Premiership outfit around, had quickly waltzed into a three-goal lead either side of the break through Paolo Di Canio, Trevor Sinclair and Wanchope. It was quite a rude awakening, watching your team give their all but be easily outclassed. Welcome to the Premiership.

It all felt very unfamiliar. Partly aided, of course, by the fact I was sitting in the brand new Kop for the first time and taking up a different view point. I had made sure we arrived extra early for the game and led us up to the back of the top tier first, to take in the breathtaking view of the rest of the stadium below and the City of Bradford behind it. We wandered down to Stephen, David and Alan's seats and, after a few minutes, the urge to check out my new seat took over, so I left them. Watching the game without them felt very strange and, with a 3-0 defeat to sit through, my first taste of the Premiership was not a pleasant one.

Yet two weeks later, much to my relief and joy, I got a more enjoyable glimpse of what the Premiership was all about. Spurs were the next visitors to Valley Parade and, in what was a closely fought contest; the atmosphere in Valley Parade was the best I had ever experienced. International week had followed the West Ham defeat and the players had been worked hard on the training ground to better on their early season showings. There was a notable improvement and City battled well. The game was live on Sky in their 4pm slot and, as the match unfolded and the incredible noise from City fans reverberated around the stadium and into millions of TV viewers' homes around the world, I sat back and took it all in.

Bradford City in the Premiership, this is what it's all about.

The game itself was open and exciting. Ginola, the talented French winger, was in fine form and forced Walsh to make some wonderful saves. Spurs probably edged it, but we weren't out of it and forced some pressure. It looked like we were heading for a fourth defeat in a row, though, after Chris Perry headed Spurs in front from a corner with 12 minutes to go. Yet City kept going, forced some pressure and, in stoppage time, Wetherall headed down a Beagrie corner into the path of Stuart McCall, who planted a delicate header into the bottom corner of the net. Cue wild celebrations.

It was clear, however, that all was not well for City, especially behind the scenes. The Blake contract issue had rumbled on, meaning one of the biggest stars of last season had barely played. Before the next Premiership game, away at Aston Villa, he was publicly dropped from the squad. His cause hadn't been helped by a poor performance in the midweek Worthington Cup game at home to Reading.

The Villa away game was my first away trip of the season. It seemed a good place to start, we were obviously keen to visit all the big grounds during the season and Villa Park was a venue regularly used for big events like the FA Cup semi finals. We were desperate to get to as many away games as possible and during the summer had signed up to a new away ticket scheme, called the Gold Travel Club. Unfortunately none of us had read what the deal was properly and thought we were buying free coach travel to every away game. It was only just before the season began that we discovered joining up only gave you preferable treatment for away tickets where there was high demand and a couple of quid off coach travel each game.

When Alison (Stephen, Alan and David's mum) found out, she wrote an angry letter to Geoffrey Richmond and the T&A slamming Richmond and dubbing him 'Dick Turpin'. Incredibly, Richmond rang up Alison at work, after he read the letter, to talk through her compliant. She didn't know a lot about City, but knew enough to be shocked when her boss said, "Geoffrey Richmond's on the phone for you." To be fair to City, it was totally our fault for not realising what the offer properly was. Richmond pointed out that he had never misled fans and Alison had to accept she was wrong and rang the T&A to ask them not to print the letter. "It's the first time anyone's ever called me Dick Turpin" Richmond said to Alison. It probably wouldn't be the last.

I felt disappointed with Villa Park when we got inside. It somehow didn't feel like a mighty stadium and the away end in particular was basic. It was a rainy day, but despite being a few rows back the roof offered no protection and we got soaked. The game itself was also dismal and it was hard to believe that Villa were second in the Premiership at the time. They were certainly a much poorer side than West Ham and Spurs. Inspired by second half sub Paul Merson though, Villa sneaked a 1-0 win. We failed to create a single chance and travelled home disappointed and concerned about our survival chances.

The only real highlight for me was getting to write up my views for the local paper, the Telegraph & Argus. During the summer, they had asked for fans to sign up to write 'fans view' reports for games during the season. I applied and was asked to cover this game. I had to provide predictions for all the weekend's Premiership games for the Friday edition (I think I got them all wrong!) and on Sunday after the game rang up a copywriter who typed up my match report as I read it out over the phone, which appeared in the paper on Monday. I wrote, "For City the problems that had blighted their season so far remained – scoring goals. City remained solid in the back and in midfield but once again there was little up front. Three goals in seven games is not good enough by anyone's standards." Looking back, that seems a fair summary of our slow start to the season.

At least we scored the following week – and won! We were away to Derby and the four of us made the trip by coach. Pride Park felt much more impressive than Villa Park and we away fans made some great noise. It helped having something to cheer; midway through the second half Derby defender Horacio Carbonari bizarrely headed a City free kick into his own net. A lucky break, but no one cared about some good fortune at last. We celebrated wildly and cheered on as a gritty defensive display made sure we held on. Derby fans began the day singing 'Going Down' at us, a chant every set of opposition fans sung at us during the season. By the end of the game we were able to sing the same song back at them. While we kept hoping that games like Spurs and Derby would prove turning points, the struggle continued. The following week we were thrashed 4-0 at home by Sunderland.

Looking back, it's clear we really struggled to adapt to life in the Premiership. The Sunderland 4-0 defeat apart, there were no thrashings, but the attacking football that had been our trademark during last season's promotion campaign was sadly lacking. Two weeks later we entertained a Leicester side 5th in the Premiership and I expected us to lose again. In the event, our first home Premiership win finally came. What's more, the performance from the players was excellent. It appeared City decided to 'go for it' more and played in that previously-mentioned attacking manner. Blake was back in the team and opened the scoring in typical style. Leicester equalised, but Mills scored for the third game in a row to put us back in front. In the second half, Blake went on a jinxing run in the box and crossed for Redfearn to prod the ball home. 3-1. There could have been more goals and the performance was easily the best we had seen from the players. Sure we scrapped, but we also played football. Perhaps for the first time, we were given evidence that the team could make a fist of surviving in the Premiership.

Leeds and Chelsea (away) – unwrapped pies and London coach tours

Our first season in the Premiership coincided with my second year of sixth form. There was a clear increase in the level of abuse I was receiving from other football fans as City's fortunes were played out in a more public arena. Previously, some friends would ask me how City had got on at the weekend on Monday mornings. I had always been tempted to lie about the score when we had lost – after all they wouldn't have known any different – although honesty always compelled me to give them a cue to laugh at us losing to

Grimsby or QPR. In the Premiership, there was no such anonymity.

I was still enjoying life in sixth form though, despite the extra pressure as it was my final year and needing to work harder. I now had a better social life and we began going for nights out in Skipton more regularly. With my birthday falling in October, I was one of the first in my year to become 18 and received a handful of free tickets for the local night-club, The Afterdark, in the post. Around 16 of us ended up going out for it on a Friday and enjoyed a fun night. We also regularly went to our local pub, the Kings Arms in Sutton, on Tuesdays. I liked going to school and being on the Media course. I was also getting really good marks and was able to have fun but find time to do my work. Going to City at the weekend remained the highlight of my week though, nothing really came before that.

I had also managed to secure a job cleaning the school for two hours at the end of the day. A contracted company, who employed students, looked after the cleaning of the school. I had a fearsome boss in John, a scouser who liked to talk about football fortunately but who was not shy about shouting at us if we weren't working hard enough. I received a huge telling off one day after teachers in the area I covered had complained about my work. I kept my head down and said I was sorry and would work harder, mindful that others who had attempted to argue back had got the sack. The job paid much better than the after school club I was working for before. I needed the money desperately, mainly to pay for away games.

During November we went on another couple of away trips, including the one we were all looking forward to the most since getting promoted on May 9th. Playing Leeds was arguably the most exciting thing about promotion for us. Despite Stephen and David's former allegiance with that lot East of Pudsey, we had developed an occasionally unhealthy hatred for our near neighbours.

We took the supporters' coach, despite the relative ease to get to Elland Road from where we lived. We had learned the lessons of a year earlier when we went to Huddersfield. We were sat in the stand behind the goal, as opposed to the corner where we held tickets for last year's cup tie. Despite a high number of friends who supported Leeds, only one of them attended this game. The fact that so many of them took the mickey out of me for supporting City, yet never actually went to Leeds games, only heightened my desperation for us to win and firmly put one over them.

There was a large City following and the anti-Leeds feeling ran even to the food bar on the concourse. We had bought a pint each and were stood near the kiosk chatting with some of David's friends. Lots of people were queuing up for food and all were disgusted when they were handed their order in Leeds United packaging. I witnessed several supporters forcibly request that the staff remove the outer packaging before handing it to them to consume.

Unfortunately the glorious win we all dreamed of didn't materialise. Midway through the second half, Michael Bridges hit a weak shot towards goal which was going wide. The ball hit fellow striker Alan Smith, changing its direction. Next thing three sides of the ground were up cheering as the ball flew into the net. Not long after, Leeds won a penalty after a poor back pass from McCall put Lee Bowyer through. Matt Clarke, who had recently been brought in as keeper after Walsh was injured, brought the Leeds player down in the area. It looked a dubious decision, although all of us were wearing our Claret and Amber-tinted glasses. Leeds put the penalty away and the game was over. Dean Windass did pull a goal back for us, at least giving us something to cheer, unfortunately it came in the last minute and there was no time for a comeback.

We trooped off disappointed, blaming the ref and the ridiculous bad fortune of the first goal. Our arguments against the Leeds fans on Monday were plotted. Of course it made no difference; those Leeds supporters, most of who had learned of the result by checking teletext, rather than bothering to watch their team, were able to laugh at me.

The following week we were away to Chelsea and on Sky again, but we still went down to London to watch it. We arrived to surroundings that felt odd and unfamiliar. Chelsea is of course in a posh part of London and viewing the number of expensive-looking restaurants and boutiques as our coach approached Stamford Bridge felt very different to going down Manningham Lane. It was even stranger to see a hotel built on the side of Stamford Bridge. We paid a whopping £3 for a programme and had a look around the Chelsea megastore. It was hard to escape the feeling that we were tourists on a day trip. We were only missing a camera.

We were housed in the bottom tier of their recently opened three tier stand running alongside the pitch next to the dugouts. The stand opposite was being rebuilt but was only half way along, so missing a roof. Although it was only recently built, the away area felt very cramped and basic. As for the game, City again lined up with just Lee Mills up front and played defensive. The plan wasn't working when Tore Andre Flo put Chelsea in front after a quarter on an hour, but we hung in there and played quite well, especially at the back.

As we drove through the streets of London on the way home following the 1-0 loss, the coach driver got on the microphone and decided to treat us to a commentary of the sights. He pointed out Harrods and other notable buildings, doing his best to tell us about their history. It was quite interesting and certainly different. It also helped to reinforce the feeling that the whole day had been like a tourist trip.

So two away trips and two narrow defeats against two of the Premiership's best teams. Performances were at least encouraging and fortunately results at home were going well. For a large part of this season, City were able to turn Valley Parade into a fortress and became very difficult to beat. You had to hand it to Jewell, who knew how to line up the team for home games so they at least didn't lose. During December, City entertained Middlesbrough, Newcastle and Everton. There was a slightly feeling of disappointment walking out of Valley Parade after drawing with Middlesbrough and Everton, but a memorable win was achieved over Newcastle. The visitors dominated the first half, but City attacked with purpose after the break and struck twice through Saunders and Wetherall. Both goals were in front of the Kop, the atmosphere that day was fantastic.

One of my favourite away trips that season, if only for atmosphere and quality of the pre-match drink rather than the football, was First Division Crewe in the FA Cup. It was quite nice visiting a familiar place away from the Premiership. We found a great bar close to the ground that was playing The Verve's 'Urban Hymns' album, which none of us had heard for a long time so we really enjoyed it. Crewe unsurprisingly treated the game as one where they could get a scalp and, after we took the lead through Blake early in the first half, they equalised with quarter of an hour to go. As a replay loomed, Jewell sent on Saunders and Sharpe and, with seven minutes to go, Sharpe set up Saunders to strike a brilliant low shot into the bottom corner and send us through to the first round.

I remember we all went crazy and began hugging some of the other City fans around us; a great moment, which felt a world away from our weekly Premiership struggle.

The only Premiership away game in December was at Old Trafford, but I missed the opportunity to watch us play Man United. It was on Boxing Day and, as was family tradition, we all went to the Alambra to watch the annual pantomime instead. Them three went and, true to form, Alan took great delight in me missing the big game. Me and Kevin decided to go and watch the play back of the game on the big screen at Valley Parade, before it was time to go to the show. We hadn't bought tickets ahead and were disappointed to be turned away at the door – the screen had broken down. I smuggled in my walkman to the pantomime and listened to the final stages of the game before the show began. City were doing remarkably well and holding United to a 0-0 draw, but then the goals suddenly started flying in. All from Man United of course, by the time the curtain opened I was sat gloomy in my seat contemplating the 4-0 defeat.

City's good home form had meant City were out of the bottom three at this stage, although a 1-0 defeat at Southampton on New Years Day saw us drop below the dreaded dotted line. Yet a few days later came another excellent home result. Chelsea were in town and most of us felt we were going to get turned over. We were as shocked as anyone when City took the lead inside a minute, Mills heading home a cross. City dug in and defended admirably. Chelsea had plenty of shots, 36 in total, as they tried to get back into the game. They did equalise mid-way through the second half, but we at least held out for a draw.

During the new millennium's fledging days the four of us were feeling very optimistic about City's chances of staying up. After a slow start, performances had picked up and we were now doing a good job of competing at the highest level. If we can start turning the narrow away defeats into draws and the home draws into wins, we were capable of achieving survival.

Sheffield Wednesday (away) – the three amigos

On a personal level, significant moments happened as 1999 became 2000 for two of the four of us, both involving love and relationships. I managed to get my first proper girlfriend, while Alan began a slow and occasionally painful break up with Bradford City.

My girlfriend is probably the easier to explain. For a few weeks leading up to Christmas I had become increasingly friendly with a girl in the year below me in sixth form. I knew her through a couple of other people and, after the usual will-we-won't-we that most people go through before starting a relationship, we got together on Christmas Eve after a night out at the After Dark nightclub in Skipton. It would be the start of an 18 month relationship that would certainly have more downs than ups. As far as relevance to the story goes, she didn't care at all for football and certainly not Bradford City. I remember on one of our early dates mentioning that she should come to a City game some time. Her response was no chance, it didn't appeal at all. As the relationship grew over the next few months, City became a disappointingly regular subject of argument. I was going to matches most Saturdays, which limited the amount of time I could spend with her, especially as she worked Friday and Sunday evenings. She would get very annoyed when I told her I was off to an away game at the weekend, even though I would usually be home by 8pm and still be able to see her.

If my getting a girlfriend came as a surprise to friends and family, the sudden falling out of love between Alan and City came as a real shock to me and his two brothers. Like the rest of us, I think we assumed Alan was enjoying the Premiership experience, with the excitement of seeing famous players at Valley Parade and trips to some of the country's finest stadiums. Of course we all wanted City to win more often and we were experiencing more regular defeats, but the general

78

mood among us was that we were doing okay and were capable of beating the drop.

The Tuesday after the encouraging 1-1 draw at home to Chelsea, City were in FA Cup action away to Second Division Gillingham. Each of us listened on our radios at home, where we were all shocked and devastated to hear City go down to an embarrassing 3-1 defeat. The performance sounded terrible and the goals conceded comical; but while I went to sleep that night feeling fed up but not completely surprised, Alan was reaching breaking point. The downside to promotion to the Premiership was seeing City lose more, and this got Alan increasingly fed up. An embarrassing FA Cup exit was too much for him to bear and he ripped down all the City posters from his bedroom walls.

I was still unaware he had reacted like this when we all met up the next Saturday to travel to Sheffield Wednesday. The poor FA Cup result had added to the pressure on the players, who were now facing a must-win game against a side below us in the league. But we were treated to another woeful display and were beaten by two second half goals. Following the Gillingham defeat, it was the worst week of the season so far.

We trooped out feeling much less confident over our chances. This game had been the second time that the Telegraph and Argus had asked me to provide the 'Fan's View' for their Monday edition. As we rode home and I planned what I would write, Alan had bigger things pressing on his mind. I didn't find out until the following Saturday's home game with Watford, but he had decided that he could no longer support City and would be reverting back to following Blackburn Rovers instead – lumbering in Division One but at least not losing as often. He still had his season ticket to see out, so would be coming to each game. But he would not be cheering us on.

Looking back years on, I still don't understand why he threw in the towel on supporting City so soon. There might have been fewer victories to cheer, but each one we achieved and even some of our draws were met with far more celebration than a Division One victory generated. We all knew it was going to be a struggle, at least in the first season. Yet even after such a bad week we were still in with a great chance of avoiding the drop and there was a long way to go.

Gradually over the coming months, Alan would become more frustrating to attend City games with. He would happily laugh at us when City lost, constantly tell us how rubbish we were and how we had no chance of staying up. We got enough of this crap from friends supporting other teams and the media; we didn't need to hear it during matches.

For the next two games at least, it appeared his decision to give up was particularly badly timed. First City beat Watford 3-2 at home, who were promoted alongside us and now sat bottom of the league. The win was more comfortable than the scoreline suggested and Watford's second only came in the last minute. The major black spot was an injury to Matt Clarke midway through the second half, which ruled out the in-form keeper for six weeks. Aidan Davison, who we had signed on loan with Gary Walsh injured, came on in the game and conceded the late Watford goal. Still the three points were ours and cheered us all up, and it was a great pleasure watching Match of the Day that night with City v Watford the main match. Who would have predicted that a year earlier?

Equally no-one was predicting a home win when Arsenal came into town for the next game. Incredibly though, City achieved their best result of the season with a shock 2-1 victory. Windass fired us in front with a quickly-taken free kick which fooled David Seamen after 10 minutes. We began to dream of an amazing win, only for Arsenal to equalise straight away through a fantastic 30-yard shot from Thierry Henry in front of the Kop. Luckily his team-mates weren't so hot that day. Midway through the second half City burst forward and the recently-recalled Gareth Whalley released a killer through ball for Dean Saunders to run onto. He just had Seamen to beat and rolled the ball between his legs and into the net. Behind the goal, we all went ballistic. This time there was no quick equaliser and we held on despite some strong pressure at the end. Amazingly we had beaten the side second in the table!

The atmosphere in the closing stages was hair raising stuff. The noise was incredible as we all sung "Are you watching Rodney Marsh", a chant aimed at the Sky Sports pundit who spent the season publicly mocking City. It felt good, although I was half-tempted to sing "Are you watching Alan Burns?"

Sunderland (away) – tabloid stars

It's the morning after Easter Monday. As usual, I'm up early doing my paper round. In better spirits than usual thanks to an amazing day yesterday, where I had travelled up to Sunderland with Stephen and David to witness City record a fantastic 1-0 win which had breathed new life into the season. As ever, I'm looking through the papers before I deliver them through each letter box and I'm more eager than usual to read the press reaction to our shock victory. As I glance over The Daily Mirror I half-notice a photo at the top of the back page which features a group of City fans looking nervous. I read the headline that accompanied it and then stare again at the photo, before almost dropping the paper in shock.

The photo is of three young lads in Claret and Amber shirts. The one on the left looks like he is praying, the one in the middle is grimacing in pain and the one on the right looks as though he is having trouble breathing. I recognise all three, in fact I know them very well. The guy struggling to breath is Stephen, the one who looks in pain is David, and the one praying is me!

I must have spent the next five minutes stood staring in disbelief. I've always been the kind of person who looks to see if I can be seen when City have been on TV. Now here I was on the back page of a national newspaper, with everyone around the country able to view my nervous face and conclude it must have been a nerve-wracker at the Stadium of Light yesterday. The three of us all look remarkably on edge and the photo was clearly taken during the closing stages when City were hanging on and Sunderland were launching long balls forward in desperation. It looked really natural, and we were clearly oblivious to any photographer snapping our faces. I don't remember praying as we desperately clung on for an unlikely victory, although I do remember wanting to.

I returned to the shop at the end of the round and go to buy more copies to take home. Alan, who didn't attend the game with us after choosing to go and watch Blackburn on his own instead, had already finished his round and seen the picture too. He had already told our boss Tom, who was sitting there at the counter studying the photo as I walked into the shop. "Why were you praying?" he asked.

Later that day my friend Michael, who lived across the road, called over. His mum has been reading the Daily Mail and seen someone she recognised in the sports section. My photo is in another paper! This time its larger although just features me and David. He let me keep the copy and my parents were off to the shop to buy another couple. The following Saturday I got a text from a friend to tell me that my photo was again in the Daily Mirror. It's the same photo, although this time even larger covering a double page spread. All three of us are in it again, and alongside, with the photo, an interview with Wayne Jacobs about how his Christian beliefs are helping him with City's relegation battle. I could guess why they chose to again include that photo of a City fan praying!

This was my fifteen minutes of fame, a moment when numerous people in the sixth form came up to me and said they had seen me in the paper. My parents and Stephen and David's mum collectively got the photos blown up large and a framed copy is still displayed in both of their sitting rooms. Even now when my parents get visitors, a glance at the picture becomes the start of a quirky talking point.

The photo was as pleasantly unexpected as the win at Sunderland. March and the first half of April had been a terrible time for City. Form plummeted badly and some vital games were lost. On Good Friday City had at least stopped the rot of six straight defeats, but a remarkable 4-4 draw with Derby felt like two points dropped considering they were one of our main relegation rivals. Throughout all of the season and even during this awful run, the three of us had kept up a strong collective belief that we would avoid the drop. If ever one of us had doubts, the other two would soon talk them round. Part of our belief stemmed from how well we had performed at times during the campaign; the run-in which featured home games against relegation rivals also gave cause to remain positive that we could gather those vital wins needed to finish fourth bottom.

The six defeats had chipped away that belief and the draw with Derby felt like the end. We didn't talk much of football travelling on the coach to the Stadium of Light for once, all probably mindful that belief had now gone. We were away to a side who had only lost twice at home all season, who had striker Kevin Phillips scoring at an incredible rate and who knew a win could put them in with a great chance of European qualification. What chance did we have?

The run of defeats had begun in the most painful of ways with another narrow defeat to Leeds. After the previous two derbies had taken place at Elland Road, we felt very confident of beating them at Valley Parade – after all, we were unbeaten at home since October. In the build up to the game we were further buoyed at news the outstanding Clarke had recovered from injury and could continue again as keeper. He had been out since the Watford win and although the on loan Aidan Davison had done okay, he was no Clarke. His return seemed especially crucial as City's attempt to sign Aidan permanently fell through. Still who cared? Clarke was back and we were very confident as we made our way to Valley Parade for the Sunday kick off (the game was on Sky). This is the moment we had been dreaming about.

No sooner had we walked onto the concourse of the Kop when some terrible news reached our ears from one of Dave's friends; Clarke had fallen down the stairs the night before and was on crutches. He was out of the game, so instead we were going to have to play our goalkeeper coach. Okay this was Neville Southall, a legend for Everton and Wales, but he was now 41 and had not played for at least 18 months. The pre-match optimism seeped out of all of us and we instantly feared the worst.

(We heard later that Southall was called upon when the ageing Welshman had told Paul Jewell that the junior's keeper, Danny Taylor, was shaking in fear in the dressing-room at the thought of playing. City had had a bid of £180,000 accepted by Leeds for their second string keeper, Paul Robinson, but the Elland Road club wanted a clause that Robinson would not play in the forthcoming match which was refused by Geoffrey Richmond).

To be fair Southall performed okay, although I felt Clarke would have saved both goals he conceded. Those two strikes Michael Bridges netted put Leeds in a strong position, despite the fact we were playing well and dominating for long periods. Beagrie did pull a goal back for us with a wonder strike. Unfortunately we couldn't force the equaliser. Leeds had recorded their third straight win over us, our five month unbeaten home record was gone. Can I have Monday off school, Mum? I can't face those Leeds fans again.

After that debacle, Davison changed his mind and signed the contract to join City. He was needed the next week at Coventry as Clarke was still injured. Unfortunately Aidan and many others had an off day and we were thrashed 4-0 by a team sitting in mid table. We were thrashed 4-0 again the next Saturday despite Clarke finally returning, although there was no disgrace to it. We were playing Man United, who played a strong team at Valley Parade and performed really well.

As much as no one likes City getting thrashed, the quality of Man United was something to admire. When Paul Scholes met David Beckham's corner and crashed home a stunning first-time volley from the edge of the area, I joined other City fans in standing up to applaud. The strike was special and, years on, remains a famous goal often shown on TV. It was a pleasure to be there that day and, as I met Stephen, David and Alan after the game, we could only talk of admiration for the master class we had seen from the European Champions. It seemed cruel to attempt to find fault with City's efforts.

Through all of these defeats, the belief remained largely due to a run of three winnable home games against teams near us at the bottom of the table. A week after we lost 2-0 at Newcastle, Southampton became the first of these visitors and put a huge dint into our confidence by taking all three points. On the day they were too strong, although luck was typically against us when, early in the second half, Chris Marsden hit a tame shot that would have rolled behind the goal, but instead it hit Dean Windass and the ball changed direction, completely wrong-footing Clarke and rolling slowly and painfully into the net in front of us. It ended 2-1 to Saints. Belief was now slipping away and wasn't helped the following week when Everton thrashed us 4-0 at Goodison Park.

Next up was Derby on Good Friday and the second of the three winnable home games. After six defeats, it really was now or never for us. Derby scored within 30 seconds, then again after six minutes. It was then that Windass, a player who had won around most of us after much improved displays since October, cemented his place as a Valley Parade cult hero. He came up towards the Kop and signalled to us to feeling gloomy and make some noise – the team needed us. Within six minutes Deano had reduced the deficit with a cool finish. Six minutes later he latched onto a loose ball and fired a shot low and hard from distance which flew into the bottom corner. 2-0 to 2-2, we were certainly roaring now. The game was only 20 minutes old.

Just before the half hour Robbie Blake was put through and finished with a lob over the keeper, but our celebrations were cut short when the referee blew up. He disallowed the goal, only to award us a penalty after Rory Delap was tugging Robbie's shirt. He then sent Delap off and Beagrie coolly finished the penalty. Now it was 3-2! Unfortunately defensive frailties remained at the fore with Westwood conceding a penalty. 3-3. Just before half time, Windass completed his hat trick after running onto a through ball. Half time and 4-3, confidence returned. Pause for breath!

It was unfortunate that soon after the break Derby were level again with another penalty. The game was now on a knife edge with both teams having chances. It looked over for us though when the ref incredibly gave Derby a third penalty. This time Clarke pulled off a save to keep hopes alive. But we badly needed the win and were desperate for another goal. In stoppage time substitute Saunders was presented with a great chance. He blew it and we all quietly travelled home believing the 4-4 draw was probably it for our hopes.

So the three of us were quiet travelling up to Sunderland three days later, and tried to keep the conversation away from football and City's chances. We were on the ropes in the first half as Sunderland pressed, but defended really well. Midway through the second half, confidence began to grow and we started threatening a goal. When Beagrie crossed the ball from by the corner flag and John Dreyer met the ball and headed the ball low into the bottom corner, we all berserk. Suddenly there was something to hang onto and the players continued to dig in and defend for their lives.

Sunderland launched plenty of balls into the box as they tried to come back, but Wetherall and Andy O'Brien were outstanding. We chewed our nails to death (some us apparently prayed!). Eventually the referee blew full time and a 1-0 win. As we walked out of the ground celebrating what we hadn't dared hope, we talked about what it meant to the league table and became even more excited. We were third bottom, and now only two points behind fourth-bottom Wimbledon, who were playing awful and had lost seven games in a row. Next week's opponents at Valley Parade? Wimbledon.

Who put the ball in the Liverpool net?

From the moment the 1999/00 season kicked off to the last final whistle, the whole season was played out in gut-wrenching nervous tension with our survival hopes in the balance. There were times when it had looked hopeless, and there were also periods where survival looked very possible. Yet largely we lived right on the edge with every corner kick, every goal and every result mattering greatly.

With the Premiership title race easily won by Man United, the national media spotlight turned towards the battle at the bottom of the Premiership and our bid for survival became the big story. The impact of this was felt beyond those of us right in the middle of the battlefield. It was great to be able to pick up a national newspaper and read stories about City. It was nice that we regularly became the main match on Match of the Day and our results were naturally one of the big topics of conversations among friends in the sixth form lounge. What was surprising was how much it impacted on other people.

It's easy to forget that, as we walked into Valley Parade, there were eyes peering in from over the walls of the four stands. We weren't the only people studying the bottom of the table on Teletext for hours. I would say bye to my parents as I left to go to matches and they would always know the result by the time I got home. But they were taking more of an interest than just whether I would be in a good or bad mood when I got home. They began to care about results as well and hoped City would win. When even my girlfriend's dad – who seemed as indifferent to me as he was about football and barely uttered two sentences to me during the whole time I went out with his daughter – began paying attention to City's results, it felt like a measure of how much my life was impacting on others.

As I sat at Valley Parade for the final game against Liverpool where our fate would be decided, probably more nervous than I had ever been in my life, my mum was listening to the game on the radio feeling equally edgy. She even made my dad take her out for a drive in the car while continuing to listen, to do something about her nervous tension. For a few weeks at least, City became a larger part of my friends and family's lives than usual.

The first signs of the hysteria came before the Wimbledon match the week after the season-turning with at Sunderland. The significance was huge. A win and we would be out of the bottom three with just two games to go.

The points were everything and it was with great relief that City managed their biggest win of the season, 3-0, to overtake the Dons. It was certainly wasn't the best performance and Wimbledon were probably the better side. We also received two pieces of extraordinary luck in the first half. First Jason Euell managed to miss an open goal that would have put the visitors ahead. Then, just before half time, City won a soft-looking penalty when Saunders' cross hit the arm of a Dons' defender. Beagrie coolly slotted it away and scored the second with a good run and shot just after the break, though even that had an air of fortune – Wimbledon players claimed a handball by Wayne Jacobs in the build up. Still who cared? We were 2-0 up and that was what mattered. John Hartson got himself sent off for complaining too aggressively about Jacobs' suspected handball but, despite being down to 10 men, Wimbledon continued to press. We held out well and broke clear at the end to score a third through Windass. We travelled home feeling elated at the result, though I was a little disappointed with City's display.

So we were out of the bottom three and Wimbledon proceeded to sack their manager Egil Olsen. The twists and turns weren't over, however; not that I witnessed the next major moment. Our penultimate game was away at Leicester while Wimbledon entertained Aston Villa. We didn't go to Filbert Street, in fact I didn't even listen to the game at home. My girlfriend had begun losing patience with the number of away games I was going to and how much of the Saturday it took up. I decided, as another huge argument flared up about me going to the Sunderland game a few weeks previously, that I would miss the Leicester trip. So my Saturday afternoon was spent with her as we walked her dog. Out in the countryside, I was unaware of events at Filbert Street or Selhurst Park. In some ways it was a good thing, although my mind was never far off thinking about what was happening. Should we win and Wimbledon lose, we will have definitely survived. As desperate as I was for City to stay up, the idea of missing on them achieving it felt somewhat unsatisfying.

I needn't have worried. After saying our byes I took the bus home with anticipation and fear reaching fever pitch, to discover we were back in the bottom three. City had lost easily at Leicester (0-3) while Wimbledon had stopped the rot by scoring an injury time equaliser to claim a 2-2 draw. That tied us both level on 33 points, but the Dons goal difference was better. Now it would go to the last game of the season, with Wimbledon down at Southampton and City preparing to entertain Liverpool. We had to better their result.

I remember little about the build up to the final Sunday, but I'm sure it was hell. During the same period I was studying for two A Level exams and finishing off my GNVQ coursework – how I concentrated I don't know. In the end the day of the big game arrived and we were travelling nervously to Valley Parade. Liverpool were going for a Champions League spot and desperately needed to win, they were near the top of the Premiership with the England strikers Michael Owen and Emile Heskey, a young-up-and-coming Steven Gerrard making a name for himself and the strong Sami Hypia rated by some as the best defender in the Premiership. The size of the task was huge.

Perhaps that explained why Dave was so subdued before kick off, he looked a bag of nerves and barely said a word. We had our usual pre-match pint, Dave spoke about me and Alan swapping seats so they could sit with me, as both he and Steve wanted to sit by someone who'd experienced the highs and lows and still cared. I could see Alan didn't want to and couldn't blame him, so I didn't push it. He had already purchased a season ticket for Blackburn next season and this game would be his last sat with his two older brothers.

The game was live on Sky and it felt great to imagine how many people around the world were tuning into watch what was about to unfold at Valley Parade. They included several of my Leeds-supporting friends. They were away at West Ham and were desperate for us to beat Liverpool so they could secure the final Champions League spot. Whatever rivalry exists between the two neighbours we were joined in one hope that day, for a Liverpool defeat.

The game kicked off with City attacking the opposite Bradford End and, for 10 minutes, nothing really happened. I remained nervous and on edge, but the game was slow and uneventful. Then we won a free kick out wide. Gunnar Halle swung the ball over and David Wetherall met it with a perfect header that flew powerfully into the corner. A moment of disbelief at what I was witnessing; then I leapt up and down wildly in celebration. We were in front! A lead to hang onto and confidence raised. Disappointingly, no one around me had a radio to keep in touch with events hundreds of miles away on the south coast but I was sure The Dell was aware of the scoreline at Valley Parade. If it stayed like this we would survive, only 77 minutes to go!

City began knocking the ball around confidently and showed some nice attacking moves. Jamie Lawrence seemed to be enjoying himself on the wing and, whenever Liverpool attacked, our defence held firm. The noise was terrific and we all became more excited when some cheering broke out just before half time. No confirmation around us of Wimbledon falling behind, but they must be or why else would people be cheering? Checking the monitors on the Kop concourse at half time revealed it had been in fact a cruel joke started by someone. It was still 0-0 at the Dell. In between that false hope and the interval, Liverpool had almost equalised when Owen broke clear, skipped round Clarke, but saw his stabbed shot at goal scrambled off the line by Halle. Half time and it was so far, so good.

The second half felt long, Liverpool were desperate for the three points and must have been aware that their Champions League rivals Leeds were only drawing, meaning an away win would secure them the coveted 3rd spot (this was in the days when only the top three qualified for the Champions League). Then another cheer broke out around the ground that seemed to be louder than the false alarm before. People nearby, like me no doubt, wishing someone had brought their radio, remained cautious and didn't dare believe. Soon after, another loud cheer went up around the ground, again even louder. This time we all seemed to relax more and believe Southampton had definitely scored, probably their second.

As the minutes ticked by it felt strange knowing that City didn't even need to hold on for the win to survive, a draw would be enough. Not that anyone wanted the added nervousness of a Liverpool equaliser. The players were magnificent, defending for their lives and throwing their bodies in front of any shots heading towards our goal. We moved deep into injury time and were whistling loudly and pleading for the referee to finish the season. Some fans prematurely believed he had and ran onto the pitch to celebrate when he had actually awarded a throw in. Once they were cleared back into the stands the full time was blown and thousands of us raced on to the pitch in jubilation.

It was a wonderful sight, and the tannoy announcement of Southampton 2 Wimbledon 0 was music to my ears. We had done it! I ran to the front and was soon on the pitch, and then headed towards the other end of the Kop to find Stephen, David and Alan. They weren't in their seats and must have already run onto the pitch. I looked around but it was impossible to find them in the sea of happy fans. Then suddenly someone jumped on my back and forced me onto the floor; it was Alan, with a huge smile on his face enjoying the moment. The four of us looked at each other in amazement and there were knowing glances between myself, David and Stephen. We had always kept each other's spirits up and collectively believed we would stay up. We now felt vindicated, happy we had kept faith, even in the face of apparent hopelessness at times. Yet we also couldn't believe it!

The players had wisely ran off the pitch as soon as the referee blew for time, although Lawrence was still out there and we realised that the claret-haired person in a City shirt nearby us was him. I quickly ran over and gave him a pat on the back while others hugged him. Then we all walked towards the Liverpool fans and both sets of fans jointly sung 'You'll Never Walk Alone'.

No one wanted to leave, not the pitch or the stadium. But soon we reluctantly headed off for to a pub to celebrate and then catch our train, still with huge grins and in amazement. We were soon back in Sutton with family and me and Stephen and our parents went to the local pub and spent the night having a few pints to continue the celebrations, only going home to watch the highlights on Match of the Day. The following day at school I received warm appreciation from many. The day's big news story and I had been a witness – everyone wanted to know what it had been like. Even Leeds fans congratulated me and had huge respect for our achievements. Not least because our victory had meant Leeds had qualified for the Champions League. For the second May in a row I walked around with a permanent dopey smile, which couldn't be removed.

It truly was a great achievement and I had huge respect for Paul Jewell, his coaching team, Geoffrey Richmond and the players. The Premiership had proved to be every bit as tough as everyone told us it would be. But all those people who wrote us off so easily – and so ignorantly – were proved wrong. Fellow football fans who belittled us were now talking of their admiration for our achievements.

There were heroes throughout the team who given everything for our cause – Matt Clarke, Gunnar Halle, David Wetherall, Andy O'Brien, Wayne Jacobs, Jamie Lawrence, Stuart McCall, Peter Beagrie, Dean Saunders and the media star Dean Windass. Others also played their part and battled hard when called upon.

As hard as it is to believe now, considering the decline which would follow, at the time the achievement of staying up was knocked by some City fans who believed we should have done a much better job of surviving. We were lucky they claimed; maybe so, but I don't think the efforts of the management and players deserved such little respect. We were up in the best league in the world, facing world class players week in week out. It was always going to be a struggle, but everyone gave their all and never could their efforts be questioned. Sure there were some poor performances, bad mistakes and naive moments; but City had taken on the best that English football had to offer, and survived. That season had been an exhilarating experience. Some brilliant matches, great grounds visited, world class players witnessed and unforgettable victories achieved.

And the whole experience came with a happy ending that we would never forget – who says fairy stories are always made up?

Chapter Six

2000 - 01
Failing to get comfortable

The temptation was to believe the hard work was over. Throughout the previous campaign, we'd been repeatedly told how the first season promoted to the Premier League would be the toughest. Should we survive, the money coming in would enable us to attract better players and then progress even further. After a year feeling so stressed out about whether we would stay up or go down, I guess it was natural we would want to go into the next one believing we would have no such difficulties maintaining our place among the elite. How wrong we were.

What in fact we were about to discover is second season syndrome. The Bantams were probably the pioneers of this. As after we were relegated somewhat feebly in our second season, a succession of other newly promoted clubs enjoyed a great first campaign before unexpectedly crashing back down the following year, just like City. As we finished bottom of the table this season, newly-promoted Ipswich were heading for a top five finish and European football. A magnificent achievement – but that still didn't stop them going the same way as City a year later.

It is quite simply a huge challenge just to stand still in the Premier League, and the relegation zone is more like falling off a giant cliff than sliding through a trapdoor. Even with the cushion of parachute payments to ease that fall back into the Football League, financial problems quickly follow. City's second season syndrome can be put down to failed attempts to improve the playing squad and playing style after it was widely accepted we could play in a certain way during the first season, in an attempt to grab any point going. Just as we thought we could get comfortable and start to have a level of expectation when travelling to places like Old Trafford and Anfield, it was quickly taken away.

But even if we had stayed up again, the long-term prospects would have doubtful. Just how far could City have gone over the subsequent years? We would never have competed for the title; we would have had no chance of ever making a Champions League spot. The best to aspire to seemed to be mid-table, year-on-year of getting to 40 points as quickly as possible, while hoping for a memorable cup run. So much about football-supporting is the anticipation of success, but what type of glory could we have realistically dreamed of at the start of a new season – a memorable victory over Manchester United? Perhaps we'd have adapted and loved it, but I do sometimes look at supporters of Wigan and Bolton – success stories that other newly-promoted clubs aspire too – and wonder if they enjoy effectively making up the numbers at a party where they'll never be allowed near the VIP section.

And that's where the dream all lower league supporters apparently have of being in the Premier League is clouded. Sure, it was amazing to see City take on the best and to witness some of the World's finest players on your own turf, but is it worth paying those excessive ticket prices year on year when the prospects of achieving much beyond a 10th place finish are so limited? I can't say I missed the Football League during our two-year stay among the elite; but looking back years later now, I don't think I'd ever want City to leave it again. There's something nice about approaching the start of a new campaign and realistically believing we can win the division we are in. Only a minority of Premier League supporters feel the same way.

Manchester United (away) – leaving home

The summer of 2000 was a crossroad, both for Bradford City and myself. While the Bantams were changing manager, entering Europe through the Intertato cup and spending big money on big names, I was preparing myself to go to University and move away from the area.

My destination was Sunderland. After completing sixth form I was keen to continue my Media Studies education by undertaking a degree in Journalism. I looked around and visited a couple of places, but Sunderland was my first choice. I visited the City and Campus in February with three other friends and the place seemed nice enough. Students wanting to go to University were encouraged to apply to up to six Universities and I received two offers; one from Lincoln, a place I had never visited, the other Sunderland.

Of course there was a downside to moving away. I was going to be moving 100 miles away from my family and my friends. My girlfriend was also upset at me relocating and couldn't understand my motives. I was going away to a strange town where I didn't know another soul. It was a scary prospect and I knew it wouldn't be easy. But still the reputation of what student life is like, plus the fact that so many of my friends were also setting off to different parts of the country as well, meant I was going through with the move no matter the nerves.

Not surprisingly, one of the biggest drawbacks for moving away was no longer being able to watch Bradford City. I hadn't renewed my season ticket for obvious reasons, and Stephen and David were facing a season not just without their brother, Alan, by their side, but with me absent too. I didn't want to give up going to watch City each week, but had to be realistic about the bigger picture. Getting my independence, studying for a good quality future career, experiencing what life was like in a different part of the country; they were all really important to an 18-year-old on the verge of adult life. Whatever happened in the next three years, Bradford City would always be there to come back to. Right?

Moving away made me think more about the future of City and I thought about not just were the club might be next May, but in three years time. It left me feeling fearful. Given the rate of progress during the last five years and the excellent leadership of Geoffrey Richmond; I could only imagine City would progress strongly during my time away. Already work was starting on a new stand and there was talk of doing up two more. I pictured the Bradford City in three years to be an established, decent Premiership club. Crowds would be very high; we would have some fantastic players. During those three years there would be some magical moments; we would beat Leeds at Valley Parade, probably even Man United too. There would be a memorable cup run where we would reach a semi-final, big money would be spent, transfer records commonly broken, high league positions achieved. This all sounded wonderful, but at the same time not something I wanted to miss out on. I was fearful that, as the club continued to progress, I was going to be left behind. When I returned home in three years time clutching a degree, would I even be able to get a ticket to matches?

If all of this sounds a bit paranoid, the progress of City that summer alone left me with anxious feelings that the club was moving on without me. It was certainly eventful as we basked in the glow of Premiership survival and watched the tape of highlights from the Liverpool game again and again. First came news that we were going to be entering the Intertoto Cup. City in Europe? This was something I had dreamed about. Then Paul Jewell resigned as manager and in came Chris Hutchings. He had been Jewell's assistant and his appointment followed the previously successful formula of promoting from within which had seen Chris Kamara and Jewell deliver City high rewards.

Meanwhile, a period that would be later described as 'six weeks of madness' was in its infancy. Richmond was sanctioning player buys for money unseen before at Valley Parade. It began with free transfer signings of Peter Atherton and Ian Nolan from Sheffield Wednesday, then a club record £2.5 million was spent luring Leeds midfielder David Hopkin to Valley Parade. The next two moves blew those out of the water. First Dan Petrescu was signed from Chelsea in exchange for £1 million. The Romanian international was a classy player who had been very popular with Chelsea. Then the website announced that City were on the verge of "the most exciting signing in the club's history".

Naturally expectation was high and it was actually slightly disappointing to discover it was Italian playmaker Benito Carbone who was about to sign and who came with a good reputation. Still, it was an intriguing signing and seemed to signal that City's status in English football had reached new heights. Carbone was a free transfer signing from Wednesday, (last season he had been on loan at Aston Villa), but his wages were a mind-boggling £40,000 a week. As future Chairman and at the time board member Julian Rhodes would later comment, City were paying Carbone more than Man United David Beckham at the time. Ashley Ward's £1.8 million arrival from Blackburn was barely newsworthy alongside such extraordinary developments.

I was on holiday as the news of Petrescu and Carbone broke, which helped add to my uneasiness that the club was leaving me behind. I had been attending the home Intertoto Cup matches, which had felt very comfortingly Bradford City. The games were like pre-season friendlies, only slightly quicker and more meaningful. Our first round game was against Lithuanian side FK Atlantas. Having already won the away leg 3-1, the home leg was always going to be comfortable. We soon raced into a 4-0 lead and the whole European experience seemed very enjoyable. Even when Atlantas scored it was one of the funniest moments I have ever experienced watching City. It was a free kick to the visitors in the last minute, with the aggregate score 7-1 to City. The player curled an effort low around the wall and into the bottom corner and went mental in celebration; first charging over to the substitute bench to hug the manager, then running towards us in the Kop and goading us. Finally he raced to the far end of the Midland Road Stand where a handful of Atlantas supporters were housed, jumping into the crowd and continuing to hug fans long after the referee had blown for full time. I don't think I have ever seen a player as pleased to score at Valley Parade as this guy was!

As I was going to University in September, I had to get myself summer employment to save up money to get me through it. It took me a while to find something, but I eventually got taken on by McDonalds in Keighley. The advantage of this was I would be able to transfer to a Sunderland store and have a job at University – but what a horrible job! The work was simple but at a fast pace. Some of the managers were nasty people clearly enjoying their status too much and going to great lengths to exercise their power. In general, the atmosphere wasn't great. I was working in the kitchen, usually in charge of cooking Quarter Pounders. During the interview my hobby of watching Bradford City was raised and I was asked if it would affect my availability.

Desperate for the job, I had to say it wouldn't. I don't know if the manager in charge of setting the shifts, who had conduced the interview, was aware of City's fixtures; but as I was scheduled to work at the same time as City's opening three Premiership fixtures I felt like I was being tested. There were only a few games before I moved to Sunderland, but as City kicked off the season with a narrow 1-0 defeat away at Liverpool I was flipping burgers and getting a dressing down for forgetting to wear the right footwear.

Of course this meant I had to also miss the first home game of the season against Chelsea. While a healthy crowd packed into Valley Parade to see Carbone mark his full debut with the second goal in a shock 2-0 win, I was getting in trouble for not cleaning the toilets to an appropriate standard. The Chelsea game is considered the high water mark of City's elevation, the night when it looked like the expensive signings were going to pay off and lead City to the promised land of midtable. The quality of the performance, the fact we were up against one of the favourites for the Premiership, the brilliance of Carbone...I was to discover all of this just after midnight as my shift came to an end. Left behind? City were seemingly already out of sight.

Looking at the schedule for the next two weeks, I realised I was not going to get to watch City before I left for University. Action had to be taken and I was able to swap shifts so that I could attend the next two Premiership matches. I was finally able to look forward to my first league game of the season, the small matter of Man United away. Stephen and David were both on holiday so I ended up travelling on the supporters coach by myself.

The significance of going to watch City at Old Trafford wasn't lost on me. It felt unusual to be visiting a place I had known quite well from several visits to the Old Trafford Megastore a few years earlier. Now United were the opposition and I was hoping for a shock away win. I wandered around the new superstore before kick off, much larger than the old one was. Inside the ground felt different with the stand behind the goal where we were near now having a second tier. I imagined the visit as like seeing an ex-girlfriend while with a new one. You wanted to secretly impress and make the old flame feel jealous, while subconsciously confirming inside

97

that you had made the right choice. I hoped us fans would make a brilliant atmosphere so that everyone in the stadium knew of our presence, I dreamed for a victory that would really make them sit up and take notice.

Yet United couldn't have acted more dismissively than if their fans had turned their backs during the match and munched on their infamous prawn sandwiches. Sir Alex Ferguson picked an almost entire reserve team, with many big names rested or on the bench. City were of course considered nothing more than an easy home victory to United and, while there would have been nothing better than to prove them wrong, the task proved beyond our players. Within ten minutes Andrew Cole hit a shot which deflected off Atherton and looped into the net over Matt Clarke's head. Ten minutes later, we were on the attack and should have won a free kick when Gary Neville fouled. The referee ignored the push and United broke to make it 2-0. Early in the second half they scored the third through another deflected shot. It was hard to take, we were 3-0 down but United had been fortunate with all three goals. If only the referee could have blown for full time then, instead the home side scored three more goals. United reserves had beaten us 6-0. Oh well, I still preferred the new girlfriend.

I was also able to get to the Arsenal home game a few days later, though felt a little pushed into the corner. I could only get a ticket in the Midland Road stand, right at the far end from my old regular place in the Kop near to the Arsenal fans in the Bradford End. The ticket cost an incredible £28, quite a hike from the £5 I was paying three years ago. Still it was a much better performance and I had a good view as Stuart McCall fired us into the lead. Arsenal equalised with a first ever goal for Ashley Cole in the second half, but we held on for a credible draw. The highlight of the game had been watching the first half duel between Carbone and Lee Dixon. The Italian showed some breathtaking skill in regularly beating the experienced full back. Unfortunately he was guilty of two bad second half misses that should have won us the game. It would arguably sum up his whole City career.

Still at least I had got to a couple of games and the following weekend, as City lost 2-0 at Aston Villa, I was packing my stuff and moving to the North East. I was going to miss family and friends; I was going to miss watching

Bradford City. Still at least I was confident we would survive the drop again and be a Premiership team for years to come.

Southampton (home) – from a distance

The following week City entertained Southampton in a game that most assumed would be easily won; thus propelling us up the league following a difficult start. In the event, the 1-0 defeat was the first signal that the season was not going to go as hoped. But while 17,000 City fans had an uncomfortably good view of Gunnar Halle's own goal which lost us the game, I was 100 miles listening to football scores on the radio.

It was a strange experience, being so far away with the game going on. I'd missed more home games than I would have liked since starting to watch City, many through being on holiday and hundreds of miles away, yet this felt different. It was a Saturday and I had nothing to do, but I wasn't at Valley Parade which is how I had spent most free afternoons for the last 34 months. Meanwhile, life at City was carrying on as normal. Thousands of fans had turned up with the usual mixed range of optimism and nerves, the players had taken part in what sounded a dull game of football and manager Chris Hutchings had attempted to the lift the team with substitutions. The tea bars served refreshments, Lenny (the City Gent mascot) threw sweets into the crowd, the scoreboard flashed up the latest scores and Stephen and Dave were sat in their usual seats in the Kop.

Life went on as usual, but I was no longer a part of it.

It was a feeling I would soon have to become used to, but nevertheless wasn't a pleasant one. Since my first game against West Brom in 1997, I hated missing any match, especially games at home. There was the fear of missing something utterly memorable and it didn't even necessarily have to be a good memorable. Of course not witnessing a brilliant win or fantastic goal is hard to bear, but equally there is something unsettling about missing dismal defeats or wretched performances. Good or bad, I wanted to be there for it. In the second half of last season in particular, I had missed few matches and experienced the full highs and lows of the relegation battle. To a supporter not there, the 4-0 defeats to Coventry and Everton just appear like woeful defeats they are glad to have missed. Yet, having been there, I have fond memories of the incredible atmosphere among the away support and how different each game might have been had we scored during our good spells.

Now all of that was gone, for three years at least. I heard the final score that we had lost 1-0 at Southampton and, apart from viewing the match report on teletext and later on a couple of websites, I knew nothing of how the game was. Were we unlucky? Were we outclassed? Was the game at least good to watch? Are we going down or was this a blip? I was now back to the kind of supporters' role I had when I was a Manchester United fan. Relying on other people to tell me how good/bad games are, who the best players were and what Hutchings should be doing to improve things.

Can you just continue living the way you have for years – without making changes that might enhance it – just so that you can keep going to Valley Parade every other week? Other opportunities, be they other people or career chances, come along and no matter how important City are it can't rule your life, can it? I went to University because I wanted to experience life in another part of the country. I needed to have a stab at living independently and was keen to further my education in the hope of a good career. In my own world, this was more important than attending Southampton home – or Man United at home for that matter. So I had to stop going for a few years, and I had to somehow learn to get used to it.

Not that this made my life unhappy. After a couple of days, I quickly adapted to life at University and began to make friends. The feeling of being alone on that first Sunday evening was horrible and I feared I wouldn't make any friends. After my parents left and I had called my girlfriend, I was ready to explore and find people. I went downstairs and quickly discovered the student bar which was full. I ordered a pint and stood there, waiting for people to come up and say hi and for friendships to begin. It didn't work out like that; the bar was already packed with small groups of friends. Whether they were an established groups in their second year or people who had met that afternoon, they all looked happy and no one was going to walk up to the stranger in the corner nervously sipping a pint and ask them to join them.

So I quickly disappeared into the Sunderland night to wander around the city, trying not to get lost, before returning to my room deflated. Just as it approached midnight someone knocked on my door and I found that mythical group looking for strangers to join them. They invited me to hang out with them and, within an hour, I was sat on the floor in someone's room taking swigs from a bottle of vodka and introducing myself to a circle of people. Pretty soon I was drunk with the room spinning, and so stumbled back to my room to sleep. The next morning I woke up to find my bed and wall covered in sick. Welcome to University.

Monday was all about induction classes with people on my course and tours of the buildings where we would have lectures and seminars for the next three years. Again I found myself on my own and this felt more awkward when we were taken to a room full of food for a welcome party. Eventually a few of us got talking and, almost in an effort to break the ice, someone suggested we all went together to the Freshers' Party at the student nightclub that night. We all agreed and bought tickets from the bar. We then arranged to meet up in a couple of hours, and went back to our rooms to get ready.

It was the start of proper Uni life. Around eight of us went out and, while some people that night disappeared into the background and weren't part of our group of friends, others became good mates with whom I would share the next three years. The nightclub had an indie covers band playing and, with us all loving that sort of music, we had a great time. We then retreated to a flat where three of the group lived together and stayed up drinking for hours. One particular character was a Geordie named Paul, who had the strongest Newcastle accent I had ever heard. He also spoke ridiculously fast making him impossible to understand. As he ran through his repertoire of anecdotes I struggled to catch what he meant and laughed when others did so, out of politeness. I later discovered that everyone else listening was doing the same. I went to bed that night much happier, feeling like I was making friends. Thankfully I also woke up to a sick-free wall.

This loose group remained for the next few nights with more people gradually brought along into it and others finding different friends. I was living on the eighth floor of a building that resembled a tall block of flats and gradually got to know everyone else on my corridor. Several of us became good friends and would live together in the second and third years of University.

Socialising was top of the agenda for me, with University work coming very much second. I didn't enjoy a lot of the lectures and lessons and found that the days were an unwelcome distraction from the important nights out. To be fair, in the first year the work was less important and everyone around me felt the same. We soon had a routine of going out. Monday was a big student night and we headed for a club on the opposite side of town called The Palace. Tuesday was about recovering and maybe going for a couple of pints in the evening. Wednesday was another big night with a trip to the 70s/80s night at the Student Union nightclub, Manor Quay. On Thursday we would head to the City Centre and visit Pzazz, a nightclub infamous for being slightly rough with the potential for trouble. At the weekends we would stay in; Sunderland would get packed with locals in the evenings and they weren't exactly keen on students.

I also had a part time job. Having applied for the local McDonalds, which I was able to get in to easily given I had been working at the Keighley store. There were three stores in Sunderland but I had the misfortune of getting a job at the one on the opposite side of town – not only was it a long walk to work, it was next to the Sunderland FC's Stadium of Light. I usually worked Saturday and Sundays which meant I had to get up very early at weekends. I hated every second I was there, extremely resentful of losing my free time. I would be at work for 7am on a Saturday morning and finish around 4pm. Usually I would return to halls to find friends were just rolling out of bed. Saturday was everyone's sleeping in day and I felt very bitter to be up early and doing a horrible job.

Working on match days was sheer hell as the store was so busy with hungry fans on the way to the game. Burgers were ordered much faster than we could cook them, managers would shout at us all to hurry up without doing anything to help us. It was good to get to 3pm when the 40,000 Mackems who descended on this part of the city were inside the stadium watching the game.

Working Saturday's meant I also missed following City's fortunes. I signed up my mobile phone to receive score flashes from games so that I could at least sneak off and check my phone. After that Southampton defeat results continued to disappoint. A late Dan Petrescu equaliser to claim a draw against West Ham was as good as it got. City then lost 2-0 at Man City and at home to Ipswich, both teams were newly promoted. The Ipswich defeat sent alarm bells ringing and left City lying second bottom of the league. Geoffrey Richmond publicly warned Hutchings that if results didn't improve he would lose his job. He then sanctioned the signing of Stan Collymore. City offered him a good salary and another opportunity to revive his career. It was another gamble by City in the wake of the big summer spending. Collymore would prove the last big name signing.

Leeds (home) and Newcastle (away) – new angles

I had two main fears with going to University. The first was that I wouldn't make any friends and be lonely and miserable in a strange place. The second was that I would find a group of friends, but they wouldn't like football.

I certainly had no worries on either front. A group of us 10 males became firm friends, and six of us were particularly close. We also soon had a network of other friends, including plenty of females. We had a busy social life with two or three big nights out each week. Would always hang out together on evenings we stayed in and were having a great time bonding. There were also some big football fans among the group and watching football became one of the things we did.

James, one of the first people I met but someone ultimately on the outside of the six, was a Wolves fan. In truth rugby was his main interest, but he did go and watch Wolves infrequently when at home. He had been at Molineux on the day City were promoted to the Premier League; in fact he was in the tier above where we away fans were located. We both spoke fondly of that day with James saying he still enjoyed it, particularly watching us celebrate. Dan was a fierce Blackburn Rovers fan. He had been going to watch them regularly for a couple of seasons before they were relegated from the Premier League in 1999. Out of the group he had the most difficult background with his parents splitting up and money tighter than for the rest of us. There was no doubting his fierce loyalty to Rovers and, in particular, his passionate hatred of Manchester United.

Which meant there were plenty of arguments with Simon and Alex, two supporters of the Red Devils. Simon was from Spennymoor, just down the road from Sunderland. Despite the strong passion of Newcastle and Sunderland fans nearby, Simon had been heavily influenced by his United-supporting older brother and, to be fair, he was no glory fan. He had begun following United as a kid in the late 80s, when they were a mid-table team considering sacking a struggling Alex Ferguson. He had also attended many United games over the years. I didn't tell Simon or Alex about my dark past of supporting their team; they wouldn't find this out until years later.

Then there was Martin, a Nottingham Forest supporter. He was born near the city, although lived in a town called Long Eaton which had a Derby postcode. Given the close rivalry of the two East Midlands clubs, this was a great snippet of information to tease him for. Like me, I suspected Martin was later into football than the rest and seemed to only start liking it from Euro 96. He did go and watch Forest semi-regularly, although it was only after leaving University years later that he got really passionate and became a season ticket holder. There were other big football fans that I was friends with, notably Simon a Newcastle fan who I'll come back to. But in our little group conversations rolled around Man United, Blackburn Rovers, Nottingham Forest and, of course, Bradford City. Naturally football was a source of plenty of banter.

It was part of this banter, and the fear that comes with it, that led me to sit in our student bar on my own to watch the Sky screening of City v Leeds. I had quickly impressed on my new friends the level of dislike I had for our near neighbours. It wasn't a rivalry that they were really aware of, which meant I could unfairly get the Bradford City viewpoint across to them. Luckily I found willing ears as none of them had any time for Leeds either. But still this derby game which, in light of recent results, worried me and I wasn't sure I could cope with losing badly and their taunts.

I was pleasantly surprised to find the bar heaving with a notable number of fellow City fans present. I had decided to wear my City shirt so others could identify my team and unexpectedly fell into conversation with a number of people I had never laid eyes on before, but who were from places local to me at home such as Keighley. It was a very unusual feeling to be watching Bradford City play at home on TV in a pub. I was grateful Sky had put this game on TV so I could at least watch the game, but it just wasn't the same.

The game kicked off and the rain was pouring down. I guess my fellow supporters freezing in the stands wished they were in a warm place like me. They soon had something to cheer though as, 20 minutes in, debut boy Collymore hit a sensational overhead kick from a Benito Carbone cross which flew into the bottom corner. I instinctively stood up and cheered, as did several others. It was clear that there were even more City fans here than I thought. What a goal! What a way for Collymore to become an instant hero; you can't do better than score a wonder goal against Leeds in your first game!

There was still a long way to go and Leeds always looked a threat. City were battling hard and defending well. It seemed comfortingly familiar and a reminder of last season. There was strong criticism coming out of Valley Parade and Hutchings was under pressure, but the players were giving everything today. Unfortunately it wasn't enough as, with 10 minutes to go, Mark Viduka found half a yard pulling away from Peter Atherton to head home an equaliser. The game finished 1-1. A decent result and at least they hadn't beaten us for the fourth time in a row. But having been in front for so long, the opportunity of a famous victory being taken away was disappointing. I went back to my halls to find everyone else playing poker. I almost wished I hadn't been so scared and dragged them to watch us play.

If I felt sad about watching City from afar, I was comforted by the fact that I would be seeing their next game in the flesh. With three North East clubs in the Premiership, I knew there would be opportunities to see City when they were in the area. City had drawn Newcastle away in the League Cup and Simon, the Newcastle-supporting mate, asked if I wanted to go along with him. Of course I did, even though it meant I would have to sit with him in the home end. It was Halloween on the night of the game and, while all of our group prepared themselves for a themed night out at the student nightclub, me and Simon caught the bus to Newcastle. It was interesting to be alone in his company for the evening. Most people choose their University on the quality of the course or reputation of the nightlife. For Simon though, the main reason for selecting Sunderland was because it was the closest place running the course he wanted to do in relation to St James Park.

Simon was from Birmingham but a passionate supporter of Newcastle. He had chosen them because his mum was originally from Newcastle and over time had become fanatical about them. Unfortunately for him, he lived hundreds of miles from St James Park so never got to go to games. His decision to study in the North East was an easy one, for it meant Newcastle United was in easy reach. While we were all making nights out and cheap fruit vodka drinks our priority, Simon was making sure he had enough money to watch the Toon and became a regular at home games.

As we chatted on our way to Newcastle; it struck me that whilst I had moved so far away from Valley Parade that I couldn't go any more, and was still coming to terms with coping with such a big hole in my life; Simon was just starting out going to the football. His life was now dominated by watching his team, just as mine had been before. It was as if we had swapped lives. I was now him, frustrated at being so far away from my team and ultimately not feeling like part of things. He'd become what was me, living for Saturday afternoons and the excitement of watching his team.

We sat in the Gallowgate End to watch the game, the main home stand. I felt slightly worried being surrounded by Newcastle fans. Would they be able to tell I was a City fan? Would they even care if I was? What if we score, can I trust myself not to jump up and cheer? What if Newcastle score, can I convincingly pretend I'm happy? It felt very odd, peering across the ground, to see a small band of City supporters located in the top corner of a huge stand opposite us.

The game was a classic. Newcastle looked very confident and quickly took the lead. I stood up and clapped, which I felt was a safe reaction that wouldn't arouse suspicion. It was soon 2-0, our defence is shocking. Time to stand up and clap again: 3-0, for god's sake! As I stood up and applauded again I began to fear a six or seven-goal hiding. We've only played half an hour and were getting slaughtered. Then, unexpectedly, we scored. Shearer of all people played a weak back pass and Ian Nolan ran through on goal to slot home. Under the plastic chair, I clench my fist in silent celebration. It doesn't feel much better though; we're surely still going to concede three or four more.

Incredibly, the goal changed the atmosphere – from being surrounded by happy Geordies rubbing their hands at the prospect of a cricket score, everyone went quiet. This atmosphere translated onto the pitch and suddenly those in black and white looked nervous and edgy. Each poor clearance and bad pass increased the level of groans and, as the referee blew for half time, it didn't feel like I was sat in the home end of a team 3-1 up.

Hutchings' showed his displeasure at our first half display by hauling off Carbone and Collymore and replacing them with Ashley Ward and Dean Saunders. And City started the second half much better, taking the game to Newcastle. The nerves around me remained, Newcastle were struggling a little this season and it was clear the crowd didn't trust their team to perform. Their fears were soon realised when some terrible defending allowed Ward to score for us, his first goal in a City shirt. I clinched my fist underneath my chair again and struggled to keep calm. 3-2. Are we going to come back from 3-0? Ward has finally scored a goal, so anything's possible!

Minutes later it happened. More slap stick home defending allowed Ward in. He made the faintest of contacts on the ball pinging about in the area, but it incredibly rolled past the keeper and into the net. 3-3! I can see a couple of hundred City fans going berserk at the opposite end of the ground. I wished I could have joined them. Instead I covered my mouth and pretended to look devastated, but it was only so I could smile in disbelief at what I'm seeing. I tried not to look at Simon, who had gone very quiet. How will he react to this? Will he suddenly turn on me and 'out' me to the fans around? No, surely he is too nice for that. Hey, what happens if we score again? How can I seriously keep my emotions in check at what I'm witnessing?

I had no need to worry, within two minutes Newcastle went up the other end and scored from a corner. 4-3, now I felt gutted again. Everyone around me was jumping up and down and I had to muster all the strength I could to stand up and politely clap. Finally the Newcastle players sorted themselves out and killed the game off in the final 10 minutes. City didn't get near to scoring a fourth and were out of the cup. Hardly a surprise result, but the scoreline and performance was unexpected.

The whole experience felt unsettling. It was nearly two months since I last saw City in the flesh and life had progressed, both for myself and for the club. Tonight we met again, only I'm still watching from afar. Sat in the home end, I feel as though I'm still observing Bradford City without me. I'm watching the away fans, when last April I sat in that part of the ground among them. I'm seeing familiar players, although there are some I don't know as well. But Bradford City, players and supporters are oblivious to my presence. I felt the urge to shout out in support of Carbone, as he attacked towards me during the first half. I wanted to tell Aidan Davidson he's unlucky as the fourth goal flew into the net in front of me. I wanted to loudly shout in support of my team and help them, my natural urge. But I couldn't do or say anything and at full time we passed our separate ways into the night. It was great to see the players again, but I left feeling more left out than ever.

As we travelled back to Sunderland, Simon was full of enthusiasm and talked non-stop about the game. He said, "all credit to Bradford for your performance" repeatedly, and I had to sportingly return compliments about his team. Despite the excitement of the game, I couldn't imagine any other Newcastle fans are feeling as happy as he did. After all they had laboured to overcome a struggling team near the bottom, blew a three goal lead and defended woefully. They were lucky, which Simon acknowledged; but he wasn't interested in talking about his teams failings and moaning. He had seen a thrilling cup tie, probably the first of his life.

We arrived back in Sunderland and I rang one of our group to find put where they are so I could catch up with them on the night out. I asked Simon if he was coming too, but he said he was going home, "I want to watch the highlights of the game on TV." I knew exactly where he was coming from, thinking back to last season and the number of night outs I had missed on Saturdays, preferring to watch the highlights of the game I had just been to on Match of the Day.

We parted company and I thanked him for getting me a ticket and taking me along. As he walked away I felt envious of his enthusiasm. He was ultimately at the proper beginning of supporting his team, experiencing all the excitement I did three years ago when I first started going to City. Newcastle United was the most important thing in his life now and it's a journey I'm familiar with.

The start of a great adventure for him, but for me I've gone slightly off the rails and know I'm unlikely to get back on board for a few more years.

Everton (home) – enter the judge

Three out of four games. If that was a striker scoring about his recent goalscoring record, he'd be rightly pleased. I was also feeling proud that, after watching the Leeds game on Sky and the Newcastle cup match from the home end, I was now sat on the Kop about to applaud the players onto the pitch for the home game with Everton. In between, City had lost 2-0 away at Charlton, prompting Geoffrey Richmond to sack Hutchings. We were still second bottom with just the Chelsea home win and a few draws to show for our efforts. Hutchings had only lasted 12 matches and, in a caretaker capacity, Stuart McCall was now in charge having suffered the only sending off in his career in the last minute at Charlton. It was a good time to come back in some respects and, as I gazed around the familiar sights and sounds of Valley Parade (just the Main Stand without a roof and a new corner stand in-between it and The Kop in the process of being built were different to usual) I felt glad to be back.

It was reading week at University, which meant a week without lectures. I had come home for a few days, which gave me the opportunity to get to Valley Parade. It wasn't my first weekend visiting home since leaving for Sunderland, I had come home for my birthday in October when it was international week, this visit also wouldn't be my only one between now and Christmas. Yet I would not see City live again until January.

Why was this? My girlfriend. Just before I left for Uni, we had temporarily broken up with the pressure building. The thought of me moving away was something she struggled to cope with and added to the difficult moments of when I left. In the meantime, things had got worse. She had continued to struggle to handle me leaving and things showed no sign of improving. We were now having huge arguments over the phone at least once a week. There she was at home, moping about a little and missing me. Meanwhile I was going out three or four nights a week and having the time of my life. It was hard for her to handle, being in her final year of sixth form, to speak to me on the phone on a Monday night and knowing I was going out to a club that night. As she went to sleep, my evening was just getting started. I would be getting in at 3 or 4am while she would be getting up a few hours later. By the time I had woken up the next day, she would have been at college for a few hours and it would be getting close to lunchtime. It was understandably difficult for her to get used to. She could only picture what my life was like in Sunderland, and in that kind of situation most of us would see something far worse than the reality.

When it came to going home for a weekend, the pressure was firmly on. I had so many demands on my time. My family obviously wanted to see and spend a decent amount of time with me, and then there was my girlfriend demanding more time than there were hours in the day. Satisfying everyone was very difficult and led to upset at times from both. I would arrive home early evening on the Friday and go back around tea time on the Sunday. In between there was a constant need to be spending quality time with everyone. Other things, such as seeing friends and of course Bradford City, unfortunately had to go out of the window.

So when I came home for a week on this occasion, I knew that I would have time to go and watch this game. This still wasn't enough for the girlfriend, who was extremely upset when I told her my plans for Saturday afternoon. I couldn't make her understand how important this was to me, she resented me going to watch City when I was still living at home and she certainly didn't understand now. I had to hang in there, put up with the flak and remember the end goal. After all, I was going to be witnessing the first ever match with Stuart as manager.

It was great to get away from the pressures and be with Stephen and David again. I was even able to buy a ticket next to them as Alan's old season ticket position had not been taken up. In fact, with ticket prices ridiculously steep, Valley Parade wasn't filled to capacity during the first half of the season. Stephen and David had continued following City in my absence and were still making away trips too. They had recently seen us lose to Man City and were planning to go to upcoming away matches against Derby, Middlesbrough and Newcastle. They weren't too impressed with performances so far and agreed Hutch had to go. They spoke glowingly of Carbone's performances and of Collymore's sensational debut goal against Leeds.

The match ended in disappointment as City lost 1-0 to a very late Everton goal. Being away from Valley Parade for what felt like an age, I was probably more immune to the pain than others. It was a pleasure simply to be there and I had enjoyed our performance. Several good attacks were foiled by good Everton goalkeeping or defending. We had played very well and deserved the win. The late Everton winner felt like a kick in the teeth and made the future look even gloomier. The old rule of winning the next match after sacking a manager hadn't happened. We were still second bottom with only Derby below us. The following week's fixture was Derby away.

We lost that one too, 2-0, to go bottom. Watching in the stands that day was Jim Jefferies, the former Hearts manager who had recently resigned but had done a great job for the Edinburgh club. He was to be our next manager and met the players in the dressing room after the game. It was a surprise choice and not a name I think many of us City fans had heard of before. "The season starts here" he infamously stated upon taking over. City were bottom with one win all season, results were needed quickly.

Sunderland (away) – local passions

One of many reasons for going to University was to experience life in another part of the country. Football played a huge part in that and I was interested to learn more about how football is consumed elsewhere. Moving to the North East was a great place to see this and I became quickly aware of the strong passion locals had for The Game. Early on at Uni, I put myself forward to write for the Students Magazine called 'Degrees North' along with Martin, Alex and James. We wrote articles about music and sport; the music stuff particularly was a great perk as it meant we received free copies of new albums and singles to review prior to their official launch, which we could keep.

Talking to the sports editor, I first learned that the date of the derby between Sunderland and Newcastle was November. He was keen to do a special feature about it and the topic of the derby became a regular part of conversation with people around Uni, weeks before it was due to take place. I was especially aware of the derby build up working in McDonalds alongside Newcastle and Sunderland fans. This game was huge and the keenness of the rivalry was much stronger than City and Leeds, where Leeds fans professed to remain indifferent to us.

On the day of the match I was working, but for once this was a good thing. The game was at St James Park, but the Stadium of Light was hosting a beamback so we were busy with Sunderland fans eating before going to watch it. There was only one thing everyone was talking about in the kitchen, including people who didn't like football. Before the match a Newcastle fan working alongside me, who was a large butch bloke, proudly showed me all of his Newcastle tattoos on his back and legs. The game started and, while we couldn't listen to it, people were going to check the latest score every five minutes.

Newcastle took the lead, the butch Newcastle fan was jubilant while Sunderland fans looked upset. Then in the second half the Mackems equalised, cue cheers from the majority of the kitchen staff. I tried to remain impartial and didn't want to say who I was supporting. Inside I was cheering on Sunderland, my adopted home town. Suddenly Sunderland scored again; people were hugging and high-fiving, apart from the Newcastle fan. "It's a penalty to Newcastle!" was the next update, with barely anytime left. A hush descended in the kitchen. "Shearer's missed it!" The Newcastle fan ran off to the toilets and didn't come out for 20 minutes. When he emerged, it was obvious he had been crying. Did that stop people taking the mick? Of course not.

My shift ended at 5pm and I set off home just as the Sunderland fans were walking home too. Traffic couldn't get down Wearmouth Bridge, such were the throngs of people heading towards town. They were all singing and cheering; celebrating as though they had won the cup final. Well, they had won *their* cup final! I couldn't resist going out that night and dragged a few of us into town for some drinks. The atmosphere was incredible. Everywhere we went people were celebrating the result. "Who let the Toon down? She-she-Shearar!" was the chant of the night. We heard it everywhere. The passion was incredible to all of us and it was obvious what a win like this meant. I thought about City and wondered if we would celebrate like this when we finally beat Leeds? You can imagine the City Centre of Leeds after they have beaten us not been any different to usual, but would Bradford City Centre become a carnival in the way Sunderland had for the night? I had my doubts, although I'd like to find out!

People in Sunderland were hugely passionate about their team, but the rivalry with Newcastle stretched beyond football. Locals of both cities were groomed to hate the other and the rivalry was not imbalanced like City and Leeds. Despite a better history, particularly in recent years, Newcastle fans still hated Sunderland no matter which division they were in. Whenever we went on nights out to Newcastle, the taxi drivers would regularly amuse us with their comments about the other lot. Going to Newcastle, the Mackem drivers would tell us all about why the City of Sunderland is much better and what Newcastle's failings are. Getting a taxi back and, as the driver radioed the controller to inform them they were going to Sunderland; other drivers' voices could be heard on the radio laughing at our unfortunate driver for having to drive to such a horrible place. We would often be asked if we were from Sunderland. There were many occasions where it was better to pretend not to be a student, especially in Sunderland with many locals hating outsiders, but at moments like this you couldn't say, "we're students, not Mackems" quickly enough.

While it was becoming more and more obvious it wouldn't last much longer, I was pleased that City and Sunderland shared divisions and was really looking forward to the day my team visited my adopted home. In mid-January, Sunderland hosted City at the Stadium of Light and I was sat in the away end hoping to upset my new neighbours.

Our line up would not include star names Carbone, Petrescu or Collymore. Following disappointing results over Christmas, Jefferies had decided we couldn't afford the luxury of playing these players and had put them all up for sale. Petrescu and Collymore quickly left, but no one would take on Carbone with his huge wage packet and he was eventually reinstated into the squad. Jefferies' decision seemed initially vindicated when, minus all three in the starting line up, City had earned a shock 2-1 win away at Leicester. Was the great escape still on? We lost the next game, 3-0 at home to Manchester United. We were well adrift so needed to start winning more. The Sunderland game was very important.

It felt unusual to walk out of my room and, 20 minutes later, be sat in the away end for a City match. Steve and Dave had made the trip up on the coach and we met and enjoyed a pint on the concourse as we caught up. We were sat together and I was able to witness a superb defensive performance as City earned a clean sheet and creditable 0-0 draw. It should have been a win really as Windass missed a sitter in the second half. Still everyone left in a good mood and, as I said bye and watched the supporters' coaches depart, I had the equally unusual short walk home from a City match. I tried to conceal my happiness as I made my way through a sea of disappointed Mackems muttering that they should be "thrashing teams like Bradford."

This result failed to inspire the sort of revival last year's match at Sunderland had. City lost their next three matches without scoring a goal - away at Arsenal (0-2) and Southampton (0-2) and at home to Villa (0-3). I had tried to remain upbeat about City's chances of survival, yet these three defeats were enough to convince me we were going down. Players were also departing quickly with Peter Beagrie and David Hopkin following Collymore and Petrescu out the door.

Other sold included young Andy O'Brien (sold to Newcastle £2million) and Windass (Middlesbrough £1 million). At one stage it seemed a player was departing every day. I worried for the future and hoped that new faces would be coming in during the summer.

Relegation

Throughout the 2000-01 season, I displayed a squad photo of City on my bedroom wall at University. With the exception of Ashley Ward and later Stan Collymore and Robert Moleanaar, every member of the squad featured on it. I often studied the picture long and hard, especially as a distraction when talking on the phone. And there was one question that popped up again and again in my mind that left me feeling frustrated.

Was this the most talented Bradford City squad in the club's history? Of course City were once one of the top teams in the country before the First World War, on one occasion finishing fifth and winning the FA Cup in 1911, but football must be better now than it was in those days. Player for player, is this the best City squad ever assembled? And, if it is, why is it failing so badly? Each position in the team had two and sometimes three players talented and capable of playing there. At the back we had David Wetherall, Andy O'Brien, Peter Atherton, Andy Myers and later Moleanaar to choose from as centre backs. In the middle of the park new signing David Hopkin was competing for places with Stuart McCall, Gareth Whalley, Jamie Lawrence, Lee Sharpe, Peter Beagrie, Dan Petrescu and Gareth Grant. Lee Mills and Isaiah Rankin might have been sold on that season, but both Hutchings and Jefferies still had Benito Carbone, Ashley Ward, Dean Saunders, Robbie Blake, Stan Collymore and Dean Windass to score goals. There was equally strong back up options at full back and in goal. So again, why did the squad fail so badly?

Time would tell that the squad was built with finances that were not really there, but surely they should have been able to make a better attempt of fighting relegation than they did. It was hard for me to know why they fell so badly short, I wasn't able to watch them regularly enough. We all knew the Premiership is tough, but what was undoubtedly a much stronger squad than the season before put up a pretty feeble fight to stay up. Why were we basically relegated by February?

On Good Friday City won for the first time since that Leicester game on New Years Day. The second goal of the 2-0 triumph over Charlton was scored by Carbone with a beautiful lob over the keeper. While a win was a rare moment – only City's fourth of the campaign – it was just another of many brilliant Carbone goals during the season. For me though, this was the most special and meaningful of the lot. I was their, sat in the Kop behind the goal where he struck, celebrating with everyone else.

It was the Easter holidays and, being home for two weeks, I knew I had to get to a City game no matter how much it upset other people. This was only the sixth City game I'd seen live all season, a really disappointing total which was well below my worst fears when I left for University. There might not have been much to cheer supporting City this season, but what there had been I had largely missed. This included the talented Carbone, who many other fans were calling the most skillful player to wear Claret and Amber they had ever seen. So far, the best I had seen from him was some great play in the Arsenal home game last September. I hadn't even seen him score a single goal, let alone a spectacular one. As Carbone's lob flew into the net to put us two ahead I felt like I was celebrating wilder than anyone else. I leapt on Stephen and David and punched the air in delight. I sang "Carbone, Carbone" like everyone else, bowing down as I did in an I'm-not-worthy type gesture.

This was a special moment for me. Until now the best I had seen all season was that home draw with Arsenal. I hadn't seen us win, not that it had been a regular occurrence in my absence. I'd had the unsettling effect of moving away and beginning a new type of relationship in the way I supported my team. I was having the time of my life at University and extremely thankful I went, but I missed some things; especially going to watch City and the little but important things such as the great feeling of the referee blowing for full time and being able to celebrate victory. This win didn't change City's season – relegation was inevitable and it was too late to escape now – but for one afternoon I at least got to remember the thrill of watching City win in the Premiership and glimpse the dream we had all shared when Carbone signed last summer, of him acting as the catalyst and scoring great goals to secure us wins.

There were six games to go and City would need to win them all to stay up, not a particularly likely prospect. In the event we beat Derby in the next game and then failed to win again in the Premiership, getting relegated away at Everton after managing to miss two penalties as we went down 2-1. Robbie Blake and Benito Carbone both had penalties that day and both missed. Neither the old nor the new could save City that day.

I was unsure how to react to my first relegation as a football fan, especially as I was not at the game. Did I lie in my bed and cry? Let's face it, relegation wasn't unexpected. It wasn't like we had gone down on the last day of the season with some sort of hope in tact. In the end I settled for playing a few particularly depressing Radiohead songs and stared at my 2000/01 squad poster again. The photo might have been taken almost a year ago, but I still thought those players should have had the courtesy to hang their heads in shame.

We then lost at home to Liverpool (0-2) in that rearranged match (I had to get a refund for my ticket from the club) before ending the home campaign with a 1-1 draw against Middlesbrough. There was just two games to go, one being away at Leeds. I was home for the weekend yet again for that one, with the pressures on my relationship with my girlfriend showing no signs of improvement. I was desperate to go to Elland Road, though in the end was almost glad I didn't. With loads of injuries in defence, City fell apart with McCall and Andy Myers scrapping on the field at one point. The final score was an embarrassing 6-1 to Leeds. Back at University, my friends knew how much that would have hurt me and quickly stuck the knife in with numerous wind up phone calls and texts. I just wanted to hide in my room and not come out for days. Thank goodness the season was almost over.

As City played out a 0-0 draw at fellow relegated Coventry I breathed a huge sigh of relief. A difficult season had finished and hopefully we could rebuild in the summer and challenge for promotion back next season. On a personal level I was hugely dissatisfied at how I was supporting City. I knew I couldn't go every week – and I was happy accepting not doing so as I enjoyed University life so much – but I still needed to see them more often that this. When I went home for the weekend, it had to include attending a City match. I felt like I was getting left behind and, if my fear a year ago of the club progressing to such a level I wouldn't be able to get a ticket to watch them was already looking unfounded, things had to change next year or I could lose them even more.

There were still a few more weeks of University before the summer and I continued to enjoy some great nights out, have fun with my friends and argue weekly with my girlfriend. The day after I came home for the summer we broke up. I looked forward with huge excitement to single life, to full responsibility of living at Uni without anyone else telling me what to do and of getting back to Valley Parade more often.

I was already longing for next season.

Chapter Seven

2001 - 02
"What else is on?"

After jealously watching the Premier League get rich off TV money, in 2001 leading Football League clubs mistakenly believed it was their turn to ride on the wave of football's increasingly popularity. TV was evolving through the early stages of moving to digital broadcasting. The consumer choice of either five basic analogue channels or an expensive satellite TV package was widening. As the key market players looked to steal a march, the Football League was seemingly well-placed to benefit. Sadly it was an expensive lesson in the limitations of what consumers will pay to watch the sport.

ITV Digital was rolled out in the summer of 2001, with a popular marketing campaign that featured a puppet monkey and Johnny Vegas. To tempt consumers, they had snatched the rights to show live Football League matches from Sky's ever-expanding portfolio. The deal was worth a colossal £315m over three years for the 72 clubs, a significant increase from what Sky had previously been paying for the rights. But it was to prove to be a fatally over-priced deal, which would have significant consequences for the Football League and especially Bradford City. Within a year, ITV Digital had collapsed due to lack of customers.

And I had a close up view of this implosion. Now in my second year of University and having moved into a rented house with six friends, there was one especially important decision we had to make at the beginning of the academic year. Given there were six of us sharing the house, the additional monthly cost of getting digital or Sky TV seemed

119

minimal, and we talked excitedly about the prospect of having hundreds of channels to keep us entertained over the coming months. In choosing the right service, football was obviously an important factor. And while we debated which would be best over email during the summer, Martin and I stole in and took advantage.

With both City and his club Nottingham Forest now in Division One, we were determined to ensure that we could see live games involving them. ITV Digital was the perfect solution. And so a charm offensive highlighting the benefits of us getting it, instead of Sky, began. For Russ, the only non-football fan, there was the lure of having MTV and various comedy and music channels. For Simon and Alex, the two Man United supporters, winning them round with the promise they could see every Manchester United Champions League group match – rather relying on which ITV select for live coverage on their terrestrial channel – won them round easily. Now five of us were all on board and me and Martin quickly rushed out and got a Digital box. Only Dan, the Blackburn Rovers fan was unhappy. Still it worked out extremely well for him, as the additional live League Cup games coverage offered only through ITV Digital meant he was able to watch each round of Rovers' progress, as they went onto to lift the trophy.

There was a sense of urgency about getting the Digital Box set up – because that evening's live game was none other than Nottingham Forest v Bradford City. On the afternoon of the game we were at home trying to get the system to work, but had no luck. Afternoon quickly became evening, and with it the realisation we were not going to get the system working in time. We needed telephone assistance, but with the help line closed we reluctantly grabbed our coats and began a fruitless search for a bar in Sunderland that would be showing the game.

Given that Sunderland, Middlesbrough and Newcastle were all in the Premiership, the chances of a pub opting for ITV Digital over the more lucrative option of screening live Premiership football on Sky was slim. We quickly realised there was no hope and, when we bumped into some female friends, we opted to go for a few drinks with them, keep an eye on our phones for the latest score updates and make the most of a disappointing evening. A few hours later when back home we suddenly got ITV Digital to work, typically one wire was in the wrong place. So we settled down and watched the re-run of the second half. We already knew the result, sadly, that Forest had beaten us 1-0 with a goal from their rising star Jermaine Jenas.

Even though we were ITV Digital customers, it was easy to see why it failed so miserably. In the early 90s Sky had been close to collapse but it had exclusive rights to the newly formed Premier League and it was only this that rescued it as interest in football soared. ITV Digital had gone down the football ticket too, committing huge funds to a Football League package it hoped could entice viewers and rival Sky. But it put the football watching consumer in the position of having to make a choice – live Premier League action on Sky or Football League games on ITV Digital? Manchester United v Arsenal on a Sunday afternoon or Coventry v Stockport County on a Sunday evening?

When it came to live Football League games involving City or Forest throughout the season, in our house we would be guaranteed to be sat on the couch watching. Not just me or Martin either, the opportunity to view (and, painfully for us at times, take the mick) out of their friend's football team was sufficient entertainment for the rest of the group. But when it came to live games involving other clubs that none of us had any direct interest in, the TV would be off or on a different channel. I suspect we were the norm among ITV Digital customers across the country.

ITV were reliant on the loyalty of Football League clubs' supporters signing up to ITV Digital to watch their team in action, but a Football League fan is generally a different beast and their interest in the division is usually more limited to their own club. And so pretty soon stories of ridiculously low viewing figures for live Football League matches emerged. That game between Forest and City apparently had less than 1,000 viewers – one later fixture was revealed to have had zero viewers and another to have so few it would have been cheaper to take all those watching to the match rather than screen it. Given how much money ITV had paid for the rights, the resultant fall in advertising revenue quickly made it unsustainable.

Not that this means lower league football isn't enticing to TV viewers. Soon after ITV Digital collapsed, Sky bought back the Football League rights and has retained them ever since. But as much as nothing beats watching your own team, the reality is that from an entertainment point of view the Premier League is much more exciting to watch. And that's what watching football on TV largely is when it's not your team in action – entertainment. Years on I love watching some televised lower league games, but I wouldn't view them all the time. Whereas there are far more Premier League fixtures which I would choose to watch when shown on TV.

Above all, this costly misjudgement by ITV and the Football League showed where its place belongs on the nation's screens. ITV tried to set up the lower divisions to compete with the top flight, but ultimately there was only going to be one winner. Later on in the season, Sky Sports became available on ITV Digital and we paid the necessary extra couple of quid per month to view their live Premiership games. We subsequently rarely missed a Premiership match, no matter who was on, as the season came to a climax. Yet we probably only bothered to watch two other live football league matches which didn't involve City or Forest all season. I imagined this must be the same scenario for many others.

ITV Digital was doomed from the moment the season began. And for City, the ramifications would be felt for many years to come.

Barnsley, Coventry, Burnley, Gillingham (home) and Sheffield United (away) – bouncing back

Despite the relegation from the Premier League, there was no doom and gloom about Bradford City as we prepared for life back in Division One. Two years in the Premiership were great; but with City permanently battling the odds, every point gained and victory earned felt like a huge achievement. Frankly, I think we were all sick of getting beaten so often. In two years City had won a grand total of just 14 Premiership matches. Given that in 1998-99 we had won 26 games to earn promotion, it just showed how rare victories had become.

Ultimately our first season back in the Football League was a hugely topsy-turvy affair that ended far worse than any of us could possibly have envisaged. We began as one of the favourites to go up and a belief that our squad, whilst worryingly thin, was capable of achieving at least a play off spot. We were to end the season in the bottom half of the table and with a huge question mark hanging over the very existence of the club.

On a personal level, the summer of 2001 felt frustratingly long and dull. Back from University for 12 weeks I knew I couldn't face going back to Keighley McDonalds, so found a new summer job. I was working as a cleaner at the local NHS hospital; a role which largely involved cleaning the same section each day and spending my time with the other cleaners, who were mainly old women. I had to be in early, but at least finished by 3pm so the rest of the day could still be enjoyed. It was certainly a more pleasant job than working at McDonalds and the money was hugely helpful.

Elsewhere, being single meant that I could turn my attention to a wholly neglected area of my life, my friends. Given that I had to balance my time away from Uni in the first year between my demanding girlfriend and family, not to mention attempting to get to a City game if possible, friends had unfortunately and grossly-unfairly fallen to the bottom of a priority list which I would never get down to. True, most of us had now spread our wings around the country and my return home at weekends didn't necessarily coincide with others; but there were still friends around who never went to University and I also missed the big reunions at Christmas and Easter. I had a lot of catching up to do.

So my weekends during the summer were largely spent in the nearby village of Silsden, drinking with my old group of friends in local pubs. We also had a few nights out at the local club in Skipton. There were new people who had become part of the group for me to get to know. With others, it was just great to catch up and see them regularly again.

I was desperately looking forward to the new football season and getting to see the first few matches before returning to Uni in mid-September. In early August I joined Stephen and David in watching the season kick off at home to Barnsley. It was an afternoon where pre-season optimism was at its peak and many of us believed City would go straight back up. During the summer there had been little transfer activity, with all those players shipped out before transfer deadline day last season meaning there was no one else to leave. The biggest bit of business was securing Rob Molenaar, Eion Jess and, thankfully, Stuart McCall on new contracts. Geoffrey Richmond also announced midway through the summer that the playing budget had been increased from £5million to £7.5 million. This was so a certain Benito Carbone, with his huge wage packet, could stay. We had all expected him to leave with relegation. In First Division terms his wages were far too high and we had assumed he would want to continue to play top flight football.

So on a hot August day City came out onto the pitch against Barnsley for the big kick off with Carbone in the starting line up. It was still hard to know how good we would be at this level, but in the first 45 minutes we got a good idea. City went 2-0 up though a penalty from Ashley Ward and a great finish from Eion Jess. In the second half, Ward scored another penalty and the day was really capped off when Carbone scored a stunning overhead kick to complete a 4-0 rout. We caught the train home feeling very happy. A great performance against a side who we might expect to challenge for promotion with us, and Carbone scored a stunner.

The good start continued with a 2-1 League Cup win away at Macclesfield and a 1-0 league success over Portsmouth – the only two games up until I went back to Uni which I was unable to get to. After an exciting home win over Coventry, Andy Myers and Gary Locke scoring our goals, the next match was at home to Burnley – a fixture we were really looking forward to. Living in Sutton, there were a high number of Burnley fans around. As we would walk past the local pub to the bus stop in our City shirts for home games, we would often receive abusive comments from Clarets fans sat outside. Geography is a huge factor in rivalries and, while we all disliked Huddersfield, we didn't know any Terriers' fans living our way. Burnley was a different story and this was a local derby the three of us were desperate to win. Confidence was sky high with our 100% record, but Burnley provided the first doubts about our chances of going up. They took the lead three times in this match, often thanks to some very poor defending on our part. City could only equalise twice and lost 3-2, the winner coming in the last minute.

The defensive worries continued in the next game away at Sheffield United. We took the lead through Jess after two minutes, but the Blades came back strongly to lead 2-1 after quarter of an hour. Both goals were down to poor defending and at times the Blades threatened to tear us apart. We held on and scored an equaliser just before half time through Andy Tod – an on-loan Scottish defender (not to be confused with the Bolton player of a similar name) who had been shifted to emergency striker for a few games after Ward was injured against Burnley.

My final game before heading back to the North East was Gillingham at home on a Friday night. As if to ensure I remembered them, City produced a five star performance to thrash the Gills and leave me feeling cautiously optimistic about their chances of challenging for promotion. It was a masterful display, one of the best I have ever seen. David Wetherall gave us a 10th minute lead and the only surprise at half time was that it remained only 1-0. Tod then quickly scored a second, Jess a third and Carbone a fourth. Robbie Blake made it 5-0 before Marlon King pulled a goal back with Gillingham's only attempt on goal all evening. The attacking football was great to watch and the performance of Carbone the icing on the cake. Defenders couldn't handle him as he produced what was surely his greatest-ever performance in a City shirt. The evening showed what City were capable of and what Carbone could do to drive it forward.

As me and Dave went for a drink after the match we both chatted happily about the game, how wonderful Carbone was and how we had a great chance of going up. My thoughts were also turning to my move back to University in two days. And while feeling happy, I was also a little sad to be leaving City behind again. I had enjoyed a great run of watching them and the signs were that it was going to be a memorable season. I knew I would still see quite a few more games this season – all weekend visits home would be timed to coincide with a City match – but I also anticipated many great moments ahead in the next few months which I would again be observing from a distance.

Wolves (h) – that Jonah feeling

No sooner had I left them behind, things began to collapse for City. The 1-0 Forest defeat that me and Martin had expected to watch through our new ITV Digital Box proved to be the start of a slump in form. The warning signs were loud, as in the next game City crashed to a 4-2 defeat at home to a dismal Stockport team who up to that point hadn't won a game. A 3-2 win at home to struggling Grimsby barely put a dent into the growing doom and gloom, but it was significant for me.

No one else noticed, thankfully, but after a year and a month at University this was the first time City had won a league match while I had been in Sunderland. Each of the five league victories achieved the previous campaign had either been achieved before I started Uni, when I was on holiday from Uni or when I had visited home for the weekend from Uni. This season had begun well with some impressive wins, but as soon as I crossed the North East border the poor form began again.

The Grimsby win was the first time I could say to my flatmates that City had won today, the first time I could bask in the glory of victory while in their company. I never mentioned it to them for fear they'd think I was a geek for noting such an unusual stat, and because they weren't exactly short of reasons to take the mick of out of me for supporting the Bantams. That evening I watched highlights of the victory on ITV Digital with a quiet sense of satisfaction and relief.

But joy from City was short-lived. Form continued to drop in October starting with a 4-1 defeat to Watford in the League Cup. I was at home for the next weekend meaning I was able to attend our game at home to Wolves, but a crushing 3-0 defeat meant I was far from a lucky mascot in making my first return since the Gillingham thrashing. The team as a whole seemed desperately short of confidence, and I slumped in my seat in the Kop – turning my phone off for fear of James the Wolves supporter at University ringing me up to gloat, I was already deeply concerned that a promotion push was going to be beyond this team.

Carbone played but was frustrated by a decent defence. Things just didn't go for him and, following rumours City were keen to get him off the wage bill, this provided his final game before a three-month loan spell at Premiership Derby County. The loss of such a skilful player felt like a further hefty blow to our hopes, and there was no sign of any reinforcements. City lost their next three games shipping in nine goals and scoring just once (2-0 at Palace, 4-0 at Birmingham and 3-1 at Millwall). Stephen and David had travelled to Birmingham and I rang them straight after for the verdict, it wasn't pretty. The pressure was now really on and fortunately City temporarily picked up. We played Watford at home and were cruising 4-1 with a Jess hat-trick. Frustratingly, we let Watford come back to 4-3, although held on for the win. Three more goals were conceded at home to Wimbledon the following Tuesday, although thankfully City at least came back from 3-1 down to take a point.

I was fortunate enough to be able to view our next game in our University house with ITV Digital choosing to cover our trip to Crewe. Dan, Simon and Martin all sat there with me and enjoyed supporting Crewe. We should have won, going in front twice and looking much better on the ball. Blake and McCall both scored crackers to make it 2-1. Deep into injury time, our keeper Aidan Davidson flapped at a corner and Crewe stole an equaliser. Cue celebrations from three people in the room. I tried to ignore them by swearing at the City players on TV. Still form was improving and continued with wins against Norwich and Walsall plus a draw at Preston.

Not that my life was consumed by football at this time. University was now in full swing and I had settled back into life up their comfortably. Our social life in the second year was certainly more different. Towards the end of the first year, Dan and Simon had discovered a brilliant club in Newcastle called Shindig and re-focused their priorities towards heading their most weekends. Shindig was devoted to house music and they quickly became immersed in the music and culture of that scene. Martin quickly followed but, while I went along on a couple of occasions, I failed to enjoy it so rarely joined them. I was heavily into my music and did like some aspects of dance music, but I didn't 'get it' – yet.

The day stuff – lectures and seminars – still failed to excite me, although the work was at least a little more interesting. We studied radio and news journalism more and were required to visit a local radio station and put together our own news piece.

Other parts of the course, such as studying media law and ethics, were less interesting and I was usually jubilant when the day's lectures were over. I didn't go back to McDonalds; I simply couldn't stand it any more. I was jobless, but had saved money up during the summer and had my student loan to support me.

Life sharing a house was largely brilliant. Sharing each other's space properly for the first time did cause conflict, mainly about the cleanliness of the house. We had extremes of Alex who liked everything spotless and Dan and Simon who couldn't care less. We had a washing up rota, but people would often wait two or three days before doing their turn. I was somewhere in the middle – not keen on messiness but not caring as much as Alex. The lounge became a tip with dirty plates, old magazines and stolen traffic cones littered about. By the end of the year we had rats under the skirting board in our lounge and kitchen, it was a good job the landlord didn't care.

Sheffield United and Crystal Palace (home) – the judge loses out to the Law

I was a fraud. There was little doubt about it. I stood in front of the camera, told the man what I thought and prayed I was speaking intelligently and accurately. I knew there would be no further questions, so little chance of being caught out now, hopefully. Still I felt like there should be a caption underneath my face when this is shown letting people know the truth. 'He's not a proper fan; he's not been to a game since October'

It took place at Valley Parade on Sunday 23 December. I had stopped off with my parents, having been Christmas shopping in town, to buy tickets for the two Christmas fixtures against Sheffield United and Crystal Palace. City were playing Coventry away that evening and I was looking forward to going with David and Stephen to a pub down the road in Steeton to watch live coverage on ITV Digital. After buying my tickets a film crew had approached me and asked if I could speak on camera to share my views for Yorkshire TV's Calendar News. "It's about the resignation of assistant manager Billy Brown and if you think Jim Jefferies is about to quit," explained the interviewer. I tried to conceal my surprise, Brown had left? Jim Jefferies might be about to be sacked? I knew things were bad, but...I didn't want to let on that I knew nothing of these breaking developments, and shared my views on camera. I believed Jim was unlucky and hadn't been given funds to strengthen the team but had to sell lots of players, I said I hoped he'd stay on.

Why did I feel like a fraud? Well here I was facing up to the prospect of appearing on regional news as a representative Bradford City fan, when I hadn't even been to a game for over two months. I was hardly the most appropriate person to use and, if YTV's budget stretched to background checks of people being interviewed, they would quickly discard the footage of my views. Did most City fans agree that it would be sad if Jim left, or would the 10 second clip of my views be sandwiched in-between other City fans saying good riddance and they'd be happy to help him clear his desk?

That evening I nervously watched Calendar and sure enough my face appeared. I was the first fan to be vox-popped and three others followed. Fortunately their views were in line with what I said. I knew that, with it being local news, some people who knew me will have seen it. This included City fans and, before the Boxing Day game with Sheffield United, we met Dave's friend Shaun in a Bradford pub, who told me that he had seen and agreed with what I said. Given he won't have seen me at a City match since October; he could have loudly screamed across the busy pub that I was a fraud for being on TV. The fact he didn't made me feel very grateful and even a little pleased with myself for spouting an apparently intelligent view. It was perhaps a good job I hadn't criticised Jim!

After the Calendar news bulletin ended that evening, I raced to catch the bus and met Stephen and David as we went to the pub showing City match at Coventry. It was two days before Christmas, and the pub was packed with City fans. There was a nervous edge in the air, recent form had been poor and it looked as though Jim was about to walk. City had recently lost to Millwall at Valley Parade, defeated Rotherham at home and then lost away at Man City.

With stories emerging of a training ground bust up between Jefferies and McCall, it looked like the Coventry game would be the manager's last. It was a strange game to watch, knowing what the result would ultimately mean. The game was fairly even until, five minutes before half time, Ashley Ward missed an open goal for us. Less then a minute later Coventry scored. They added a second before half time. An injury to Davidson meant that Gary Walsh had to come on at half time, but the game continued as it left off with Coventry scoring twice more. During the closing stages the TV pictures cut to the miserable, scowling face of Jefferies on the touchline. I tried to imagine what was going through his mind. Had he decided that's it and was taking in one last glimpse of life managing City, or were the rumours rubbish and he was going to battle on to turn City round? In a season of too many lows, this felt like rock bottom.

The following day Jim Jeffries quit.

As a supporter who had witnessed just seven games of his 13-month reign, I felt slightly unqualified in judging if his exit was a good or bad thing. He came in midway during the Premiership season, but so much ground had been lost that even then it would have been a miracle had we avoided relegation. He had been forced to ship out players as relegation became more and more of a formality. In the summer he might justifiably have believed he would receive decent funds to rebuild and mount a promotion push. But the transfer budget had been sacrificed to allow City to keep Carbone, it seemed, and then the Italian was shipped out on loan two months into the season. It was a situation that left Jim without his star player or funds to bring in a replacement.

Youth team coach Steve Smith was made caretaker manager for the next two games. I was very excited to be able to go to both and it seemed odd, that, given the lack of matches I had been to over the first 18 months, that I was back to witness the in-between of two managerial reigns – just as I had a year ago when McCall was caretaker boss. On Boxing Day City played Sheffield United, but the old rule of winning the next game after losing a manager didn't apply. We deservedly lost 2-1 with Ward scoring. Defeat left me even more hoping for a win three days later as Crystal Palace came to Valley Parade, when you get to go so little you certainly want to see their better days. City lost again 2-1 sadly, although the performance was much better. In the second half we battered Palace and their keeper made a string of superb saves. As I walked home with David and Stephen looking especially downbeat I tried to lift their spirits, and mine, by talking up how well we had played. Ultimately, it was small consolation.

I would have also gone to the next game, Burnley at Turf Moor, but icy conditions meant the game was called off on the morning. That was especially disappointing as I knew I would not be around to attend the re-arranged fixture. It was announced the day before that Chesterfield manager Nicky Law was taking over in the Valley Parade dugout. He came with a good track record after leading the Spireites to promotion. Although not a name I was familiar with, his distinctive bald head and likeness to The Adams Family's Uncle Festa made him quickly-recognisable. It appeared that the aim for the remainder of the season was consolidation. Just like when Jim was appointed, I was back at University for the beginning of the Law era. The problems still persisted and a 2-0 FA Cup defeat at Walsall was a miserable start. Things could surely only get better.

Wolves (away) – Losing bragging rights

There are certain pleasures connected to football which are to be treasured. Beating your mate's football team is right up there. The friendly rivalry leads to the odd argument through the rose-tinted glasses view of your own club, but there is nothing quite as satisfying to settle a debate of who is better than the result when you play them. So when Wolves v City was moved to be shown live on ITV Digital, I knew I had the chance to obtain ultimate bragging rights off my Old Gold-loving friend James; the one with the anorak knowledge, who would be sure not to forget this particular result.

I invited him over to watch the Wolves game and the fact it was some sort of grudge match between two friends was enough to drag all of my housemates out of bed for the Saturday lunchtime kick off. Where I got my optimism from I wasn't sure. Wolves were going well near the top of the league and beat us 3-0 at Valley Parade last October, meanwhile our own form had only slightly improved. Nicky Law's first league match in charge had seen City come from behind to beat Portsmouth 3-1. This was followed by a 3-3 draw at

Barnsley where we had been 3-1 behind with eight minutes to go. Then we lost at home to Preston and all hell seemed to break loose.

Carbone's loan period with Derby had come to an end and he was back at the club, but Law decided to put him on the bench for his first game and play defender-converted-to-striker Andy Tod instead. The Italian reacted badly and refused to be a sub. He ended up watching the 1-0 defeat in the stands. City fined the Italian two weeks wages, £80,000, Carbone publicly apologised and returned to the starting line up for the next game at Grimsby, where he scored the winner from a free kick. Then he was loaned to Middlesbrough for the rest of the season.

But still the slightly improved form and need to show face meant that I hid any fears of defeat to Wolves through bravado in front of James. This only increased when City took the lead after half an hour through Ashley Ward. I leapt up in my chair and clenched my fist in his face. "Get in! ha ha ha!" was my less than sporting reaction. Ignore the fact Wolves had dominated, it had been our only chance of the whole half and there was still half the game to go; I was feeling very pleased with myself as James sat quietly in a chair at half time.

In the second half City badly let me down. Wolves continued to press hard and equalised. James didn't jump up and goad me, he sat in his chair with a quiet smile and a comment of how well taken the goal was. James might have had a statto-like knowledge of football, but he didn't possess the same level of passion that the rest of us had for our team. That and he was more sensible than me.

Now a face-saving draw seemed the best I could hope for, but even that looked unlikely. With 15 minutes to go Wolves scored again with a brilliant run and shot from Shaun Newton. Brilliant if you're a Wolves fan or my flatmates now sniggering at the look on my face, bloody horrible to a City fan left wondering why on earth no one was able to get near Newton and tackle him. I tried to avoid eye contact with James, but I could feel his smile smugly pointing in my direction in a provocative manner. "What a great goal, he took that so well. Your keeper had no chance with that one," he said in a tone of voice that betrayed his attempts to hide his gloating.

Maybe we can still get a point; I won't celebrate in his face if we do this time, I promise.

3-1 Wolves. And now I want to throw this guy out of my house.

Great game, but I'm sure you agree that we deserved to win it," stated James in his best pundit voice. I tried to muster the words "well done" but I couldn't allow him the further glee of my humbleness. So I took the only sensible option that any male football fan in my position could, I sulked. James was now the unwanted guest you couldn't get rid of quickly enough and I grabbed the remote to find the most offensive or dull programme that he would hate, so he would be encouraged to leave. I wanted to go to my room and not speak to anyone for the rest of the day. Yet I had invited James over, foolishly, so I was the last person in the house able to make excuses and slope off. James looked settled and tried to engage others in conversation. "What did you think of our performance? I thought we played really well. We deserved to win." My flatmates were only too happy to agree, while laughing in my direction. Eventually James got up to leave and I summed up my last ounce of strength to say goodbye. Door shut, I'm off upstairs, music on loud and do not disturb. If only we could have beaten Wolves with a last minute winner live on TV I would have invited James to stay for tea.

It was an important lesson I learned about games against your mate's team. Don't be too boastful until the result is a sure thing (and with City there's never a sure thing). Try to show as little sign of emotion as possible if you do lose. And, as the years continued with more similarly painful defeats to your friends team, don't rely on City to win on the big occasions. They let you down. Too often.

When City did beat a friend's team a few weeks later, Martin's Nottingham Forest, the result was much less of a celebration. As it wasn't on TV, we followed the progress of the game by checking teletext every so often. While Jamie Lawrence's last minute winner for us allowed me to gloat a little, the result had less impact on our lives and therefore meant little.

Despite this defeat, City's form did appear to slightly improve, although it was probably fair to say that expectations were now lower. From being disappointed at Jefferies for not being able to get City challenging for promotion, everyone seemed satisfied that we could do no better than mid-table as Law settled in. It wasn't his fault, all that had gone on before, so it felt like the season was now all about preparing for the next. Players were coming and going, with promotion hero Robbie Blake disappointingly sold to Burnley for £1 million and Danny Cadamarteri arriving, initially on loan. The one-time Everton starlet had suffered a wayward time and had recently appeared in court for punching a woman. Cadamarteri was born in Bradford and it had felt he had been linked with us repeatedly over the years. He scored on his debut in an impressive 4-0 win at Gillingham and was quickly signed up permanently. City then beat Forest, much to my satisfaction, and things seemed great.

Then it all went wrong again and City were beaten surprisingly 2-0 at home to Sheffield Wednesday. Worse, the following Tuesday we lost 1-0 at rock bottom Stockport. The Hatters were enduring a woeful season and this March win was only their third of the season, but two of them had now been against us! Not surprisingly my mates gave me plenty of stick for that result. More defeats followed against Man City and Birmingham before a 1-1 draw at Rotherham at least stopped the rot. Ultimately the season became all about avoiding relegation, which we managed to achieve with a few games to spare finishing a disappointing 15th overall. I saw two home games while back in Yorkshire for Easter – a 2-0 home win over Crewe and 1-0 loss to Norwich.

But for supporters the unrest was growing. While at Uni I kept in touch with City events on the internet daily by visiting the library. I also still eagerly got hold of each issue of City Gent. Fans were now turning on Geoffrey Richmond and the fact that no money was being spent. What was going on? I found the whole situation slightly bewildering. Ever since starting to support City Richmond had been worshipped by fans, yet now many were questioning and turning on him. There certainly seemed to be good reasons for doing so and it appeared our chairman wasn't reacting well to the criticism. Surely money will be spent during the summer so that we can challenge for promotion next season?

All of this was troubling, but in reality a distraction for me. University life felt especially good after Christmas and I was really enjoying my lifestyle. I was bonding closer than ever with my flatmates and enjoying some memorable night outs. We had a widening circle of friends and rarely seemed to be short of things to do. Even the lectures and seminars didn't seem as boring as they had before. The end to the season was also to provide a glorious, unexpected moment, when James' Wolves, seemingly out of sight and about to cross the finishing line to promotion to the Premiership, managed to blow up spectacularly and lose a 10 point lead to end up in the play offs, where they then lost in the semi finals to Norwich. To make matters far worse for them, the team who managed to pip Wolves were their biggest rivals, West Brom. As Norwich scored their clincher in the play offs we decided to call up James to taunt him loudly and cruelly down the phone.

I bet he wished he could swap that win over City for a less painful end to the season. That'll teach him to have acted so smug.

The collapse

When I first heard the news I didn't know what to think. I knew it was bad, but I didn't fully understand what it meant and where things would go from here. As I sat nervously in my room watching the BBC News in the evening – a rare occurrence – I knew the fact there was a national reporter stood in front of the familiar sight of Valley Parade at ten past six was certainly not a good thing.

Bradford City had gone into administration. To a large proportion of football fans, me included, the word 'administration' meant very little before May 2002. I had heard the term before and knew that it was associated with businesses going broke, so it certainly wasn't a word I was comfortable with being associated with my Bradford City. What does this mean? Are we about to go bust? Is this the end of City? I spent the evening at the campus library anxiously studying stories on the internet in an attempt to make sense of it all.

As the details of the story broke, the horrible and shocking realisation of the mess City were in emerged. We were £36 million in debt and the collapse of ITV Digital, plus our continual failure to offload the high-earning Benito Carbone (after a pretty successful loan spell at Middlesbrough he failed to agree terms for a permanent deal and was back) had put the club in real trouble. These were debts we seemingly had no chance of paying back. We had been placed into administration to freeze them and attempt to work out a solution to continue operating. It remained questionable if this could be achieved, and whether the club could continue to exist.

A week or so later, Alex rang me with news of the first step taken. I had a day off from lectures and myself, Simon and Dan had managed to turn a leisurely stroll to the shops into an afternoon drinking session. Alex explained that we had sacked all of our players. Simon and Dan offered their words of sympathy about what was happening to us. Just like when the news broke over the original administration, I was left feeling confused about what it meant. I stumbled to the library again and did my best to read the screen as I loaded up City's website. The full details of the incredible move were there for all to see. Just five players had not been sacked. As I scanned through the list of those dismissed I felt a mixture of sadness and shame. Gary Walsh, David Wetherall, Wayne Jacobs, Jamie Lawrence…all had been great servants to the club and who were now being treated like this. Apparently most players found out the news from the media or through reading the website. It was a shocking way for the club to act and the whole situation was growing increasingly desperate.

The PFA stepped in to fight for the players' rights and the move was ultimately ruled illegal, with the players reinstated. It meant that for the most part of the summer players were in limbo, advised by their union to sit tight and wait for the matter to be resolved, but that they were also free to talk to other clubs. The Rotherham United manager Ronnie Moore sensed an opportunity to get some talented players in on the cheap and made moves to sign Andy Myers, Robert Moleanaar and Wetherall. They all refused after being offered contracts much less than what they were on at City. When Moore discovered what they were earning at City he publicly spoke out, demanding Bradford City be kicked out of the Football League.

His point, which was valid, was that we had sought an unfair advantage over other clubs in the division by paying higher wages for players that we ultimately couldn't afford, when it had failed we were now trying to ditch the contracts instead of honour our commitments. What Moore didn't think about though, as he made his demands for City to be expelled, was that the club's supporters would be the real victim of any such action. It wasn't our fault City had taken players on well beyond their resources and it wasn't our fault £36 million worth of debt had been racked up. To the supporters, worried about the future existence, Moore's attack was upsetting and hurtful and few City fans will ever forgive Moore's thoughtless and ill-timed attack on our beloved club, when it was on its knees.

As the summer dragged on, the news began to look more positive and talk of other people putting money into City began to circle around message boards. Deals were starting to be put in place with some of our biggest creditors. With the exception of Eion Jess, Carbone and Lawrence, the players returned for pre-season training and were told their contracts would be honoured and that they would eventually be paid again. New players were brought in on trial and took part in pre-season friendlies. The final stumbling block was to get a Creditors Voluntary Agreement accepted, where those who we owed money would agree to receiving only a fraction of what they are entitled to. Talks were taking place with some of these biggest creditors and the administrators' seemed optimistic about reaching a deal. Just like every other City fan, I anxiously checked for news each day. It was a helpless position to be in, there was nothing us ordinary fans could do. We just had to pray for positive news.

As the crucial CVA meeting approached, news came through that deals with some of our biggest creditors were far from agreed and looked hugely doubtful. Two days before the meeting, the players decided to go on strike and all pulled out of a friendly against Hull. They took this extraordinary action because they don't want to risk picking up an injury if they had to look for a new club. The players had attracted widespread sympathy after City tried to sack them, but this move upset most of us supporters and saw their status go down.

137

I was working the day of the critical CVA meeting and – back home for the summer and back in the cleaning job – my mind was certainly not on the work. I felt panicky and worried. I couldn't concentrate on anything but events at Valley Parade. As I cleaned a corridor, my club could be going out of business. I was desperate to hear some news and the day passed by awfully slowly. When work was finally over I rushed to the hospital's Internet Café and anxiously loaded up City's website. What was I about to read, that something I thought I was going to be doing for the rest of my life was no more? That the club I had stumbled upon just under five years ago, fallen in love with and spent countless hours cheering, worrying, thinking, and despairing over was gone? I prayed for good news and I stared in disbelief at the news which had loaded up in front of me. The CVA has been accepted - BRADFORD CITY IS STILL ALIVE!

The CVA had been narrowly approved and we could carry on. We knew that City would still have financial problems for years to come and the days of big name signings were certainly over. Indeed one of the club's biggest creditors was Carbone, who agreed to write-off a substantial part of the money he was owed saying he didn't wish to see us go under. He returned to Italy where he signed for Como. Jess signed for Nottingham Forest and Lawrence, who originally refused to return to training until the mess was sorted out, returned. Law, who had so much to put up with during the summer, could start properly planning for the season ahead. A few days later me and Stephen went to watch City draw 1-1 at home with Middlesbrough in a friendly. It felt great to be inside the stadium again and to be worrying about a game of football.

Now that the dust settled, the blame and recriminations for the mess we landed in could begin. Richmond was under fire from fans and held his hands up to apologise. He blamed the events of two summers earlier when City had gone on that unprecedented spending spree and signing the likes of Carbone, Ashley Ward and Dan Petrescu. Richmond infamously described it as "six weeks of madness". Now many supporters were demanding he exited the club and stated they would not watch City again until he did. As City had dropped from the Premiership to near financial oblivion, Richmond had paid himself and the board huge amounts of money in dividends and, in this darkest of hours, he refused to commit any of it back into the club while expected to carry on leading it.

For my own part I felt a mixture of anger and sadness. Of course I was frustrated by how badly he had mismanaged the club and where it had left of us. But I also admired him for his previous achievements. He had taken over City when they were a mid table Division Two team and delivered Premiership football within five years. He masterminded the rise of the club, including the development of Valley Parade and our fanbase. If it wasn't for him doing so, would I have ever gone to watch Bradford City? So while I was hurt, angry and upset at what he had done to my club, I was also thankful that he had made City my club. I was a Richmond kid and that at least I would never forget.

Days after the Middlesbrough draw Richmond did leave the club with his position untenable. That the club could strike deals with creditors to settle the huge debts was completely down to the club's other shareholders, Professor David Rhodes and his son Julian, and a new partner in Gordon Gibb, owner of local theme park Flamingoland. City prepared to begin the 2002-03 season after one of the most eventful and traumatic summers possible. We made our way to the opening game against Wolves just thankful we still had a team to support.

Chapter Eight

2002 - 03
Living as paupers

The Bradford City that emerged from the rubble of those summer events felt very much like an elderly relative who'd suffered a fall or stroke. When it happened you naturally worry if they will be okay and then about their future. And, after they do recover, your expectations of what they can now do are much less. The shock also makes you realise that you can't take anything for granted and things will probably never be the same again.

For City, the next few months were all about recuperating from the unexpected trauma of administration and getting back on its feet. Even as we came out of administration, warnings that it would take years to recover from the financial woes came with it, and expectations had to shift downwards. The best we could all hope for in the season ahead was to avoid relegation – and even that looked a tough feat. After spending a year bemoaning the lack of new signings and wishing we could be chasing better quality players, we knew Nicky Law had very little money to spend and those coming in would not be the sort the club would have been looking at not so long ago.

All of which left a rather flat feeling as the new season began. Sure, we were all happy there was a still a club to support, but when just a few months earlier we had been hoping City could reclaim its place in the Premiership, to merely be hoping they stay up in Division One felt slightly disappointing. We had to be realistic, those dreams of the Premiership were just dreams again and unlikely to materialise for sometime, if ever, now. It felt like the next few years would just be about treading water and, while we were grateful to still have a club to support, it wasn't the most exciting of propositions.

Such feelings were soon to become commonplace around the Football League. Bradford City's 2001 implosion was hardly the first time a club and experienced financial difficulties – indeed the club itself almost went bust in 1983 – but prior to ITV Digital's collapse it was more of a rarity. Geoffrey Richmond had suggested several other clubs would follow City's lead of going into administration, and he was soon proved right – within a year 12 clubs had followed.

Since 2000, 30 Football League clubs have gone into administration or receivership. And it didn't take long for the Football League to instigate punishments for those who did. While it's easy to dismiss a 10 point deduction for a club in dire financial straits as harsh, it's equally unfair on clubs who paid the bills and kept within parameters, if their rivals have spent money they can't afford to gain an on-the-field advantage. But football's inequality doesn't help. While the Football League learned the harsh lessons of the ITV Digital fiasco, the TV deals for Premier League clubs continued to get larger. Worldwide TV audiences were impressively growing, and the revenue coming in even to clubs near the bottom of the top flight has become colossal. If you're an ambitious Chairman of a club in the upper echelons of the Football League, it can be very tempting to believe that pushing out the boat a bit more and gambling on promotion to the Promised Land could lead to receiving those same rewards, quickly making enough money to cover those larger bills. However if it doesn't work out as planned, the recriminations begin. Competition is distorted by money. To succeed you largely either have to have lots or be prepared to gamble. And while ITV Digital caught many clubs out cold given no one could have predicted what would happen, even years on clubs are still overreaching themselves and later having to pay the price.

Or at least the long-suffering fans do. Placing a club in administration can effectively mean removing your responsibility and hoping someone else will come in with the money and sort out the mess. But the very nature of going into administration – to pay only a fraction of your bills, can hurt the very community you are in and later cause difficulties obtaining sponsorship and corporate hospitality. At City, one of the creditors was a local newsagent to whom the Bantams owed £943. Going into administration meant City only had to pay back a fraction of this bill – seriously hurting this small business. Shamefully the St. John's Ambulance charity was left owed thousands of pounds by football clubs because of the way administration works. The loss of goodwill can hurt attendances and your reputation, and it's a difficult thing to restore.

Bringing more balance to football – i.e. getting the Premier League to share some of the money they receive from TV – would help to reduce some of these problems. But the financial difficulties in the lower leagues have largely been ignored – save for the introduction of solidarity payments to the tune of £60 million a year from the Premier League to the 72 Football League clubs. In the 2009/10 season, Portsmouth became the first Premier League club to go into administration, causing some obvious embarrassment to Premier League Chairman David Richards. But he was still able to largely dismiss it, and Pompey's relegation ensured it quickly wasn't his problem again.

Wolves (home) – new beginnings

In truth the highlight of the 2002/03 season took place before a ball was kicked. It came at the start of the first game against Wolves; it was the normally-routine sight of the players coming onto the field for kick off. It's the kind of moment when attending a match that you usually take for granted, but looked questionable whether we'd ever see it again during that horrible summer. Bradford City in action – pinch me. The Wolves game was a Sunday lunchtime Sky kick off. It was still the holidays from University, so I was able to go. As the players ran onto the pitch for kick off, emotions were running high in the Kop. I felt relieved and grateful for what I still had. It could have been very different and I could be facing up to living the rest of my life without City. During the dark moments, you just hoped we'd see this day.

Wolves had of course blown promotion spectacularly last season, but this year they would get it right and be promoted as Champions. Therefore a 0-0 draw was a decent start for the new-look Bantams. Wolves dominated most of the game and we were grateful for the form of Gary Walsh and David Wetherall. City then drew 1-1 away at Crystal Palace with Andy Tod scoring, before losing 2-1 at newly promoted Stoke in a game where Walsh made a terrible blunder after kicking the ball straight to Stoke striker Andy Cooke who slotted home. This proved to be Walsh's last game for City and it was a sad way for a hero to end his time with the club. One would have hoped for some fitting send off – a packed Valley Parade offering him a standing ovation perhaps – but this was the typical reality of how unsentimental football clubs can be towards its heroes.

I missed both these away trips and the next home game, against Grimsby, because I attended the Creamfields music festival with Martin and Simon. City drew 0-0 in a game marred by a serious injury to promising midfielder Tom Kearney, which would rule him out for the rest of the season. It was a slow start to the campaign and, while we had to keep expectations low, one that caused a degree of concern. With a trip to relegated Ipswich following two days later, the prospects didn't look good. Yet City recorded their first win of the season – and first ever at Portman Road – with recent signings Paul Evans and Michael Proctor on target in a 2-1 success. I listened at home in the radio in delighted disbelief.

I was able to get the next game, at home to Rotherham United, before I returned to University the following week. The game with the Millers had become a grudge match following Ronnie Moore's comments in the summer. Happily we raced into a 3-0 lead with goals from Ashley Ward, recent signing Gus Uhlenbeek and Proctor. Although Rotherham pulled two goals back, Ward added a fourth to seal an excellent win. Two wins in a row – maybe we can start dreaming of mid-table!

On the weekend I returned to University City made it three straight wins with a 1-0 success at Walsall. I had enjoyed my summer back at home and hanging out regularly with my friends, but I was glad to be returning to University. My enthusiasm for at least coping with working had waned towards the end and I found my motivation severely lacking during the final few weeks. I was keen to get back to the student lifestyle, hanging out with my flat mates. During the final few months of last year, the urge to have a proper girlfriend had also come back again.

I'd spent a large part of the summer daydreaming away about what the third and final year of Uni would be like, now was the time to see if I could make my hopes of getting a good degree and a girlfriend reality. From what I'd seen of City, I felt reasonably confident they would be okay this season. At the same time, I didn't feel as though I was going to miss much while I was away.

Derby (home) – a very happy 21st

During my first month back at University Bradford City had some serious competition in holding my attention. Over the last year my musical tastes had slowly altered and was really taking over when I returned to Sunderland. I also got into a relationship and quickly found I was falling in love.

Both require a bit of explanation, so let's do them in order. Music's importance had grown thanks to the influence of my flat mates. For years I had been an Indie guitar music fan and enjoyed bands such as Oasis, Embrace, Blur and Fun Lovin' Criminals. I have always had a passion for music and regularly bought CDs and went to gigs. I've been into all sorts of different styles of at certain points as I grew up – from heavy metal to happy hardcore. I'd also enjoyed dance music although had got bored of it just before I entered University life.

Towards the end of the first year, Dan and Simon had gone out in Newcastle and discovered Shindig, which was the coolest nightclub around and where every Saturday night one of the world's top house music DJs would play. Dan and Simon came back with excited tales about seeing Carl Cox which rubbed off on myself and Martin. We both ended up going along with them, but while Martin enjoyed it I initially found it boring. I left the three of them to it and the more that Simon in particular visited Shindig, the more he got into the music. By the second year he had bought his own pair of decks and quickly had a substantial CD collection of house music. At the same time, he and I became much closer and I hung out with him more and more. I soon became familiar with his

144

house CDs and began to enjoy them more. When I understood the music better, I was ready to venture out and try it again. Towards the end of the second year I went clubbing three times and found I enjoyed it much more. It was a huge learning curve, getting to appreciate how the music works and understanding how to enjoy dancing to it for hours on end. Creamfields that summer, an event both Martin and Simon had been to a year earlier, was another great experience. Watching Underworld performing live while the sun was setting proved an exhilarating and spine-tingling moment – one which almost competed with Wolves and Liverpool.

Part of my urgency to get back to University during the final few weeks of the summer was to go out to Shindig and experience more great live house music. I even returned a day earlier than I usually would so that I could go along with Simon to see Steve Lawler. For the next few weeks I went to Shindig every Saturday and had some wonderful nights, far greater than any I had experienced going to regular nightclubs. The crowd was really friendly and were there simply to enjoy the music; there was no need to drink loads and no worries about looking to pull. We went along to see the DJ and the DJ only, and the experience was phenomenal. Compared with watching City, there probably were quite a few elements better. For one thing there was no worry about where my emotions might be. I knew I was going to see a DJ play music I should enjoy; the worst case scenario being it would prove a poor performance. Watching City, I left myself open to up and down emotions which depended on the result – something I had no control over. The crowd at Shindig were happy people having a great night that most will have looked forward to all week, a contrast to being surrounded by people moaning and booing which often occurred at City games.

It probably wasn't like this at all house music clubs, but Shindig was truly a special place at this time. The layout of the club was excellent and it was a venue not quite as well-known and so not pulling huge crowds. We had to travel on the metro train to get from Sunderland to Newcastle and this ride felt exciting, with all of us happy and looking forward to a good night. The walk from station to club also felt really special, as special to me as the walk from Forster Square station to Valley Parade along Manningham Lane. Just like that walk it was one that signified I was close to arriving somewhere I was hugely excited about visiting, and was about to experience something I would find hugely enjoyable and memorable.

Like Simon a year earlier, my CD collection was quickly boosted by more house ones and for my 21st birthday I received my own decks. I was getting quite good at them too. For the first time since starting to watch City, my weekend's mood was no longer dependant on how City got on. The day City woefully lost 3-2 to Brighton I went to Shindig to see Satoshi Tommie. I woke up Sunday morning feeling very happy.

Away from going to Shindig though, I was still attending student nights where I was more hopeful of finding a girlfriend. Within two weeks I had succeeded in an unexpected but exciting way. I met Rachel, an American who was attending Sunderland University on a study abroad programme. She would be going back in December so I knew it couldn't get serious; but could enjoy it for what it was and have a great time along the way.

Or so I thought. Being in a relationship where you don't worry about it becoming serious is not so simple when you suddenly realise you've fallen for the other person – but more on that later. We met a week or so into the third year on a specially arranged student night out at a club in Newcastle. The Student Union had laid on coaches for us to get to and from Newcastle and I was introduced to Rachel, through a friend, before we set off. The night itself is something of a blur as Alex and I downed a huge amount of shots beforehand. When I sobered up a little to the point where I knew where I was, Rachel and I were kissing on the dance floor and it was the end of the night. It doesn't sound like the most promising of beginnings, but we arranged to meet again the following night and again the night after. We were soon a couple and I was feeling on top of the world.

Rachel was from Georgia, in the south of the USA. She had taken part in study abroad with a Uni friend named Meghan, who my other flat mates were all now taking an interest in. Rachel was a sweet-talking woman, who clearly loved and missed her family but had been determined to experience life in England. I was really enjoying her company and she eased into my Uni life and my circle of friends. Importantly, she also seemed to like football and told me how she used to play it at school. She was soon joining me and my flat mates on our regular trips to the pub across the road to watch the live football on TV. Of course she hadn't heard of Bradford City, but I promised I would take her to a game.

My 21st birthday followed a few weeks later and was marked with a big night out across town that saw around 20 friends come along. I felt really happy and pleased with how my life was turning out. I had a great set of friends, plus a girlfriend I was happy with. I still relished the freedom of Uni life and the excitement of going out. City were also doing okay, drawing a lot of games but rarely losing as well. It felt as though they would comfortably achieve the season's aim of avoiding relegation and I could take in their results relatively stress-free. I still felt grateful that City were still in existence and happy with their achievements, however minor.

As it was my birthday I went home for the weekend to see family. It meant I was able to go and watch City play host to Derby County (a 0-0 draw). As usual I went along with Stephen and David, but there was a gloomy feel to their mood. David had recently lost his job and was finding the realisation of unemployment difficult to cope with. He had been happily working for a bank and seemed to enjoy the work and his group of friends, although it was also apparent, from talking to him, that he had taken it a little for granted and started to believe himself more important than the work he was assigned to do, so he neglected it. Still it was sad to see him, as we had a drink in the pub before the game, looking so miserable. He kept talking about how much he was looking forward to 2003 beginning as it would herald a new start. Yet it was October and a long way from the end of 2002.

Stephen was also quiet. He was still at college in Shipley, where he had been since leaving school at 16 – five years ago. Stephen was also looking to get himself a job but it was very difficult to find anywhere that would take him on, hence he stayed at college. He dreamed of being a chef and at least had a part time job washing up at the local Chinese takeaway. Still it was hard to imagine him being given the opportunity to realise his ambitions. I looked at them both and felt both sorry and guilty. I had become a good friend of them both in recent years, but for the last two-and-a-half years I had hardly been around for them. There was little I could do to help them in their respective predicaments, but I felt bad that I was unable to at least be there to offer words of encouragement and companionship.

It was impossible to be in two places at once and I wouldn't have swapped being at University for anything. But just as I had learned to live with and take for granted the match day experience of Valley Parade going on without me, I had also taken for granted that Steve and David would both be happily enjoying the games. I followed the scores on a Saturday afternoon and felt jubilant and sad like every other City fan, but then I could turn off the TV or radio and try to focus on other things. You forget that everyone else is leaving and travelling home from Valley Parade and won't be able to take their mind off it as quickly; you even forget that they have lives outside of football. In truth I rarely thought about Stephen and David other than when City were in action. I never wondered what they were up to on a Saturday night in the same way I did about my other friends, or what they were up to during the week. I gauged how they would be feeling entirely on how City were doing. Seeing them both looking sad and miserable made me realise that life wouldn't seem wonderful for them even if City won today.

The following day I made my way back to Sunderland looking forward to seeing Rachel and my flat mates again and going to visit Shindig the following Saturday. Still I was left pondering the future and realising that my time at Sunderland was coming to an end. Soon I could be moving back to Yorkshire or maybe even another part of the country. I now had to start considering what I would be doing next and thinking about applying for jobs. The great run of going out and sleeping in during the week was no longer far from over. What next? It wasn't difficult to imagine sitting grumpily with Stephen and David in a year's time experiencing similar problems.

Wimbledon (home) and Nottingham Forest (away) – defences down

A month later I was back in Yorkshire, this time with Rachel in tow. She was going to be meeting my parents and see where I lived. This kind of situation can be a nerve-wracking affair with plenty of pressure but, for me at least, there was little. Firstly, we were approaching half-way through Rachel's three month study abroad programme when, I assumed, the relationship would be naturally over, so there was no need to worry about what the parents or Rachel thought of each other. Secondly, the trip felt more about showing Rachel another part of the UK. Her thirst for tourism had already seen her visit Paris for the weekend and she had trips planned to visit London and Scotland (twice) before the end. I knew that the hilly green landscape of where I was from would be attractive to her and that she would think I had grown up in a beautiful part of the world.

There was one part of the weekend trip that did leave me feeling nervous though. As usual I wanted to ensure my visit home included a trip to Valley Parade so was taking Rachel along with me. This did feel worrying because it was one element I was unable to control. It's not so much that City could be awful that concerned me (although at the same time a 5-0 drubbing would have felt shameful) more that the game might be boring. I was introducing her to an important part of my life, one which I had talked often about and which I had tried to explain how much it meant to me. She liked American Football and she enjoyed watching Premiership football in the pub with us all, so I knew she got that it's not always about the winning. But I didn't want her to watch a dull and cagey game with neither team playing with much quality, so that she went away thinking City played a boring and low standard of football.

On that score I needn't have worried as we went to see City entertain Wimbledon, as less than ten seconds into the match City took the lead. Right from kick off the ball was crossed in for our new loan signing, Delroy Facey, to head home. I felt relived that at least it wasn't going to be a 0-0 and hoped we would now go onto win comfortably. 10 minutes after taking the lead, Wimbledon equalised after some poor defending. A few minutes later we were back in front as Michael Standing curled a brilliant shot into the far corner.

Are you okay?" I kept asking Rachel, looking for reassurance that she was enjoying the cold November afternoon. "Yep" was her reply, as she sat their wrapped up in her new Bradford City scarf. Wimbledon equalised a second time after a mistake by Standing, but just before half time the midfielder struck again so we went in 3-2 up. "We'll finish the job in the second half", I confidently predicted. Rachel's view was one that could have come from any long standing City supporter worn down by years of cynicism, "I'm not sure, they've scored twice and our defence looks weak." Why did she, in her first game that I secretly, even though it seemed completely improbable, hoped would be the beginning of a life long-love affair for her, have such a wise view while I, who had seen City fail so often, was so foolishly optimistic?

Not for the first or last time, she was right and I was wrong. Wimbledon quickly equalised in the second half but this time we failed to take a fourth lead of the game. Instead it was the visitors who scored next, then added a fifth. Again our defence was all over the place in gifting Wimbledon the goals. Standing must have gone in at half time feeling happy after scoring two goals. He was awful in the second half and his performance probably signalled the end of his City career.

I asked Rachel if she had enjoyed the game and she said she had, though I don't think City had bowled her over and didn't hold out any hope for her ever wanting to go again. Still the opportunity would probably never occur again, so I took the consolation that at least she had seen this part of my life – and at least knew how much misery it was capable of inflicting on me.

During the week, back up at Sunderland, we went out for a drink together. Rachel was going to Spain the next day to visit her best friend, who was also taking part in a study abroad programme, until Sunday evening. It was study week, so no lectures and I was looking forward to a relaxing couple of days with my flat mates, before a weekend in Nottingham with Martin. As we walked home, knowing we wouldn't see each other until Sunday, the dreaded conversation unexpectedly came up. Rachel asked me what would be happening after she went back to America and believed we should carry on as we are. I said I didn't want to and told her I didn't want to be in a long distance relationship, especially one so far away. She cried, and we both agreed we needed to talk again next week.

I felt sad and didn't want to end the relationship, it was by far the best one I had ever been in, but I couldn't see how it could work. She was going to be thousands of miles away in a foreign country, how could we have a future? I might never see her again after this. There was no point in keeping it going, was there? With Bradford City I already had one long distance relationship successfully on the go...

Such thoughts were still dominating my mind as me and Martin made the journey to Nottingham a few days later. There were many reasons for the weekend visit to Martin's home; to see where he lived, to go clubbing and watch some decent DJs – but the main one was to attend the Nottingham Forest v City fixture at the City Ground. It was a tough fixture for City, after our decent start to the season we were now struggling and the Wimbledon reverse was the latest in a succession of defeats, a run which would eventually equal a club record. Injuries and lack of finances were playing a big part and Forest felt like a new low. In desperation because of the lack of players, Nicky Law had signed one time City striker Graeme Tomlinson on loan – from a non-league side. He was an unused sub against Forest, though the game did see the debut of young right back called Simon Francis who quickly showed his promise which would cement a place in the team. He would eventually go onto better things.

In contrast Forest were flying high up the league and on course for a play off finish at the end of the season. Manager Paul Hart had assembled a team of promising youngsters who were doing the business. It looked highly unlikely we could get anything more than a point out of the game and as we parted company outside the ground – me going into the away end and Martin joining the home fans – I knew that when we met up at the end he would probably be the one feeling triumphant. Martin deliberately bought a ticket for the section of the home section nearest the away fans, which was also the area that housed the most vocal Forest fans. I could see him among them and he could see me, so as Forest quickly took the lead I had a great view of him celebrating. Soon after it was 2-0 Forest, then 3-0. We had played barely half an hour and a real battering looked on the cards. I could sense Martin smiling in my direction and did my best to ignore him. I knew that if the roles were reversed I would be gloating, probably more, so wasn't too upset at the half time text he sent me.

In the second half we played much better and at least prevented Forest scoring again, although we didn't really look like coming back. I met up with a smug Martin at the end and could only offer words of praise for his team and tried to avoid talking about City's failings, we were poor and the bet I had again made with him over who would finish higher was looking foolish.

We went out that night in Nottingham and I had an okay time, but my mind was more and more on the Rachel situation. I chatted it through with Martin, who had just started going out with Rachel's friend Meghan. She had arranged to stay at Sunderland for a full year so it wasn't an issue for him yet. If you're really happy and it's working well why not give it a go, was Martin's advice. Perhaps one day Rachel might want to move to England, perhaps I might one day want to move to America. I couldn't see the latter scenario, but you never know. Still, I was falling for Rachel and didn't want to give her up. I wished she could stay but that seemed impossible.

By the end of the night I had come to a decision, I was going to give long-distance a go.

The following day we were travelling North to Sunderland on the National Express, both listening to music on our Walkmans to pass the time. Suddenly Martin received a voicemail from Meghan which was for me. I paused my music and listened as Meghan let me know that Rachel was not going to be home that evening. She had been making her way to the airport in Madrid when her handbag was stolen on the train. This included her phone, plane tickets and passport. She was stranded and alone without a way of getting home. She'd made it to the US Embassy, who were trying to sort her out. She'd been able to speak to Meghan and arranged to stay with her sister who also lived there, but there was now no way of getting in touch with her.

Naturally I panicked. "Is she okay? How and when is she going to get home? I can't believe I can't speak to her!" That feeling of helplessness was bad enough, but sat on a National

Express coach which I wouldn't be getting off from for another four hours felt a hundred times worse. The journey became hell and no music or words of comfort from Martin were going to help. Even when I got to Sunderland, there was nothing I could do. I felt in limbo.

It wasn't until the following morning that I got to speak to her. When Meghan's phone rang she instantly passed it to me. Hearing Rachel's voice was such a relief. She was heading back and was due to arrive at Newcastle late in the evening. I instantly volunteered to meet her at the airport and felt excited but still scared. That evening I was supposed to be going to watch The Doves at Newcastle University with Dan, Martin and Alex. I managed to sell my ticket to another friend, there was no way I could go feeling the way I did. Later that night I was hugging Rachel in arrivals and she told me the whole nightmare story.

We then talked about our future and I told her I was prepared to try long distance with her. We spoke about her one day moving to England, which she raised and said she was prepared to do. She had two years of University back in America to complete first. That felt like a dauntingly-long time, but worth trying at least. Maybe the Wimbledon game won't be her last City match! Happy she was safe and that there was some sort of future for us, my mind now turned to sadness at the fact there was less than a month to go until she returned to America.

Stoke City (home) - depression

City's losing run showed no signs of letting up. After the Forest defeat we were stuffed 5-0 at home by Sheffield United, then a 1-0 defeat at Millwall. Gillingham then beat us 3-1 at home and the team had equalled a club record of eight successive defeats. It was a miserable period for every City fan, although highly appropriate for me.

The last few weeks with Rachel before she returned to America were Hell. The Madrid episode had only reinforced how much she meant to me. After a short period of time, the feelings had crept up inside me and I felt I'd taken too long to realise. Now time was running out and I was scared I hadn't made the most of it. It was as though I now had to make every second left count. This was tricky as she had things lined up each weekend, such as visiting Edinburgh with Meghan. Her Mom and Grandma also came to visit during Thanksgiving and they cooked a wonderful meal for all of our Uni friends.

To my own disgust, I stopped spending quality time with my flat mates during those weeks as I was determined to see Rachel whenever I could. It was unfair on them and I knew, from in the past, how much it had annoyed the rest of us when one of us gets a girlfriend and starts ignoring us. I had to do what I had to do and hoped they would understand, in a few weeks I wouldn't be spending any time with my girlfriend.

The dreaded day of her going back quickly arrived and I struggled to keep it together. The first semester of the third year had been largely awful. We started the year with housing problems after our new landlord messed us about, and this created an atmosphere of conflict. Alex moved out at one stage and then came back; Martin and I were both guilty of spending too much time with our girlfriends, away from everyone else. I felt under more pressure doing my degree, as it was my final year, but still wasn't enjoying the course enough. I'd stopped going on student nights, which meant I'd stopped seeing a lot of my regular friends. Nights at Shindig were much more expensive and quickly became rarer. We were all hardly going out, but also hardly spending time together as a group. I was no longer enjoying Uni life.

The one positive was Rachel. The more I disliked my Uni life, the more important Rachel seemed to become. Now she was going away and I would have little left which made me happy, just an empty feeling. I went with Rachel to the airport to see her off, it was a hugely difficult moment and tears were shed. Rachel's flight was in the middle of the night so I took the early morning Metro train home, tried to sleep for a few hours and then got up and caught the bus home to Yorkshire for Christmas. I didn't want to see anyone, I was still too upset, so said my goodbyes to flat mates by text. Being back home was barely any better. I was back working at the hospital, more in need of the money than ever. Christmas felt empty and largely joyless. I ended up working on Christmas Day morning, the opportunity to earn money too good to turn down. Returning home at 11am to open presents with the family felt as un-magical and un-Christmassy as I had ever felt on the big day. Even a phone call to Rachel in America did little to lift my gloom.

Boxing Day was the highlight though, as I got to watch City play Stoke. After the record of successive defeats was equalled, we had gained a much-needed win over Notts Forest of all teams. Me and Martin hadn't gone to it as planned because it was the same weekend Rachel was due to go back. The win eased pressure on Law but was followed by a 1-0 defeat at Watford, courtesy of a last minute goal. The Stoke game became vital, so not so good when we were 2-1 down at half time. City had looked poor and it was worrying as Stoke were near us at the bottom. Still I felt glad to be there and happy to be able to focus on another problem instead of how to cope without Rachel.

Whatever Nicky Law said at half time worked a treat. Kicking towards us, City began to really take the game to Stoke and were soon level through an own goal. Then a Claus Jorgenson's header and an Andy Gray low finish earned City a 4-2 win. Such is the gap between watching City games that it had been a long time, last September, since I last saw City win a match. Being able to see such a rousing fightback cheered me up for a few hours and gave me the sort of hope that I knew I had to try and input into my own life. City's form lifted at just the right time for me, the Forest win launched a run of five wins from seven. Feeling so gloomy about life and missing Rachel – the idea of also having City sinking into relegation trouble would have felt unbearable.

But still when I got home and went up to my room I quickly felt empty again. I'd decided I was going to spend New Year's Eve back in Sunderland so that I could go to Shindig, meaning my Christmas holidays were cut shorter than usual. Not being particularly well off, it probably wasn't the wisest decision. But going back to Sunderland and only having Simon around, meaning I could mope around without the guilt of making my parents think I was unhappy to be home, was a relief. New Year's Eve failed to live up to expectations, typically, and I spent the evening looking forward to 7am, so that I could call Rachel and wish her a happy new year. She had an interesting proposition to make and one that left me shocked. Her dad was offering to pay for me to fly to America in the summer so that I could meet the family and see her!

I'm not the sort of person comfortable to accept such a charitable offer, so I spoke to my parents who, hearing that a person they had never met was willing to pay for me to fly 4,000 miles, weren't too sure. In the end a compromise was made that they would pay for me to fly to the states in May and I would be spending five weeks with Rachel and her family. It felt like a happy beginning to 2003. A few weeks ago I had tearfully said goodbye to Rachel at the airport, fearing I might never see her again. Now I would be seeing her again in five months. In fact I soon after discovered I'd be seeing her sooner as she decided to come back to Sunderland for a visit during her spring break.

There was a target. Something to work towards. A goal. Now I had to get through those few months, while in the process ensuring I worked hard enough to get a good degree.

Ipswich Town (home) – loneliness

By February I was convinced I was suffering from depression. I'd had a few weeks of feeling low; waking up in the morning and feeling very unhappy that I had to face reality. I wished I could have just hibernated until Spring. Life felt miserable and unbearable, I'd rather shut down and wait until it felt good again.

I went through it all in my head and come to the conclusion that there were three things making me feel so down. The first, and more obvious one, was missing Rachel. When she left I had been desperate to get away from Sunderland for Christmas, but as soon as I got home I was anxious to hide away again in the North East. Back in Sunderland I realised that it was no better. I walked around the streets and all I could think of was times I'd walked these streets with Rachel. Songs on CDs and TV programmes reminded me of her. Everywhere I went I saw Rachel, but she was now back at University in Valdosta, Georgia, and I was reduced to speaking to her on the internet late on in evenings and calling her every other day. She was coping much better than I was, which I was pleased by but also sad. Why am I, in comparison, struggling to cope so badly?

Then there was money. Two and a half years of Uni, a year and a half without a job, were now taking its toll. I could afford to eat and pay the bills, which was more than some of my flatmates. But as my January student loan came in and I noted how long it would be before the next instalment I quickly came to the conclusion that there would be little or no chance of doing much. Luckily my flat mates had similar problems, so none of us were going to Shindig anytime soon. But such luxuries as a trip to the pub, or buying a CD were now rationed. I would largely be staying in, night after night. I had a crap portable TV and my video machine had packed in. It was going to be a long semester.

The third problem was my flatmates. As the new term started a new American moved into Rachel's room in her halls and, to everyone's amusement but mine, was also called Rachel. She was soon hanging out with us as Meghan became friends with her. Simon quickly made his move and they became an item. As we walked home from a rare night out, minus Simon who was walking home with Rachel, I realised that all five of us flatmates now had girlfriends. The odd one out was me, as mine was living thousands of miles away. I knew this would mean there would be nights I would be on my own and initially even welcomed such a prospect. What I didn't realise was that this would be the case five or six nights a week, every week, for the rest of my time at Uni.

So I was now close to poor and hanging out on my own every night, desperately missing Rachel. It was one of the hardest times of my life. I felt bitter at my friends who seemed to ignore how unhappy I was and spent every night with their partners. Martin, Simon and their American girlfriends would go off for foursomes, even cooking meals together in our house. No one asked me along. I felt like I was penalised for being on my own.

There's never a good time to receive bad news, but receiving a phone call from my mum to tell me my Grandma had died was especially upsetting. She'd been ill in hospital for a few weeks and things weren't improving, but still it came as a shock. I went home for the funeral which involved seeing family I hadn't seen for years. It was a tearful experience as you'd expect, though the most upsetting part of the day was after everyone had gone and we – my mum, dad, Kevin and I –

spent a few hours with Grandpa. We asked him about things like the war and memories of Grandma. He'd taken it all badly as you'd expect, and was crying often. Eventually though we had to go home, leaving him there in an empty home felt horrible. We lived 40 miles away and, while mum and dad would go and see him again in a couple of days, it felt awful to leave him in bits and by himself. At least it put my own problems into perspective, though contributed to making me feel even more depressed during this difficult time.

The one bonus was I began to throw myself into Uni work. I had a project of creating my own magazine to work on so would spend seven-eight hours a day sat at a computer putting it all together. I stayed out from home all day, feeling the satisfaction of working on a meaningful project and enjoying writing stories. Then the day would be over and I would have to go home. The misery and loneliness would quickly return. Often Dan would hang out with me for the early part of the evening, Martin would make the effort to have a night away from his lass on occasions. I wasn't on my own all the time, but it was something I had to get used to.

In such a situation, there was little Bradford City could do for me. Of course their results affected my moods, but I spent Saturdays watching score updates on TV and there was little indication of performances. My daily routine always included checking out the latest City news on the various websites, but I was still very detached. If only I could be going to games so that, win, lose or draw, my mind could be consumed by something else. Lack of money meant that weekends going home and going to watch City were ruled out. I became more and more consumed by football on TV and would watch anything that came on. Monday nights were the best with an hour-long Premiership review show, Champions League weekly and Nationwide League extra programmes all on one after the other on ITV. I got glimpses of City's goals for and against, but it wasn't enough.

I did get down to Valley Parade in February for the visit of Ipswich. I was making that trip home for the weekend that needed to be made every so often, and although it wasn't the wisest thing to do paying to watch City, it felt essential. It felt great to be there with Stephen and David again and I couldn't help but think back to six months earlier when they had both sounded so depressed about life and waiting for better things. They didn't seem any further along the circle of returning to happiness, but the chance for the three of us to go to a game together appeared to lift us all, albeit temporarily.

I certainly picked a good game to come back for. Ipswich were faltering in their bid to get promoted back to the Premiership, but were favourites as we had numerous injuries. After that great run of five wins in seven, there had been a couple of set backs and it was important we got a win to stay above the relegation battle intensifying just below. City had just one fit senior striker, so Nicky Law had to turn to youth and handed 18-year-old Danny Forrest a full debut after his attempts to sign veteran Adrian Littlejohn on a £350 'games only' contract was unsuccessful..

After a goalless first half in which Ipswich dominated, the game sprung into life with the visitors being reduced to ten men following Pablo Coungo's head-butt. Playing towards us in the Kop, the team raised their game and began creating chances. Claus Jorgenson put us in front and then Forrest scored. The youngster had missed a few chances before, but was able to slide home a loose ball. It was a fantastic moment watching the young kid's reaction to scoring in front of the Kop. Later, in an interview, he revealed how he had grown up on the Kop watching City like the rest of us, he even named the same heroes of Mills and Blake that I had. It left me with such a warm feeling to think that a supporter who has spent years occupying the same spot as me, cheering and despairing with us all over City's fortunes, was now playing in front of us and scoring. His mates were still in the Kop celebrating an extra special goal. The strike also left a warm feeling over the future of City.

After a difficult period, a few kids were now emerging. Forrest joined Simon Francis and Mark Bower in youth players making names for themselves, and there were reports of other decent players ready to come in. The future felt bright and I got home feeling fantastic that, for once, I'd been able to forget my problems. Being back in my spiritual home, cheering on City to a great victory while sat alongside two great friends, with the scorer of one of the goals as big a City fan as I – for a few hours I was no longer lonely.

North East passions

I was now approaching the end of my three years of living in Sunderland. There were lots of things I appreciated about living in another part of the country. The culture was notably different to what I was used to and I felt as though I stood out for my accent, which sometimes felt strange but also help me to realise and be proud of where I was from. Of course a lot of the time locals would be muttering 'bloody student' to themselves when I was out around town, but I felt proud of my Yorkshire accent and knew it was at least more tolerable to them than the more whiny southern student accents they were also hearing.

I also really appreciated living in a City madly-passionate about its football. With Bradford there isn't even a local radio phone-in for supporters after games, up here there was a phone-in show on for three hours every weekday evening so that Sunderland, Middlesbrough and Newcastle supporters could air their views. I often listened and found the passion and arguments fascinating. It wasn't that I felt we City fans cared any less; it was just the sheer number of them. With City I tended to think of only us fans who go to matches as really caring about the club and that's largely true. Up in the North East there was a huge army of fanatical supporters going every week, and then thousands of others who don't go to games but who equally cared. In 2002-03, Sunderland were feebly heading for relegation with Howard Wilkinson as manager, they would set a record for low points and suffer financial problems. It was an interesting time to be witnessing it all. There was huge unrest towards the Chairman, Bob Murray, anger at star striker Kevin Phillips who had gone off the boil and frustration at several expensive flops such as Tore Andre Flo and Marcus Stewart.

Of course living in such a hotbed of football, I should have taken in some matches during my stay. I'd only been when City had played them in the Premiership a few years back. Right on my doorstep, well 20 minutes down the road, some of the world's best players were in action every other week and while I kept up to date with developments, I never went along. When Dan, the Blackburn Rovers supporter, said we should all go along when Rovers were playing at the Stadium of Light, it was a great opportunity for the rest of us to see a game of football; and so the four of us attended the Premiership clash, at the end of January.

It was a nice change for us to do something together; we were now at the beginnings of spending so much time away from each other – those three with their girlfriends. It was great fun sharing in some old banter as we walked across Wearmouth Bridge towards the stadium. We had tickets for the home end, not exactly ideal for Dan. After going through the turnstiles we had to make our way up the stairs to the concourse, where we each bought a pint. It felt really nice, not just to be out with my friends at the beginnings of a depressing period, but also to be at the football on a Saturday afternoon. The pre-match routine of going to watch City always included a pint on the Kop concourse before I went away to Uni and, even when I go to matches when I'm home, we still always go to the pub for one. We were all enjoying it and began openly questioning why we hadn't been doing this before. A quick glance through the programme I had purchased showed that the likes of Chelsea, Charlton, Arsenal and Newcastle were still due to visit before the season was over. We spoke about going to other matches, even getting carried away enough to think about going to every game. I knew in reality the expense would rule this out, but it still felt nice to imagine going to watch football on a regular basis again.

No one was considering changing allegiance to the Mackems. In fact none of us were too bothered about who won today. Except for Dan of course, who we were slightly worried would give in to the passion and reveal himself to be supporting the away side in front of Sunderland fans. The game was soon underway and the tension on the field and among the fans we were sat with was notably high. Sunderland were struggling woefully and couldn't see to buy a goal, never mind a win. Attacks quickly broke down, possession surrendered easily, defensive clearances hurried. Rovers weren't much better and neither side were able to break the deadlock. Dan kept quiet and only seemed to shout out when Sunderland fans were making noise themselves, so unable to hear him. Sunderland had put on some pressure in the second half and I think the three of us (not Dan of course) had silently begun to want Sunderland to win, but there was no breakthrough. The final whistle blew and the 0-0 scoreline was greeted with mutterings and groans around us. We made our way home feeling happy to have attended, but also a little unsatisfied that we hadn't seen a goal.

Three days later we were back, this time just a few rows behind the goal at the Sunderland end of the ground. It was Bolton Wanderers who were the opposition for an FA Cup 4th Round replay. Ticket prices had been slashed and, having enjoyed Saturday, we had quickly decided to go along. Alex, our fifth flat mate had also come along with his girlfriend. With no worries of upsetting Dan by cheering the opposition of his team, we spoke more of wanting Sunderland to progress and earn the opportunity of a cup run.

Just like Saturday, Sunderland laboured to get going and lacked confidence. Kevin Kyle, a young striker who never seemed to score, was playing up front and missed a couple of decent chances. Bolton were physical and their recent signing, former Real Madrid man, Ivan Campo, was laughably overweight. Sunderland were clearly the better side but didn't possess anyone able to put the ball into the net. Extra time beckoned, 0-0 again. We had now watched over 180 minutes of football at the Stadium of Light and still not seen a goal. 15 minutes of extra time followed and still no goals, was the game going to penalties?

Then, finally, Sunderland scored. Right in front of us as well. Instinctively, the six of us rose from our seats and cheered. It felt great to finally see Sunderland score after our three hours of willing them to. None of us were going to become Sunderland fans, but the idea of going to watch a team and cheer them on appealed to all of us, so we were all prepared to adopt them as a second team for a while.

But after the goal nothing. We sat back in our seats and I personally didn't feel any happier than before. When City score and go on to win it gives me a warm glow that lasts so much longer after the initial cheer, often well into the next week. Yet here nothing had changed, was I really that bothered that Sunderland were heading through to Round Five? Not really. I didn't want Sunderland to take over City, they never could, but the idea of having something else in life, a purpose, such as going to watch a football team and cheering them on, appealed. Plus I'd now lived in Sunderland for nearly three years, I had a right to have some feelings for the place. Sunderland scored again, this time I didn't even cheer. I realised that there is only passion for one team in my life, nothing comes close to City. Nor do I want anything to. I've spent nearly three years away from watching them and learned to deal with it, but the idea of replacing them with someone else, even if only temporarily, suddenly held no appeal. Feeling this way was unexpected and the realisation meant I actually felt sadder for Sunderland winning.

The walk home was quiet and I felt that the conclusions I had come too had been reached by others as well. It's probably different to going to Uni somewhere and watching a smaller team, had I gone to Lincoln I would probably have watched Lincoln City with no problems. But going to the Stadium of Light isn't as good as going to Valley Parade for me, or for going to the City Ground, Ewood Park or Old Trafford for them. No one bothered to scan the programme after to consider the next Sunderland game to go to. We didn't watch another Sunderland match.

Goodbye Uni

I was now in the final few weeks of Uni life and counting down the days with relish. I still had plenty of work to get stuck into, but the end was in sight and I was relived. I was still unhappy with how things were now with my friends never around, still on a tight budget so living on basic food and never doing much. I was bored, fed up and miserable. I also began to feel guilty that, while I was working hard now in pursuit of my degree, that hadn't always been the case.

In the middle of the term the University had held a careers open day to help us all consider what we want to do after Uni and how to achieve it. One speaker was a local newspaper journalist from Stoke. Those of us interested in being a local journalist rushed over to hear from her, but the story she told was not pretty. She had applied to over 60 papers, was lucky if she got so much as a rejection letter back. Having finally landed a job, she moaned the pay was really poor, hours were very long and that she was not optimistic of further climbing the ladder.

This talk had a life-changing effect on some of the students I was on the course with. A handful decided there and then to pack it in and not bother even trying to get a related job. They would finish their degree, but look to do something else. Our tutors tried to talk them round, while at the same time probably making a mental note not to invite this dour lady back next year, but minds were made up. Me? I was still up for the challenge and had always been under the impression it would be tough to get a job. Besides, if these guys are giving up then there's less competition...

I was now considering the next stage of life more and more, something which made me feel happy given my current predicament. As I did, where I would end up living became more of a consideration. In a month's time I will be going to the States for five weeks, but then what? For a long time I'd wanted to stay living in the North East, especially as my flatmates would still be there as none of them, other than Alex, were going to graduate this semester due to falling behind. Perhaps this option was less attractive now, but I equally didn't want to give up my independence. I was prepared to move to another part of the country for the right job and was trying to brace myself for shortly stepping into the unknown.

When I had left home for Uni three years ago there had been some things I was going to miss – family and friends was high up there. I had learned to adapt to this and speak to my parents on the phone once a week, plus just see my friends on weekends I visited. I had also been dreading giving up City and found this one of the toughest things to cope without. Now, three years on, I had adapted and was comfortable. Of course given the choice I would love to watch City play every week, but I had built up a life without them and, until recently, was happy about it. I got to see them five or six times a season and knew that, wherever I ended up, I would continue doing this. I didn't enjoy following City how I did now, watching teletext or Soccer Saturday on TV for score updates. I kept up with City news on the internet and always knew what was going on. But I was prepared for a new chapter of my life and nothing, not even Bradford City, was going to hold me back.

Undoubtedly I felt this was because it had been so long since I'd had a season ticket with City now. There was a time when missing an away game hundreds of miles away left me feeling torn up with guilt – I felt like less of a fan. Yet I knew that I was still a true City supporter despite not being there very often. Of course I wasn't as passionate and committed as others, but I still cared. Other things in life were more important and I was prepared to put them first. I didn't quite consider football to be 'just a game', but I knew it had its place along with everything else.

The 2002-03 ended reasonably happily for City with the objective of avoiding relegation achieved. Those five wins in seven at the turn of the year had pushed City up the table, a perfect tonic after those eight consecutive defeats. Form for the rest of the season remained inconsistent. At home, City were largely disappointing and were beaten by fellow strugglers Brighton, Walsall and Millwall. On the road results were hugely impressive as City achieved a series of excellent wins. This included victories at Coventry, Burnley and Derby. The hero was often midfielder Claus Jorgenson, the Danish midfielder scored in eight consecutive away matches, one short of equalling the all-time Football League record. Andy Gray was also a revelation switching from winger to striker with excellent effect. Survival was confirmed Easter Saturday with a 2-1 win over Watford. It was a good job too, as City lost their final four games without scoring a goal. We finished 19th with the season ending in a 5-0 drubbing at home to Champions Portsmouth.

Just like myself at Uni, for City the last year had been about surviving and getting through to the end – and now we could both look forward to a nice break. I completed all of my work three days after the Portsmouth defeat, unlike last year I wasn't staying any longer than I needed to. I had a nice final evening out with Martin, Dan and Simon, and it was also glaringly obvious that they were becoming as unhappy with Uni life as I. It had become a more horrible existence, as friends we weren't spending enough time together and resentment was growing.

So I felt nothing but relief as I left the following morning. I was home for a day before flying from Manchester to Atlanta the next morning. It was fantastic to see Rachel again, and I really enjoyed the experience of getting to sample America. It was great to be thousands of miles away from home and to forget about my problems. I knew that as soon as I returned I would have to start looking for a job, would find out the result of my degree and be back living in Yorkshire. For now I didn't need to think about the future and tried hard not too.

Rachel's family were wonderfully welcoming and we visited lots of different sights. The lack of interest in football and dance music put me off the culture of the country a little, but it was also nice to forget about those sorts of things for a while. Me and Rachel had a fantastic time, which only reinforced how much we wanted to be together. We spoke of the future and she told me she was prepared to move to England when her degree was completed in 18 months. Thoughts even turned to marriage at that point.

Once the five weeks were over I returned home feeling much better and more relaxed. I felt that my period of depression was over and that I had strength to face the new challenges in my life. It was sad to say bye to Rachel again, but we had agreed she was going to come to visit me for Christmas. Another six-month period apart awaited, but there was at least another goal to work towards.

Where I would be in six months time, or even two weeks time, was a mystery.

Chapter Nine

2003 - 04
Utter misery

The 2003/04 season was supposed to be a celebration. It was City's centenary season, a time to reflect back on the first 100 years of Bradford City with an eye on the future. But instead it proved to be one of the most miserable and stressful campaigns in our history.

Relegation from Division One looked a certainty as early as February, but that wasn't even the worst part. The financial problems that had come to a head during the summer of 2002 returned with a vengeance, threatening the future of the club like never before. As City ended the campaign with a miserable 1-0 defeat at Millwall, relegation long since confirmed, it looked as though it might be our last ever match. City had been a football club for 100 years, but it looked unlikely it would make it to 101.

All football fans have to ensure miserable seasons from time-to-time, but in many ways the bad times are worse for lower league fans. It's not just the quality of football is inevitably dismal, but the dashed expectations. While fans of Premier League clubs not part of the upper elite can begin each season dreaming of a Europa league spot at best, the main objective of avoiding relegation means in reality it's a case of finishing as high up the league as realistically possible. The spoiling of those European aspirations is hardly going to leave you moping around for long; finishing 13th or 10th isn't such a difference to define a season from average to dismal.

But lower league fans can pretty much always realistically believe their team can earn promotion that season, especially with the play off system. And when those hopes quickly look misplaced, huge disappointment sets in. Dreaming of promotion is dreaming of going someplace better, ie the division above. When that doesn't happen, the spectre of staying where you are can feel gloomy. When you're going completely the other way and heading for relegation, it becomes even more unbearable.

The fact we can dream and that promotion is not so improbable compared to Wigan hoping to finish the Champions League spots is a worthwhile trade. But when things go wrong at this level it really is spirit-crushing. The fact that only 10 of the 72 teams in the Football League can earn promotion means an awful lot of us get to May feeling depressed. But still Spring soon becomes Summer and as August comes round we dream again of glory, setting ourselves up to feel depressed all over again.

Who'd have it any other way?

Back home

City's impending relegation meant it was not exactly the greatest season to return to watching them on a regular basis, but as I moved back to live with my parents after University that was to become the unexpected reality. Now back from five wonderful weeks in America, thoughts straight away turned to the future and securing employment. I was now going out into the big wide world, starting the working life that would go on into my 60s. The era of sleeping in until noon on weekdays, drinking in the pub during afternoons and only having a few hours worth of lectures to attend was over.

Much as I had grown fed up of the student life during my final year, it was still a daunting prospect. I wouldn't pretend the life of a student is all takeaways, staying up till late and dodging taxes; but there was certain degree of comfort to the lifestyle. There were no longer any student loans coming into my bank account three times a year to live off, I now had to worry about paying them back.

At least I had a plan, well one that was enough to appease my anxious parents. No sooner had I returned from the airport and enjoyed a warm cup of coffee back on their sofa when the conversation turned to my immediate plans. "What was I going to do now?" was the question. "Well, tomorrow I'm going to begin writing letters to every local paper in the North to see if they have any writing positions going", was the gist of my reply. "And in the meantime I'm going to visit the local recruitment agency and find temporary employment." They were both satisfied and impressed. The following day I typed up a letter template and began looking up addresses of newspapers, I also visited the recruitment agency and completed the necessary forms so they could employ me. By the end of the next day, a Friday, the first few letters were in the post and the agency rang to say they had a temporary position for me at a local factory, starting Monday. Everything was falling into place and I envisaged I would soon have a journalist position and be moving on very quickly.

By the time Monday came along my mood was very different. I'd struggled to sleep the previous night, going to bed much earlier than usual so that I could get up early. I caught the 8am bus and then made the short walk from bus stop to the factory, during which I was filled with dread. My thoughts were all about how this was the beginning on an era. The first day of 'proper' working that would continue for another 45 years. All of the pleasures of student living flashed through my mind. I realised a certain part of my life, which I had taken for granted towards the end, was over. I jealously thought of my old flat mates – not a single one of them would be up right now. It was 8.20am and I was due to start at half past. 5pm seemed a long way off.

To me, a student used to dossing about, the work was awful. My first task was to shift hundreds of boxes from the back of a delivery lorry onto shelves inside the warehouse, a job which took three hours. I did this with three other new temporary starters, but the conversation was non-existent. On each of our faces was a look of shock and horror. Inside the lorry taking out the boxes bit by bit and loading them onto pallets, it was impossible to tell how far back they went. I kept thinking that we must have nearly finished by now, but more boxes kept appearing into view behind the ones we were removing. For break time we all sat in the canteen where all the other workers were. The place was silent, all around were miserable faces. No one was talking about their weekend; no one was talking about anything. One guy looked as though he could burst into tears at any moment. It felt uncomfortable and demoralising. Is this what the world of work is like? It was the longest day of my life.

The second day was thankfully no where near as awful as I adapted to the culture shock. I also realised that this wasn't the horrible existence it had seemed 24 hours ago, and that people were happy and working hard. It was clear I was going to be there for a few days, probably weeks. I desperately hoped that the letters I sent to newspapers would see quick replies containing good news, but in the meantime kept writing to others. Eventually some replies started coming in. All were polite and friendly rejections; with most saying they were keeping my details on file in case future opportunities came up. I felt encouraged, but over time would come to learn that all rejections were polite like this. Still at least they had taken the trouble to reply, many didn't even bother.

It soon became painfully clear that my strategy wasn't as sound as I'd thought and that I would be looking for a job for a while yet. How many other people were in the same boat as me? There was nothing unique about my approach and my letters and CV were probably just one of several each newspaper was receiving daily. I could only keep writing, checking relevant job websites and applying for positions and hope one would at least invite me for an interview. In the meantime I had to keep working at the local factory, feeling fed up and counting down the minutes and seconds until 5pm on a Friday. I was fed up, miserable and feeling depressed again. I needed something to enjoy in my life. I needed football.

Norwich City (home) – the two miserable men

Fortunately the new season was about to begin. I was eagerly anticipating watching a City match, especially as I hadn't been to a game since the 2-0 Ipswich win last February. Pre-season friendlies began – with City worryingly-losing a few – which included a Centenary tournament at Valley Parade. I attended the first day of this, which saw City playing Irish team Coleraine first of all. To add interest, a team from each of the four UK countries had been invited – Aberdeen and Swansea City were also in action. With Stephen and David on holiday, I went to this game on my own. It felt great to be back inside Valley Parade again after what felt like a long absence.

There were several new signings to see for the first time, including the return of a more familiar face in Dean Windass. He left at the end of the Premiership adventure to sign for Middlesbrough, but his career had stuttered a little. Other new signings included Michael Branch from Wolves and Paul Heckingbottom from Norwich. In total 11 new faces were brought in, including several youngsters released by Premier League clubs who it was hoped could do a job in Division One.

I was there for the opening day of the season, where City hosted Norwich. Over the summer Stephen had secured a job at the local hospital washing up, which required him to work weekends. My return to the area was timely for David, as without me he would have no one to go and watch City with. I hadn't seen him all summer but had heard he had recently lost another job working at a local branch of a bank. I knew in the past that David took losing a job badly, so was prepared for him to be a little down, but not to the level he was. I met him on the bus as we made our way to the train station and found he could only grunt back when I asked how well he was. A couple of further questions received short replies, so I decided to give up for a while. The silence felt a little awkward, but I gradually stopped letting it worry me. A couple of times he spoke to apologise for his mood, I told him it was fine. The silence didn't stop us doing the usual pre-match stuff and we went for a drink at the old Maestro's club on Manningham Lane near the ground. We then made our way to Valley Parade; neither of us had season tickets this season so we paid on the door. We went to the area where Dave always sat, just behind the goal in the lower tier of the Kop.

It might not sound like fun, but it was bliss to me. I was still feeling depressed about life and, although the five weeks in America had been great, the misery had quickly returned. I was struggling to adapt to living back at home and the area. I longed to be back in the easy life of University; despite the fact I knew I wouldn't really enjoy it. I now had different and more difficult problems, such as finding a job and pondering my whole future. It was very difficult to switch off from it all and relax. Every time I found myself smiling I felt guilty. My life felt like a mess and I was also badly missing Rachel. I started to go out with my friends at weekends, but struggled to make conversation and enjoy it.

Now I was hanging out with someone who felt exactly the same as me, albeit for different reasons. I found I was enjoying my day and the company of David, because it didn't include the pressure of having to make small talk, pretending to be happy or indeed say anything. I also got the impression that, after apologising and realising I wasn't worried about his behaviour, he relaxed a little and enjoyed my silent company too.

The match looked set to complement our mood as the new-look Bradford City laboured to get going. Passing moves were awkward and disjointed. Attacks were sporadic and weak, the defence looked vulnerable. Without playing much better, Norwich comfortably eased into a 2-0 lead just after half time and the game seemed lost. City even managed to blow an opportunity to claw back into it after Andy Gray missed a penalty. The game was petering out, but the performance felt very appropriate for me and David. Then substitute Ben Muirhead pulled a goal back with 10 minutes to go, can we come back? It looked unlikely as we continued to struggle going forward. The game moved into injury time with goalkeeper Mark Paston making a long clearance. The ball went into the Norwich area and in front of debut-boy Branch who, having done nothing all game, suddenly caught the ball perfectly on the volley and it flew into the net. For a few seconds me and Dave were on our feet and celebrating the improbable comeback. The final whistle was greeted with cheers and we made our way home feeling a notch happier.

Conversation was still slow on the journey home, so I was left to ponder my own thoughts, attempting to make a connection between the game and my life. Things are looking hopeless and miserable at the moment – am I capable of reaching my goals or am I going to fail? For 89 minutes it looked as though City were going to flop and weren't good enough to salvage anything. Yet they kept going, despite probably not even believing in themselves. They chased lost causes and got that bit of luck, pulled out a decent result and provided us a great moment of celebration. I was hoping that Dave was having similar thoughts about the game and his life too. For however bleak things were looking, there's hope and we both had to keep going. There was no point giving up just yet as that break could be just around the corner. Branch could be our inspiration for now; not in the game for 89 minutes, then a moment of brilliance. We both can reach our dreams, whether they happen now or in the 89th minute (hopefully not the 89th minute of our lives though). In the meantime we could look forward to more trips to watch City and long-but-comfortable silences.

Sunderland, Preston, Sheffield United and Derby (home) – free coffee and cheap goals

By September I had a different job. Not, unfortunately, a writing one as yet, but a new temporary position. I had complained to my agency that I would prefer an office role as I was fed up and miserable working in the warehouse – I respected the people I worked with, but it just wasn't suited to me. At least office work would be more relevant to my career aspirations and be more worthwhile in the meantime. Eventually they sorted me out a position at a local mortgage servicing company in Skipton. The work wasn't especially glamorous, I was required to ring up customers of a company we represented to remind them their mortgage repayments were about to go up.

The role gave me more respectability, at least in how I looked at myself. It felt good to be dressing in shirt and tie to go to work, rather than dressing down in old clothes for the warehouse. There were a few other friends from school working around the building to talk to and the working day flew by much quicker. It was a temporary position with no guarantees of length, but I was still busying myself looking for a journalism position, spending an hour or so every evening looking for vacancies on the internet and applying.

Increasingly Saturdays were becoming the highlight of the week again. I missed City's second home game of the season against Gillingham as I attended the Creamfields dance music festival again, but was back for the next game against my old home town of Sunderland. There were already worrying signs for the season ahead with some disappointing early results, the Sunderland game really took the biscuit. We were 3-0 down inside half an hour through some woeful defending and the final score was 4-0. There were increasing concerns that we were going to struggle this season and watching my former local team thrash us only added to them.

Two weeks later we played Preston and were a goal down very quickly. Preston battered us and should have gone in at the break 5-0 up, but it was still only 1-0. Their domination continued after the break but, incredibly, we scored twice to earn three points. The winner was scored by Nicky Summerbee, a new signing made in the wake of the Sunderland debacle. It was great to win and this was followed up by another victory away to Crystal Palace, but it wasn't convincing stuff.

Mid-September was a funny time for me. For the first time since I was four years old I wasn't about to start somewhere – whether it be a new year at school or University. My old flatmates Dan, Simon and Martin had all stayed on because they hadn't completed their degrees, so were about to get going with it all again. Now my younger brother Kevin was also starting Uni. He had chosen Newcastle, partly due to my glowing references of the place. As my parents were due to move him up to the city on the Sunday, I decided to travel to Sunderland the day before and hang out with my old mates and catch a lift home with them the following afternoon.

It wasn't the wisest decision as I witnessed Dan, Martin and Simon all looking refreshed and excited about the year ahead. They were back into Halls for their final year and relishing the fun it would bring and the new friends they'd make. We went out to Shindig in Newcastle and all had a great night, staying up late afterwards drinking and talking. They all slept in really late Sunday and I travelled up to Newcastle to meet my family. Kevin was nervous and excited which reminded me of myself three years ago. He was on the cusp of a thrilling chapter in his life, one that I had just completed. I felt jealous thinking of what would be in store for him and how much I knew he was going to enjoy it. Meanwhile I was on the next chapter; miserable, struggling and worried – plus going to work the next day.

The weekend I had been in Sunderland City had lost again, this time 4-0 at Burnley. Next we entertained Sheffield United. David and I were still quiet when we went to the games although saying a little more and feeling comfortable. He was having no luck securing a job either, although his sights were fixed lower than mine. He would quite happily take the role that I currently had and viewed as a stop gap.

For this game Stephen was able to come along as he had the day off. It was nice for the three of us to be together, although probably less so for Stephen who had to hang out with two miserable people. We had decided to swap positions and journeyed to the top of the top tier of the Kop as that's where all the singers were. It was great to be able to stand up and sing City songs and we could the whole pitch better. We had the perfect view of Dean Windass firing us in front, his first goal since returning to us in the summer, and could see we should have had a penalty seconds before Sheffield United broke up the other end and equalised. Unfortunately the view of the Blades' winner was too good. Of all the people to score it was our old hero, Stuart McCall – right in front of us in the Kop. Stuart refused to celebrate but his contribution made the defeat seem 10 times more devastating. This was one of the worst moments I've experienced since watching City. Stuart was – and still is – my hero and now he's consigned us to defeat. It didn't feel like being stabbed in the back, more right in the stomach so I could witness it perfectly. And then punched in the face for good measure.

Three days later we were at home again (Derby) but unfortunately ended up with same final score. It was looking like a relegation battle for City this season and, worryingly, one we could lose. Typical, as if I don't have enough things to worry about in my life as it is at the moment, I now have what I thought was the main pleasure turning into an additional cause for concern.

Newcastle v Aston Villa – signs of progress

That career day at University at the start of 2003 had left a lasting impression on me. I kept picturing and recalling the words of that dour journalist as she told us all how tough it was to get on the ladder and, even then, the struggle would likely go on for a few years. I also remembered hearing the stories of fellow students who had gotten off their backsides and done some proper writing for various publications in between midweek lie-ins and afternoon drinking sessions, when I hadn't bothered. I was full of regret at the missed opportunity, but also knew I still had the chance to put that right. I looked at what I wanted to be, a football journalist, and thought how I could gain some experience and practice some writing. A Bradford City website was the perfect opportunity.

I'd learned to rely on the internet for City news while I was at University and the first one that I would always check was boyfrombrazil.co.uk (BfB) This website, created and produced by City fan Michael Wood, was really well put together, always full of the latest City news and balanced opinions. What's more Michael welcomed and encouraged articles from fellow City fans which he would publish on the site. What better opportunity was there?

I emailed Michael over the summer to ask about writing and he replied to say that he would be happy to receive articles. Now a couple of months into the season and having become more familiar with the playing squad and standard of performances, I felt I could write more knowledgably. My first effort came after City's mid-October 1-0 home defeat to Ipswich at Valley Parade. The pressure was beginning to grow on manager Nicky Law and I myself wasn't too happy with him. Performances had been poor all season and the team looked weak in too many areas. I wrote about how it was time for Nicky to really prove himself and turn the increasingly desperate situation around if he was to keep his job. I was getting fed up of his excuses in the press and felt he had the resources to do better. In hindsight this was an ignorant view as his budget was much less than I had realised, but still I felt the situation couldn't continue as it was.

I emailed the article but never heard back from Michael, nor did my piece appear on the site. I felt downhearted and believed my work had not been good enough. Or then again, maybe he didn't receive it? Perhaps I hadn't got his email address right? Perhaps he's on holiday? No he is still updating the website each day; it must be that my article isn't that good. Still couldn't he tell me? Or was it THAT bad?

I decided that I would have at least one more go and wrote another piece following the Forest match a fortnight later, yet another defeat although City had been desperately unlucky with Forest hitting an underserved winner in the 90th minute. Martin had visited for the weekend from Uni so we could both go to the game; naturally we each sat among our own supporters.

I logged onto the website the next day and got a huge thrill. There were both my articles and an introduction from Michael saying I was a new writer for the site. I also received an email explaining there had been a technical problem with his email account and he'd just received three weeks worth of emails, including my first article, all at once. He had now put them live and thanked me. I felt proud to have my views on City published and pleased that I had done something that I could include on my CV. I didn't stop there and continued writing articles and later match reports for BfB over the rest of the season and up to the present day.

That same week I had another great bit of news as my old tutor and sports editor of the Sunday Sun in Newcastle replied to one of my application letters by inviting me up to Newcastle at the weekend to help cover the Newcastle v Aston Villa game. In their paper each week they would feature a regular match report and then an additional column with a sideways view of an aspect of the match, which different contributors wrote. They had asked me to write about who should be Newcastle's centre back pairing when Jonathan Woodgate returned from injury. This meant I would be comparing who I expected the two centre backs to be against Villa, Titus Bramble and ex-City centre back Andy O'Brien. Could I get away with bias?

I was hugely excited at such a great opportunity and arranged to stay the night at my old flatmates in Sunderland after the game. I spent a few hours doing research on each Newcastle centre back and turned up to the Sunday Sun office with a folder full of facts. I was working with Neil, who had also been a lecturer of mine at Uni. We walked to the ground together and chatted about recent Newcastle games, which helped me with my background info. The team were playing okay at the time but were yet to hit top form, at the back in Woodgate's absence Bramble was finally winning over the crowd with a series of good performances after a slow start to his Toon career. For the game Andy O'Brien was out with food poisoning so Steve Caldwell, another former City player, was in alongside Bramble. I feared this would spoil my article.

Soon it was time to go into the press box; it was well-positioned half way up the stand and offered a fantastic view. The game kicked off and it was soon obvious Villa had come to defend although they took a surprise early lead when Dion Dublin headed home a corner. We each had a monitor by our seats so we could view replays and I was able to check whose slack marking allowed Dublin in. Newcastle equalised just before half time through Laurent Robert and pressed for a winner in the second half. With 10 minutes to go they were awarded a penalty. Everyone in the press box quickly realised that it was Alan Shearer against Thomas Sorenson; three years ago Sorenson had saved a Shearer penalty while playing for Sunderland against Newcastle. Score or miss this time, the headline from the match was suddenly guaranteed. History repeated itself as Sorenson saved Shearer's effort. The game ended 1-1.

I returned alone to the Sunday Sun office to type up my article as Neil waited for the press conference with both managers. I found it hugely difficult to stick to the word limit as I tried to include views on Bramble and Caldwell. To make matters worse, in the corner of the office but with no sound on was the live Sky game of Wimbledon v Bradford City. We were the late kick off match and it was a huge game as Wimbledon were struggling even worse than City. If we lost this one, it could be curtains for Law. I tried to keep the match out of my mind as I wrote my piece, but it was difficult knowing how much was at stake. The lack of sound helped but I was aware the score was 1-1. Article finished and left with the Editor, I hurried off to the nearest pub to watch the end of the game. I was horrified to see we were losing 2-1 and the game was nearly all over. Stood alone, I attracted a few funny glances from others in the pub not interested in the game. With two minutes to go Michael Branch broke through, just had the keeper to beat but blazed wide. It was all over, what a terrible result.

The following morning I rushed to the local newsagent to buy a couple of copies of the Sunday Sun. I nervously hurried to the page where my piece would be and there it was, complete with my own by-line. I felt proud and that progress was being made. Progress that I could add to my CV and progress that saw a positive reply at last to one of my job applications. I was invited for an interview for a trainee reporter job at the Lincoln Echo. It was great to finally reach the next stage of the application progress, although it did show me I still had a way to go. I didn't interview brilliantly and didn't get the job, but things were moving forwards at last and I had something to cling onto.

Someone joining me looking for work was Law, a week after the Wimbledon defeat he was sacked. That defeat had followed two reasonable draws away to Coventry (0-0) and at home to Walsall (1-1). I left Valley Parade after the Walsall game feeling reasonably content and was shocked to hear on the radio a few hours later that he had been sacked. Still I felt it was ultimately the right decision and looked forward to a new man coming in and making a better go of things. It also gave me a chance to write a third article for BfB. After a difficult summer it felt as though things were looking up for myself and City.

Millwall (home) – new hopes

Saturday 27 November 2003, and it's former England and Manchester United legend Bryan Robson's first game in charge of Bradford City. A reasonable crowd is present inside Valley Parade for the evening kick off and the Sky TV cameras are here to beam the game live around the world. And there I am, stood towards the back of the Kop, cheering and applauding our new saviour.

There's usually nothing unusual about me being at Valley Parade now of course; until I explain that, up until a few days before, I had expected to be a 100 miles away watching the game in a pub. I was supposed to go up to Sunderland for a weekend with my old friends, still up there and finally getting on with doing some work (well most of them). I'd told them all I would be going up to see them and, slightly foolishly, promised to pay the taxi fare from Newcastle to Sunderland so

179

we could all afford a night out at Shindig. I was working now, I explained to them, so I could afford to help them out. I soon realised this promise to them was rash and that the taxi fare of £30+ on top of the other costs of a night out, train fare to and from Sunderland and eating out a couple of times was going to result in a ludicrously expensive weekend. I didn't pull out because of this, though I did feel hugely guilty about the broken promises I ultimately made.

Instead it was the lure of Robson which kept me back home. It was a glamorous managerial appointment and one some of us could barely believe. Up until now, Robson had an okay track record in management, twice leading Middlesbrough to promotion and to two cup finals. He had achieved legendary status as a player and was hugely respected in the game. We felt he could attract better players than Nicky Law appeared able too and we felt he could lift us out of the increasing mess we were in. I had known this Millwall game was going to be on Sky for weeks and could have watched it with no problems in a Sunderland pub; part of the reason why I had initially decided to go up to the North East for the weekend. But as news developed that Bryan Robson would be taking charge and this was to be his first game, I knew I couldn't miss it. So I let down my friends and paid to watch a game I could have watched for free.

To me at least, this was a sign. Up until now I had prioritised weekends back to Uni and the opportunity to see live music over going to watch City. It was almost as if I could take it for granted, the chance to go to Creamfields came but once a year and, even then, I might never go again. I always knew – the club's financial predicament allowing – there would be another City game to go to, and spending three years of not going regularly meant I had learnt to cope with not being there. Yet City were now gradually getting back under my skin and watching a new man come in and attempt to lift the dismal performances date was unmissable.

Robson's appointment followed the usual two-week period of uncertainty that always comes with a managerial sacking. In the meantime Dean Windass, Wayne Jacobs, David Wetherall and Peter Atherton were all appointed caretaker managers and looked after picking the team.

It was Stephen's birthday the week after Law's sacking and, wanting to give him a good day, I had persuaded David that we should take him to watch City's away game at Stoke and then meet Alan, who was off to Old Trafford to watch Blackburn play Man United, in Bradford after, where we could then go for a few pints. Unfortunately Dave's depression got the better of him and he was unable to lift himself to give Stephen a great day. He barely spoke, looked fed up to be there and became unnecessarily annoyed at the choice of radio station on the supporters' coach we travelled on. The game hardly helped as City, with Wayne Jacobs' in charge for the afternoon, lost 1-0 following an early goal. We barely managed a shot on goal and certainly didn't look like we could score. Thank goodness Robson was appointed a few days later. At the time we were unaware, but Jacobs and Windass had fallen out in training which resulted in Jacobs leaving Deano out. 20 minutes into the game I asked why Deano wasn't in the team, and then realised he was sat with us away fans, two rows in front of me!

We made our way back to Bradford and went around some pubs with Alan before getting the last train back. The last bar we went in was playing house music with a live DJ and, although the place was empty, it lifted us all. The music sounded brilliant and we sat near the DJ to enjoy it. Suddenly Steve could fight the urge no more and raced up to the empty dance floor. I quickly joined him and we let go of some of our frustrations and just enjoyed the music. It was a hugely uplifting moment, so good it proved the difference between a disappointing and brilliant birthday for Stephen. Even David joined us on the dance-floor towards the end.

Me and Stephen went to the same bar again the following week, this time after City's game with Millwall. How pleased I was that I didn't go to Sunderland, I would have missed the best game of the season. The first 45 minutes of the Robson reign didn't look good as Millwall ran into a 2-0 lead; we were as poor as we had been all season. At half time Danny Cadamarteri came on as sub for his first proper appearance for a year following injury. He quickly scored to put us back into it and then, with 20 minutes to go, Andy Gray fired an equaliser. We went crazy; relieved to have salvaged a draw and pleased that Robson's first game was to end in encouraging circumstances. Then came the finish we daren't hope, Robson's first signing Gareth Farrelly produced a brilliant through ball for substitute Michael Branch to run clean through onto. He kept his cool and lifted the ball over the advancing keeper which then bounced slowly into the net for 3-2. Cue bedlam as me and Stephen jumped and hugged each other and then strangers all around us. The season surely starts here!

Talk about a false dawn. We lost our next five games without even scoring a goal including being beaten by a Wigan site en route to the Premiership with Paul Jewell at the helm. It all proved too much for our Chairman Gordon Gibb, who decided to resign after a 3-0 defeat to Sunderland. The official line at the time was that he was fed up of watching City lose all the time and wasn't enjoying football like he thought he would; although a more accurate picture of problems behind the scenes would soon emerge. For now we could only worry about the increasingly-worse position City found themselves in, just one win in 18 matches was clearly relegation form. Could Robson pull off a miracle?

Coventry (home) – engaged

Christmas came early for me in 2003. A week before the usual holiday celebrations I was travelling on a National Express coach from Leeds to London in the middle of the night. I woke up from a couple of hours sleep to see I was approaching Gatwick airport and my stop. In just under two hours a flight from America would be touching down and with it some precious cargo that I was here to collect. Rachel was staying with me for Christmas.

It remained difficult for me living without her and doing long distance, but I had gradually learned to cope better with the situation since the summer. It was now a year since Rachel had left me in Sunderland to go home and I wasn't sure how I was going to survive those first few weeks. We had both since learned to live our lives without each other. I was still struggling to get a job and was not particularly happy with my situation, but I had plenty more going on in it now than when I was at Uni. At least I had friends about and was earning money so that I could do things with them. Looking for a job consumed plenty of time, as did having a stop-gap job. I still spoke to Rachel on the phone nearly every day and we shared texts regularly. She had agreed to spend Christmas in England and properly meet my family. Oh, and I was going to propose to her too.

It perhaps sounds like a rash decision – I had only just turned 22 – but it was one carefully considered. Our situation was different to the usual, not many other couples are separated by thousands of miles. Long distance is neither fun nor easy and leaves you with plenty of time to think and determine some things, not least – is it worth it? And what's the future? Not something most people our age have to start considering for a while longer.

But consider it I had too, after all what happens when Rachel finally does complete her degree in a year's time? She can't just move over here, immigration doesn't work like that. Neither can I just move over there. We would need to be married first for either scenario to work. I wanted her to move over to the UK and live with me. But where does that go? You don't just casually move to another country for a few months, you want to build a life and look for employment and a career, as well as settling down and one day buying a house. Do I want all those things with Rachel? Of course I do. Deciding to propose to her wasn't necessarily an easy decision to make, but I knew in my heart it was what I wanted to do.

The reaction I received after telling friends and family of my plans was one of shock and surprise, but seeing how unhappy I was on occasions and how obvious it was that she meant everything to me meant that they could understand. Gaining acceptance from friends and family was important and helped me realise I wasn't barmy for wanting to get married so young. I knew I would keep getting looks of surprise from other people when they heard and they would question why I wanted to get married now. "You must be stupid!" But knowing I had the support of close friends and family gave me the inner confidence not to worry. I knew what I was doing, even if I sounded a bit mad...

Rachel, of course, was not exactly unaware of this. The American culture is very different to the English with lots of people getting married at this age. In fact Rachel had already been a bridesmaid and would be another in the New Year.

There was an expectation from her and her family that I would be proposing soon. In fact our engagement that Christmas was one of the worst kept secrets going around. I didn't have to be fearful that she would say no – that thought never entered my mind. She didn't have to be fearful I wasn't going to ask, I would do at some point very soon.

In the end I proposed on Christmas Eve. With the expectation I was going to ask I was under pressure to make it special and, well, I blew that. Big gestures are not something I'm any good at so I unromantically proposed when we got home from a night out with my friends. I didn't even get down on one knee when I asked. Luckily she said yes! Even with all the lack of surprise, it still felt like a wonderful moment.

While Rachel's visit was for us to see each other, getting to know my family and seeing the area where she might be moving to; football had to come into the picture somewhere. I was desperate to take Rachel to at least one City game and had the choice of three home matches – Rotherham, Coventry or Luton in the FA Cup. In the end plans at other times during her visit meant I took her to watch us play Coventry. It proved to be a good decision as City lost 2-0 to Rotherham and 2-1 to Luton, but beat Coventry 1-0. Windass struck the winner in the first half and, while we didn't play very well in the second, we survived a penalty miss and heavy pressure to record a badly-needed win. I liked to think Rachel enjoyed the experience and at least saw City in a more positive light. I was also desperately hoping this could be the turning point for the Bantams in the increasingly desperate situation.

Rachel had to go back in early January so it was another difficult goodbye. We had talked about the wedding and agreed we should be married when Rachel completes her degree in December, so there was less than a year to go. I was also going to be visiting her in March after collecting newspaper tokens for a discounted flight voucher to America, so we had less of a gap between seeing each other again. It was still tough though and I drove home from the airport in what suddenly felt like a very empty car; back to coping with life not being great.

Cardiff (home) – from bad to worse

The weekend after Rachel left, City won again. This victory was extremely notable in that it was away at leaders Norwich City. On-loan Ipswich striker Alun Amrstrong had netted the only goal of the game, meaning we had won two on the bounce. We had two consecutive home games coming up, both winnable-looking. Is the Great Escape on?

Not exactly. Another run of consecutive defeats was just beginning, one that would see our survival hopes all but disappear. We played Cardiff at Valley Parade first, battled hard, huffed and puffed, but struggled to create decent chances in front of goal. Then a mistake by our young defender Simon Francis, who gave away a daft penalty, cost us. Keeper Alan Combe saved the penalty but the rebound was bundled home. There were still 20 minutes to go and Cardiff only had 10 men due to a sending off five minutes earlier, but it still proved game over. This defeat probably summed up our whole season; plenty of effort, but lacking in quality especially going forward, with good work ruined by defensive errors. By the end of the campaign we had set a new record for most single goal defeats in a season (21 of our 46 league games). We were only well beaten on a handful of occasions, most games were really close and we would narrowly miss out on earning at least a point, usually due to our defensive ineptitude or attacking impotence.

As a supporter watching this kind of football is extremely frustrating. Each defeat felt so agonising because we weren't far off, but to know that we have ultimately failed each time due to our own mistakes was hard to bear. We lacked the quality and you could argue that we deserved to lose most weeks because of it. But why do we never seem to get a lucky break, and why don't the opposition need to come up with brilliance to beat us? It was notable how many arguments there were raging between players when the goals went in. If everyone did their jobs properly for the full 90 minutes we would be okay. One mistake by one player ruined all the good work that they and their 10 teammates had put in. And it wasn't just one player costing us each week; the blame for the opposition goals was evenly shared over the course of the season between a number of players.

The Cardiff defeat was quickly followed by reverses to Crystal Palace (2-1) Gillingham (1-0) and West Ham (2-1). The West Ham game was a significant one for me as, in the week before, I had emailed the BfB editor Michael to ask if I could try writing some match reports for the site as well. I enjoyed the experience and agreed with Michael that I would write reports for all the other games I go to this season, so on most occasions the site could offer two match reports – his and mine – for the readers. Next we were away at Ipswich and, despite Dean Windass marking his return from injury with an all too rare goal, we were easily beaten 3-1.

Crewe were the next visitors to Valley Parade and, after five defeats in a row, it really was now or never time for City. Yet events off the field were starting to overshadow the football. In the run up to the game I had bought the paper after work as usual and being shocked to read the headline that City were heading back to financial trouble. We were going to return into Administration by the end of the week, the cause was an apparent falling out between recently-resigned Chairman Gordon Gibb and the remaining owners, the Rhodes family. The report also told of how City aren't making enough money to pay off the still large debts and operate viably. It was a depressing addition to a miserable time for City, we're beginning to look doomed for relegation but that would become irrelevant if the club can't even survive to take part in the division below next season. What else can go wrong?

At least we beat Crewe the following Saturday with goals from Windass and on-loan midfielder Ronnie Wallwork. It was a good day for me, Stephen and David. We went home after the match, quickly got changed and then caught the train back to Bradford so we could go to the Town & Country nightclub on Manningham Lane, which was hosting a house music night. We had such a blast and, after a season of such much misery with little to cheer, it was great to be in an environment with Stephen and David where we could be happy and forget about our respective troubles for a few hours. I woke up the following morning with my ears still ringing from how loud the music had been, but also with a big grin from a near perfect weekend that had involved seeing City win and going clubbing.

The following weekend I was down in Nottingham and meeting up with Martin for the Forest v City game, the day after City had gone back into administration. It was a worrying time and this fixture was vital for both clubs. Since beating us 2-1 at Valley Parade at the end of October, Forest hadn't won a single match – dropping from play off contenders to the relegation zone and in the process changing manager. This was a big game for Forest and, walking to the City Ground with Martin and surrounded by Forest fans, I heard many home fans muttering "If we don't beat this lot then we truly are crap." We went our separate ways outside the ground and I joined the City fans in the away end. After five minutes we were behind after Andy Reid was presented with an easy chance. Then, unexpectedly, Windass equalised for us with a free kick. The rest of the game was fairly even and we missed a few opportunities to go in front, and as the 4th official announced there would be two minutes injury time at the end I felt confident we could nick a winner.

But in the last minute of injury time Forest scored. I held my head in my hands, and everyone around me looked similarly miserable. Surely this was the moment when avoiding relegation became impossible. Most of the loan players who had come in and lifted us were probably going to be taken back by their parent clubs now that we were in administration, and Robson won't be allowed to make further signings. We needed a miracle.

Burnley and Stoke (home) – nails in coffin

Through all of the job application process since leaving University, I always had a safety net. Very early on when I began applying to anyone and everyone, I had received a reply from the editor of the Liverpool Echo who revealed that, although the paper didn't have any vacancies at the moment, they run an annual training scheme for graduates which involves taking on a few each year, putting them through an intensive course and then beginning them working for the paper. He invited me to apply for the next training scheme, which would take place the following summer.

In those early days when I was lucky just to receive a polite rejection letter back from my numerous applications, this had been an encouraging moment. It was an option that I knew would come around in the not to distant future. I had started to get used to rejection letters saying nice things that were ultimately meaningless, but this letter stood out as being more sincere.

So when people asked me how I was doing in my search for a writing job, I was always able to reply that, no, I hadn't got a position yet, but was applying to lots of positions and waiting to hear back (the volume of applications I made meant I was always waiting to hear back from someone). I could then also add that I had been invited to apply for a training course for the Liverpool Echo next Spring so, if nothing came up in the meantime, I would hopefully get on that. It made me feel happy telling people this, it also made me happy knowing that I had this back up on occasions where I felt down about the lack of progress.

But as Spring came around I began to think more and more about this opportunity and became more and more edgy. It would soon be time to fill out and send off that application form which the editor had kindly included in his reply last summer. I was used to filling out these types of forms, but this one felt different. I knew I had to put in lots of effort, write even neater than usual and include all the relevant details they asked for – plus numerous examples of my published work through work placements. Eventually it was time to post the form and wait to hear back.

The closing date was Friday 26 March. The following day I went to Valley Parade to watch City play Burnley. It was a local derby and always a grudge match. To add some spice, both teams were fighting relegation. Burnley were hovering above the drop zone and in need of a few more points to guarantee their survival. We were still second to the bottom, improving but still adrift. The squad looked thin and bare, but still the last few weeks had seen some of our best results of the season and some of us still believed that we could do it. One thing was for sure though; there was no room for error. A home game against a fellow struggler simply had to be won, anything less was unthinkable.

Stupidly, I invited my friend Placy along with us. He is a Burnley fan and, after going to the pub with him the evening before, the game came up in conversation and he expressed an interest in coming along. He was a keen supporter when we were at school and would go to every home game, but had stopped going years ago. For this game he sat with me, Stephen and David in the Kop. It would be fair to say he wasn't as bothered about the result as we all were. It was probably a good thing because if he had matched the nerves and tension that I was emanating, but for the opposition, we might have come to blows. I was so desperate for the points, we all were.

Eight minutes into the match, Burnley took the lead. Of all people it was our former striker Robbie Blake who ran through to score. But 10 minutes later we equalised when a delightful Nicky Summerbee cross field pass reached Danny Cadamarteri, who beat a defender and finished well. For the majority of the rest of the match we laid on heavy pressure and created numerous chances. The Burnley keeper Brian Jensen was in inspired form, saving everything that came his way. We've played well, we've battered them, but the ball just wouldn't go in. As the game headed to injury time I felt disappointed knowing a point wasn't really enough in the circumstances. Then suddenly Burnley raced up the pitch and the ball ended up pinging around the area, with some pretty pathetic attempts from our defenders to clear it. Burnley scored.

Even from such a season of such misery this was a new low. My head slumped down and I stared at the floor below me, believing I might not have the strength to look upwards again. I tried to ignore Placy who was now laughing and eventually looked towards the Burnley players who were celebrating like crazy with their fans. The final whistle blew and I couldn't move, let alone walk back to the car. I couldn't face the prospect of another week ruined by feeling miserable about City.

That's it, we're down. We can't do it now. Many fans have given up long ago but I kept my stupid optimistic hope. Where has this got me? Feeling even more miserable in the long run. How I envied those pessimistic City fans who were now slumping off to the pub, telling everyone they knew we were down before Christmas. They didn't have any hope, so don't now have to deal with losing it today. The players came over to applaud us and I wanted to applaud them back, because their efforts had deserved it, but I couldn't bring myself to anything quite so positive.

The car journey home was very quiet – well quiet that was apart from Placy. He'd picked a great time to rediscover his passion and started taking the mick loudly, singing Burnley songs and laughing about how we we're going down. By rights I should have stopped the car and ordered him to get out, but I sat there and took it. Poor old Stephen and David were as depressed as me, what have they done to deserve this annoying git making what was a traumatic time for us even worse by taking the piss? I wished the traffic would move a bit quicker, I needed to get him out of the car. During the next week I remained in a pit of despair. I went to work but struggled to muster a smile, my manager was a season ticket-holding Burnley fan, probably at Valley Parade on Saturday. At least he had the compassion not to mention the game.

My mood was made far worse by worrying about the application to the Liverpool Echo. Ever since sending my first application the July before, I'd become used to worrying about what letters the postman might bring. So I waited to receive an immediate letter back from the Liverpool Echo, hopefully saying I was successful. Monday there was nothing, Tuesday nothing again. Surely Wednesday there would be something; I got home and there was nothing, and nothing the next day, and the day after. The quickness of my interview invite I'd received, from the Lincoln Echo a few months, had taught me you're more likely to hear back very quickly if they are interested in you. Now a week had past and I had still heard nothing, how I was cursing the postman.

All I could think about was how my safety net had now gone. Through all the application process I had this back up, now if this doesn't work out I've got nothing. Nothing telling me to keep trying because there's an opportunity there, nothing to discourage me from believing I was completely wasting my time, nothing to give me the confidence that I could make it.

Getting to Saturday's post was a relief. There was still no reply, but at least I could stop worrying about it until Monday. City lost again, this time at Preston, and relegation was looming larger. During the next week I continued to be worried about not receiving a response, the frustration got so bad I decided to call them. I spoke to the editor who explained they hadn't made any final decisions but hope to do so in the next week or so. I felt hugely relived that my chances were still alive, but carried on applying for other jobs too. Over Easter City won and lost a fixture. Only mathematics was keeping us in with a chance, but even if we won our five remaining fixtures that probably wouldn't be enough.

At least we would prolong the agony another week, I thought, as we entertained bottom of the league and already relegated Wimbledon. Before the game me, Stephen and David went to Centenary Square to take part in a Supporters Trust-organised protest to raise awareness about our financial plight. The uncertainty of administration was still hanging over us and, as it stood, we only had enough funding to keep the club going until May. Should no additional money come in at the point then the administrators would be forced to shut down the club. A vital CVA meeting, where creditors would meet and be offered a settlement on their debts, was approaching. City couldn't afford to pay all their remaining debts and had to hope creditors would agree to receive only a percentage of what they were owed. As supporters we were largely powerless, a protest before the match felt as we were at least doing something. A few hundred of us turned out and some people made some speeches, including an emotive poem written by a supporter about the situation. A coffin was also put together and the local press took photos of fans carrying it. It was heartening to be there and share concerns among fellow supporters, we even went to the pub straight after with a few we met.

It was a shame the players couldn't put more effort in. Despite Wimbledon having nothing to play for and already relegated, they went 3-0 up shortly after half time. We pulled it back to 3-2 but didn't look like rescuing even a point. In the closing stages we sat slumped in our seats with our feet on their empty chairs in front. A steward came up to us and told us to move our feet or he would throw us out. Fed up, depressed and angry at the match we were watching, the threat of being thrown out was surely pushing our patience too far. I refused to move my feet, and told him he would be doing us favour throwing us out. He turned and walked away without saying anything. The final whistle blew and what we had

191

known was going to happen for a long time had happened, City were relegated.

At least the pain was over, or so I thought. Two weeks later we were due to play Stoke City for our final home game. It was a meaningless match for both sides with Stoke in mid table, but I still paid my £16 to go. Dave decided he was too full of cold so it was just me and Steve. In the morning I drove my mum into Keighley so she could go shopping and we returned home just before lunchtime. As I opened the door I noticed there was a letter addressed to me in the hall way, with a Liverpool post mark. There was no doubt what the letter was about and I quickly ran up to my room to open it alone. Would it contain great news or, more likely, was it going to be bad? I'd opened so many letters with bad news that it was my natural assumption to think the worst. Sadly this occasion was to be no different. My eyes knew not to read the letter from the start, but to skip to the middle bit after all the pleasantries about thanking me for my application were over. There were two words which signified the response, "we regret". I didn't need to read anymore.

I couldn't help it, I started crying. There goes my safety net. It's been nearly a year now since I first started applying and all I have to show for it is a file of rejection letters and one failed interview. I'd always had this opportunity to keep me going when it felt bleak, now I had nothing. Should I continue? Was I wasting my time? I've not got anywhere and it was obvious hundreds of other people are having the same problem. My application, my past experience, my Uni degree – none of it is standing out. None of it is placing me above other people. Maybe I need to face the facts; a career in writing isn't going to happen.

I tried to stop crying to face my mum, who had already guessed I'd received bad news. I struggled to eat my lunch as we sat in near silence. I had to go and pick up Stephen in five minutes, but the last thing I wanted to do was be sociable. The journey to Bradford and the hour in the pub before kick off was carried out in silence. Stephen didn't have a clue what was wrong and I wasn't interested in talking about it. He talked away to me and I tried to respond, but the best I could manage was grunts. At least there was no risk of having to be happy or cheer at the match. City went 1-0 down inside a minute and

2-0 down a minute into the second half. We barely created a chance.

As is traditional at the end of the season, we stayed back to wait for the players to do a lap of honour to thank them for their efforts. We waited for them to come out, and waited, and waited. Some 20 minutes passed and I began to get angry. In our dressing room was a bunch of players who had failed dismally this season and provided nothing but misery, but they were now keeping us waiting for them.

Why are we still here? I've never felt as stupid while at a football match as we waited for a bunch of useless players to graciously allow us the opportunity to applaud them. Eventually they came out, apparently they didn't think anyone would wait back to cheer them so didn't know to come out, was their later explanation. As we clapped them walking round the pitch, I took a long lingering look at Valley Parade and the surroundings. With the financial uncertainly, this could prove to be my last ever glimpse of this view.

Just to complete the miserable day, I returned to the car to find a parking ticket stuck on the windscreen. I was parked on the Midland Road but it turned out the wrong side of a police cone. Now I had a £30 bill for nothing, it was the wrong day for it to happen and the journey home was in even more silence. I couldn't wait to get back to my room, shut the door and not have to worry about facing the world until I was ready again.

Summer of misery

After the season finished it was obvious to the club's administrators that the proposed CVA that creditors had to agree to was not going to prove successful, so they cancelled it. Normal employees of the club staged a protest over our plight, which inspired another supporters' demonstration. I was unable to make it but heard about it later. A meeting with the clubs administrators after the protest saw a challenge posed to us; raise £250,000 to keep the club going during the summer to give the administrators' time to find a solution.

Supporters took it on and began holding weird and wonderful events to raise money, while local businesses pitched in by donating money. A charity match at Valley

Parade was organised where former City legends and celebrities would take part. It was one match I couldn't miss, so me and David went along. We paid a donation on the gate and enjoyed a cracking match which many of our heroes took part in. There was Stuart McCall, Darren Moore, Jamie Lawrence, Wayne Jacobs, and Gary Walsh among the heroes of my time, but there were also the likes of John Hendrie and Chris Waddle. It was great to see them give up their time and help the club, but the most heartening thing was the attendance. The kick off had to be delayed to accommodate everyone and a five figure crowd came along. At the end the players did a lap of honour and we all sang "City till I die". It was hugely uplifting and gave me hope that the club could survive the present troubles. The will was there.

On my own part, things were also looking up. The week after the Stoke game, with all that bad news, had seen another letter arrive. This time from the Yorkshire Post with a positive response to my request for work experience, so I got the week off work and worked at the paper instead. I was in the sports department, where I wanted to be. And, due to holidays, I was looking after the football coverage. My day would involve sourcing news, both on the internet and by ringing around football clubs in the region, then writing stories. The big news through the week was Leeds appointing a new assistant manager, Sam Ellis; which meant I got to interview new manager Kevin Blackwell over the phone about it. I also interviewed Adam Pearson and the York City chairman about a player who would join City years later, Lee Bullock. I was left with the challenge of calling Bradford City's Managing Director Shaun Harvey for the latest on City and if Bryan Robson was going to remain as manager, but Shaun would never take or return my calls.

Writing up stories and seeing my name in print the following day was a wonderful experience and I spent my final day hoping they would offer me a job. They didn't, sadly, but the placement came at a great time and lifted my morale. Even more encouragingly, it started to open the door with my job applications. The first application I made which included details of my Yorkshire Post placement under 'experience' saw me offered an interview, it was a trainee reporter position in Swindon and while I was unsuccessful it was a timely boost.

The next two applications also saw me invited for interviews, again both were down south. The first, in Gloucester, didn't go very well but I also didn't like the look of the job. The other was for a football website in London and I was really keen to get it, even if I was unsure if I wanted to move to the capital. I was disappointed to discover I was unsuccessful, but decided to write back to them for feedback on my interview performance. I was told I had been very close and should be proud; I had made the final nine from over 200 original applicants. It finally felt as though I was making progress and the experience from my Yorkshire Post placement triggered it for me. I might not have a safety net anymore, but my inner-confidence that I could make had returned.

I was also off back to America during the summer to visit Rachel and join her family on their vacation. City's supporters had smashed the £250k fundraising barrier and things were slowly looking as though they were falling into place. Bryan Robson did leave, but his assistant Colin Todd was confirmed as replacement. Then, at the end of June, the sky fell through again. Agreements could still not be reached with the creditors, in particular with our former Chairman Gordon Gibb who now owned our stadium and was owed money. Talks had completely broken down and there was no apparent hope. The day I flew to America fans were gathering outside Valley Parade for a 12pm deadline that, if no agreement was reached by, would see the club go out of business there and then. I felt in bits on the plane as I had no access to what was going on. The flight was eight hours long and then a further two hours drive to get to Rachel's home. I was scared at the prospect of using her internet and logging on to discover that Bradford City Football Club no longer existed.

Fortunately, the club was still there. At the last moment a gang of five Bradford business men had stepped in and got the different parties talking again. An agreement was reached between the creditors and City would be able to start the season. We weren't going to be in great shape again for some time, and it was obvious that any more financial problems would spell the end. For now I was just relieved that, while City would remain in administration until December, they were able to carry on. It had been a desperately stressful few months and a truly miserable year since leaving University, but the future was looking cautiously brighter again.

Chapter Ten

2004 - 05
Priced out

This was a true season of two halves, on a personal level at least. I saw 10 of City's first 11 home fixtures – then I only saw 2 of the remaining 12. This was due to personal circumstances of going through the tough, cash-strapped early days of married life. With money extremely tight, going to watch Bradford City suddenly became a luxury I couldn't afford.

Despite relegation to League One, ticket prices rose slightly to £18 and, with Rachel also to pay for, the £36 to fork out for 90 minutes of football, plus all the travel and related costs involved with the day out, became too expensive. We were living off just my very low wage and savings, and tough sacrifices had to be made. It was a strange and empty feeling not going along to watch City when I was living barely 20 miles away from Valley Parade. But sometimes in life you have to accept certain circumstances and get through them.

But even though my situation was quite extreme, it has become a fact of life that lower division football is no longer as cheap either. It may not involve the same eye-watering ticket prices as Premier League fans learn to live with, but it has stretched way beyond the easily affordable days of £9 for an adult to stand on the Kop that was the case when I first discovered the club. The fact that Premier League clubs were paying obscene wages to players – which fans had to bear the cost of through the entry price into the stadium – had a knock on effect down the leagues. Suddenly Division One/ Championship clubs were raising prices to help them have the resources to mount a promotion push. And if your rivals are charging more and gaining the advantages of bigger playing budgets, you inevitably have to follow suit. The lower leagues are still cheaper, but they are not the bargain prices that everyone can afford.

Take Ipswich in the Championship. For the 2010/11 season, visiting supporters had to pay £41 per ticket. For families who would need to buy three or four tickets for a day out, it becomes too big to justify and hardly represents the same value for money other family attractions represent. Clubs continue to rely on the loyalty of their core fan-base, knowing they will grudgingly pay hiked ticket prices and bring in enough revenue.

All of which represents a danger for the lower leagues. At a time when Premier League prices remain obscene and millions of young people especially cannot afford to go and watch their heroes, the Football League should promote itself as a viable alternative where anyone and everyone can afford to watch their local team. But that sadly is disappearing and those with a floating interest, but who could become more passionate if the team was more accessible, conclude there are better things they can spend their money on and turn their backs.

The Football League has proactively tried to attract families and young people especially, and under 11s can watch their local club for free in most places. But sadly the lower leagues no longer represent the value for money they once did, and for the second half of this season I was to feel its effects.

Big changes

It was a big season, both for Bradford City and for me personally. In December I was going to be getting married to Rachel over in America and then she was moving to live with me in England. It was an exciting and scary proposition. I knew Rachel was the one for me and that neither of us would run off scared at the altar, but it was still strange to think I was about to get hitched. I was due to turn 23 two months before and Rachel's own birthday would be eight days prior to our big day. It was partly scary because I had yet to get my life sorted. When I proposed to Rachel a year earlier I had hoped and expected to have a job, have moved out and be living wherever the job took me; saving up money for the future. Yet here I was in August, still temping and not making much from it. I was living with my parents and I had little to nothing saved away. I had four months to get my life in shape. Time was running out and the pressure was growing.

At least the scary bits were over with Bradford City. With the summer financial strife behind, the club could look forward to a more positive future. Just being around was a great achievement but there were still fears of what might happen next. The difficulties and constant uncertainty, tied with the realisation of just how close it was to being over in July, left us all with little doubt this was the last chance. We had to start making money and be able to pay off debts; we couldn't afford to go through this sort of situation again. Colin Todd was now in charge and given a small budget to bring in some players, just a handful from last season were still around. Many took up the option to leave that the club's administrators offered them when wages were not forthcoming.

The big kick off was up at Hartlepool, although it was a game I had no chance of attending. After the miserable feeling of the Stoke game at the end of the season, where that graduate scheme job opportunity had disappeared, I thought long and hard at what I was going to do. With the football season over, I decided that getting a short-term weekend job on top of the temping was a sensible idea. I popped into my local shop, where I used to have a paper round, to see if they needed any staff. Luckily the guy who was in charge when I had worked for them was still there and he took me straight to see the main boss. I was taken on straightaway and ended up working every Saturday morning and every other Sunday afternoon. As the football season approached again, however, I knew I couldn't stay working until half 1 every Saturday and face a mad dash to get Valley Parade. It was just a temporary job to help get a few extra quid and I soon handed in my notice, the afternoon of the opening game, at Hartlepool, was my last shift.

To make up for it I spoke to my manager at my office job about being taken on for a three month contract instead of temping. It seemed sensible that, as I wasn't going anywhere unless something cropped up, I should risk earning a bit more money for the sake of not being able to hand in as short a notice. He agreed and I had a contract until just before the

December wedding, I also knew it would be easy for it to be extended if need be, although I hoped I would have found my dream media position in time for the big day. Time was running out, big decisions were just around the corner.

Peterborough and Doncaster (home) – tackling the boo boys

It should have been a night of celebration, Peterborough was the first home game of the season and the first since it looked as though the club would go under. I had been looking forward to sitting inside Valley Parade, and while the Bolton friendly had allowed that, this was the real thing all over again. We'd spent the summer fearing that we would no longer have a club to support, what would we have done with the rest of our lives? A big hole would have been created and, while a non-league Bradford City might have risen from the ashes, it would have hardly been the same. So here we were, still, and about to enjoy the first game at Valley Parade since. So why is the atmosphere so terrible?

There was little singing around us, little enthusiasm, just quietness and a general atmosphere of restlessness. Perhaps, after all that had gone on, people were still upset and fed up with the way the club was being run? Perhaps seeing the lack of fans in the away stand, and in the home ends for that matter, it had hit home. We may have survived, but we've dropped a division and the reality of League One football was kicking in.

As the teams were read out I was shocked to hear Nicky Summerbee's name booed by many City fans. True, he hadn't had a great season last year and he wasn't popular, but I was still mystified as to why he deserved to be booed. Unlike many other players, at least he had chosen to stay during the summer. And while he was lazy and didn't always put in 100%, he had undoubted quality. As the game kicked off the former Man City and Sunderland winger was booed every time he touched the ball.

At least we took the lead early on. Summerbee was booed as he swung over the ball and Dean Windass met it expertly and fired home. He had opened the scoring up at Hartlepool on the opening day. That game had also seen a less than inspiring start from Ross Turnbull, a 19 year old Middlesbrough goalkeeper who we had to sign on loan as the two summer goalkeeper recruits, Donovan Ricketts and Paul Henderson, had not received international clearance in time to play. On Saturday Turnbull's mistake meant we lost the game 2-1 and, 20 minutes into this evening, he failed to keep out a weak header from a corner which allowed Peterborough to equalise. Shortly after half time they went in front and a second defeat from two games was on the cards. It looked as though we were facing a season of struggle.

The low attendance and quality of football was a real culture shock. There is of course a notable gap in standards from the Premiership to Division One (now the Championship), but League One also felt like a huge drop. City attacked sporadically but didn't look capable of coming back. Then out of nothing, Ben Muirhead hit a volley that was drifting well wide and David Wetherall stuck out his head and diverted the ball into the net. 2-2 with five minutes to go. Suddenly Valley Parade found its voice and we all came alive again, fans even stopped booing Summerbee. Incredibly in injury time we earned a penalty. Surely we weren't going to win? Michael Symes stepped up to the mark on his home debut...and weakly hit the ball well wide of the goal. There was no fairytale ending.

I left Valley Parade feeling content at a decent end to the game, but also feeling angry about the booing of Summerbee. I decided to write an article for the BfB site criticising supporters who reacted like this. I felt nervous about submitting something controversial and the risk of upsetting others that came with it, but I didn't feel I could do nothing. Our email addresses' used to be included on the site and, the evening after my article went live, I received a handful of emails from City fans. It was the first time I had received any feedback for my writing, and while there was mixed response to my piece, it was nice to read mainly emails agreeing with me and sharing their disgust for the booing.

We were at home to Doncaster on the Saturday and I was chuffed to hear some City fans singing Summerbee's name in appreciation before kick off. I didn't think for a second that my article had inspired this, but knew I had helped stir up the debate and given some sort of voice to fans who felt equally appalled by what had happened. I was pleased that I had taken a risk in writing something that might upset people and that there had been an overall positive response. I'm sure fans would have sung his name before kick off anyway in retaliation to the booing of Tuesday, but it still left me feeling vindicated for writing what I had.

My mood got even better after City went onto win the game. Two first half goals from Mark Bower and Lee Crooks were enough to claim the points, with keeper Paul Henderson impressing after finally being allowed to make his debut and new loan striker Dele Adebola making a huge difference. I'd begun to fear City might not be able to compete at this level after all the summer problems and the start hadn't been great, so to earn a comfortable win against a fancied side was a great confidence boost. I enjoyed writing a match report of the game for BfB.

Before long the season was motoring along like any other. It still took some getting used to, after facing up to no more Bradford City during the summer and adapting to League One. The fixture list felt unglamorous and uninspiring, and seemed a constant reminder of how far we had fallen. There was a notable drop in the standard of football, which helped results on the pitch at least. It was hard to imagine that some of the sides we were scheduled to face would really be playing at Valley Parade. How many fans would Torquay bring in January? Would the Colchester team bus really be parking up on Midland Road? I felt slightly arrogant in my views, but this was the first time I had seen City play at this level and it felt wrong, looking at the size of our stadium, to think we were in the third tier of English football.

But the most important thing was that things were returning to normal. City won and we were happy. When we lost we'd be sad, but it was back to worrying about things that should really matter – things on the pitch. The trauma of the summer meant expectations were low and remembering that it had almost been all over forever meant it was difficult to be too upset by a defeat. Life and City had to go on and we all wanted it to go on, so it was great to be thinking about Windass' goalscoring form rather than wondering if he was going to get paid at the end of the month. It was nice to welcome Barnsley to Valley Parade knowing this wouldn't be our last Yorkshire derby. We took things for granted once and why wouldn't we? But after the possibility of life without City had looked so real, it was nice just to be carrying on.

Sheffield Wednesday (home) – the ticking clock

I had to drop my expectations, I had little choice. I'd spent over a year hoping to secure a media job, but opportunities and chances had been limited. I wasn't giving up and still managed to keep some form of self-belief that I could make it. But I was getting married in little over two months and I had to sort things out.

I'd spent the last year with what I considered to be a very real possibility that I could suddenly be moving to another part of the country at short notice. I was prepared and confident to handle this and knew I had to do whatever it takes, but I had to admit that, as time went on, the idea of moving away became less appealing. I'd initially been desperate to move back to the North East and specifically Newcastle when I left Uni. Then I considered other parts of the country, depending on vacancies. I wanted to stay in the North and, having successfully moved and adapted to life in Sunderland, knew I would be able to cope with establishing myself in an unknown place for the sake of a career. But now I was used to my friends, settled back in the area and living a life that wasn't as ordinary as it first seemed it might be. Of course I was doing a boring job and I was keen to regain my independence, but I was now less excited by the prospect of moving to somewhere like Swindon and London when the job opportunities in these places had cropped up. I would now love to live more locally, especially as there was a certain something within easy reach that appealed.

Yes, it had me again. I had returned to watching City in 2003 believing it would only be for a short time and been fully prepared to become an exiled supporter who only saw a handful of games a season. The results and level of entertainment during the 2003/04 season were hardly a huge puller, but without fully realising it City had crept under my skin again. My job was boring and I would look forward to

5pm on Friday with great excitement knowing I would be going to watch City the following day. Then we would lose and I would be miserable the rest of the weekend and throughout the following week back at work. But it mattered more than it did living hundreds of miles away. I used to be upset back in Sunderland at hearing City had lost, but I would be largely over it a couple of hours later, if that. Now, going to the game, spending the money and seeing the action unfold with my own pair of eyes – I would be upset for days later when it didn't go as hoped.

When I first returned to the area a year ago I felt fed up and sure I didn't want to go from city living back to village life. Getting used to friends and family and adapting to the lifestyle helped me to enjoy it again, but City also played a huge part. I loved going to the football and feared the day I would have to give it up. I knew that my career was more important and that my dream job, being a football writer for a local paper, was unlikely to be for Bradford City. I was prepared to give it up and follow the Bantams from a distance again, but not before I had to.

So as I looked at my short term goals, realising that the long term view could no longer be a priority, I thought of moving to Leeds. I had to get some sort of job I would enjoy, which would also pay well so we could start our life together. Moving to Leeds and finding a Marketing job (something not too dissimilar to Media) or something like that became my goal. It would be great for us to live in Leeds and I dreamed of going clubbing with Rachel each weekend, both having reasonable jobs through the week and, of course, hopping over to Bradford every other Saturday afternoon to get to Valley Parade. It felt like a good short term goal and also one which I hoped would be a platform to reach my long term goals. If my CV could at least show a history of progress and I could take a middle step now, it had to be a good thing while I keep applying for other jobs in the future. Roots were needed and Leeds seemed to be the place to be.

While it felt like standards were dropping, I quickly learned two valuable lessons which showed I wouldn't simply settle for anything. As I scanned my usual job sites and widen the search to find related media jobs in Leeds, I saw an advert for a company boasting great wages and Marketing opportunities.

The advert said little more, but I decided to email my CV and see where it might lead. The following day I received a phone call from a manager at the company inviting me for an interview later that week. I attempted to ask him more about the role, but he just told me to come to the interview to find out. I should have become suspicious there and then.

My second clue that this wasn't the dream job for me came the night before the interview when I received an unexpected call from David. He asked me if I had a job interview at a company in Leeds tomorrow. I replied that I did, confused as to how he would know this. He then told me that he also had an interview at the same place at the same time and was calling to ask how I was getting there. I was stunned, not just because I feared we were both competing for the same job, but why he was going for a similar type of career role to me and, still, how he knew I was going for it. It turned out he had seen a job advert in the paper and called to put himself forward. When telling the manager where he was from, the manager replied that there was another person from Sutton coming for an interview, Jason McKeown. My parents had offered to give me a lift to the interview and would now be also picking up Dave on the way.

Dave had done a degree in IT, but had failed to hold down a job anywhere since. He had found temporary work like me last year, so became much happier in his life as the season progressed, but was back to unemployed again with the company he was working for reluctant to take him on. Seeing our employment searches cross over in this way left me with grave doubts about the suitability of this job for me, and whether my new direction was right. Maybe the advert he saw just said very different things, after all since when has he thought about Marketing?

When we arrived at their office it was clear that we would not be rivals, as they were recruiting a lot of people. We went into the tiny office we found, by a back road in the City centre, and were warmly greeted by the manager we had spoken to on the phone. We filled out some forms and waited to be called in, meanwhile a ghetto blaster was blearing out some naff trance music at an uncomfortably high volume. The manager decided to interview us both together, which felt wrong. Yet we were in for barely five minutes as he asked us a few questions about our backgrounds and why we thought we would be suitable for this job, even though we didn't know what the job was. Finally, at the end he explained that it would involve visiting local businesses to try and get them to buy products from us; he then asked us both back the following afternoon for a day of training with 18 others, where at the end half of us would get a job. Dave was chuffed to have made the next stage, I thought long and hard about it on the journey home and decided this was not the job for me. I felt hugely guilty, I need a job as I'm getting married in two months – how can I be choosy? Fortunately Rachel was very understanding when I told her and didn't want me to go back.

I should have learned my lesson then, that when a job advert says very little it's usually because it's invariably not an appealing position. Yet a few weeks later I stumbled across another opportunity, this time a "highly paid Marketing position" which involved working for organisations like Natwest and Asda. This sounded an interesting opportunity so I sent my CV, attended an interview later that week and was asked to come back Saturday to be shown more about the job, when they would decide there and then whether to take me on. It meant I had to miss City's FA Cup First Round match with Rusden & Diamonds, although no bad thing in the end as we lost.

I was nervous that morning knowing that my immediate future could be settled that day, but again concerned that I still knew little more about the position other than what the original job advert had said (their website was hugely vague and the first interview was very brief, with the person interviewing me not allowing me time for questions). When I arrived I discovered we were going to Rotherham on the train to visit the local Asda. It certainly was going to be finding out more about the job. I felt a little uneasy that the two people I worked with were required to pay their own train and bus fares to get to Rotherham, they didn't claim it back on expenses either, but they both kept bragging about their earnings and what a great company it was to work for, with opportunities to quickly move upwards. As we travelled out of Leeds on the train, one pointed out that he lived in one of luxury flats we passed. My questions about what the job involved were largely ignored and I became aware that, instead of me having to sell myself as the right person, the job – or at least its benefits – were being sold to me.

The answers I did get – the hours they work (7-7 on a good day) and how pay works (commission only, so if you don't sell you get nothing) – left me feeling anxious. Eventually we arrived and my questions about what Marketing they did for Asda were quickly answered, they both stood in the foyer and attempted to get shoppers coming in and out the store to sign up for a credit card! Seeing the full horror of what I was applying for quickly made my mind up. After watching them for half an hour, the manager took me to one side to offer me the job. I told her I would think about it and let them know, before leaving them to annoy shoppers as I made my way home alone. The way that she reacted when I called her the Monday evening to say, "thanks but no thanks" left me realising they must have a problem recruiting people and were fed up of rejections. She stopped being nice and simply hung up.

Both these incidents were lessons to learn, but also gave me confidence. After over a year searching, being offered a job for the first time should have been a cause of celebration. But I wanted to have a happy and fulfilling career, I was no salesman and working long hours under huge pressure was not for me. It was back to the drawing board and, while time was running out even more now, I knew this next career step was hugely important and I couldn't mess it up.

At the same time as all of this was going on, City suddenly began playing some brilliant football and won five games in a row. An inauspicious 1-0 win over Barnsley was followed by an excellent 2-1 success at MK Dons. Even more incredibly, we then went to Tranmere and won 5-4, then 2-1 at home to Blackpool the following Tuesday. It wasn't a great performance against a struggling side, but we took the lead through Dele Adebola. They equalised towards the end through a penalty and looked the more likely winners, but then deep in injury time Nicky Summerbee struck an excellent free kick from an obscure angle which flew in the bottom corner and sealed the three points and four straight wins.

There was now a real buzz growing and the next game was against Yorkshire rivals Sheffield Wednesday. Having experience low crowds all season, there were notably more supporters back for this game, plus a big Wednesday following. Just after half time we took the lead through Michael Symes' first goal for City, then Dean Windass scored a superb second with a delicate lob over the keeper. Wednesday pulled a goal back, but Symes struck again to seal a 3-1 win. The atmosphere and celebrations at the end were special. Colin Todd had lifted the team and we were now finding form, up to second in the League! Having not had any expectations beyond staying up this season, we were now dreaming of promotion. Given all we've been through the last few years, it was a great feeling just to talk optimistically of the future, to be looking at the top of the table rather than the bottom, to be looking forward to the next game instead of dreading it.

That next game for City was Luton away, the league leaders. The last time City had been involved in a first v second contest was at home to Sunderland during the 1998/99 promotion winning season. I listened to the game on the radio hoping that we could turn over a side losing their early season red hot form. Typical City, just as we began to dream of success we were well and truly brought back down to earth with a bump – Luton Town 4 Bradford City 0 with Windass sent off and a controversy over the Referee seeming to celebrate the win too. Still Colin Todd was named October manager of the month and we moved into November in great spirits at the prospects for the season ahead. Now if only I could get things right in my own life...

Dark secrets

Suddenly I heard Dan shouting my name loudly in the next room, and I knew.

The truth had come out, after successfully hiding it for all those years through Uni. Any minute now he's going to burst through the door and make it an issue. It's one that many people in the same room as me now are already aware of, but had largely forgotten. I'd been accepted, forgiven even, and they'd moved on. But now I knew it was back and I had some explaining to do to the people in the other room with Dan. I began to feel nervous and listened out for the door. Perhaps I should go into that room and face up to my awful secret? At least that way it might hopefully only come up again in one room. Yes, that's what I'll do. I just hope Dan keeps his voice down.

I knew the culprit. The dark secret I had managed to keep from my Uni friends all this time had been given away by my brother Kevin. He'd always threatened to do this, kept bringing it up when the four of us as a family were together and he knew from my uncomfortable reaction that it was a way to get at me. To shut me up; to keep me on my toes; to be used cleverly – for a situation like now, my stag do. I walked through the door and Dan confronted me straight away, I could only admit everything.

Yes it was true. I used to support Manchester United before I supported Bradford City.

Dan was sat with Martin, Alex and Simon – people I'd lived with for three years, exchanged many of my deepest secrets and felt closer to than any other set of friends I'd had. But they had no idea about this part of my past, not a clue. Simon, the big Man United fan, was naturally the most surprised. All the conversations we'd had about Man United in the past. The time me and Martin mercilessly ruined the Real Madrid v Man United Champions League game 18 months ago by taking the mick as they lost. How could I? And, in his eyes, why did I ever stop supporting Man United?

There's a strict code of conduct among football fans that you never change your team, no matter how bad things get. Yet I hadn't dropped one football team for another because they had gone crap, I'd moved downwards and, with Man United battling at the top of the Premiership while I'd been excitedly talking about City winning 2-1 at Brentford in League One the day before, the term 'glory supporter' was not branded nor considered. Yet still I had broken the code and, while there was some respect at the direction which way I'd gone, which I was now trying to justify, the most overriding question was how come I'd never mentioned this before.

Numerous drunken evenings, late night heart-to-hearts. It's not as if we hadn't exchanged aspects of our past that we were embarrassed about, me included. But I'd never dared to tell anyone about my switch. For anyone who met me after 1 November 1997, they will know me as a big City fan and nothing else. For friends who had known me longer, it was a largely forgotten fact about my youth. I supported City with a passion and people seemed to respect that, but for anyone to change their football team allows a little lessening of that respect and I was no different.

So it became my dark secret and still is. Maybe I'd done things the right way and moved in the direction you'd prefer to see. After all Man United have millions of supporters around the world who bring no value; not like converting to supporting a team with less attendances and contributing to their efforts by going to games. I shouldn't be as embarrassed as I am, but it's also something I'm deeply uncomfortable talking about. So for it to come up now – the morning after my stag do when I'm feeling hungover – was unfortunate.

My revelation came out in Manchester as me and 20 mates woke up in a youth hostel following a wonderful stag night out. Martin, my best man, had organised things splendidly. We'd gone out around the bars and then onto a club called Sankey Soap, where I had the pleasure of seeing a DJ I'd been desperate to see for a while, Jacque Le Cont. I had a healthy mixture of University and school friends present and, while going to a house club was pure hell for some of the group, it had been generally a great night. We had split into two dorms in the hostel and I was in the school friends' one; where we acted like kids in the morning by pouring water over people sleeping and conducting pillow fights. My brother had ended up in the Uni friends' dorm and decided to pick the moment to reveal my secret. Still I was quite proud I'd kept it quiet for so long.

The following week I watched Oldham beat us 3-1 at Valley Parade. Although it was a disappointing afternoon ruined by an awful refereeing performance, I still felt a sense of pride when I thought back to my previous weekend. I could have been sat at home listening to the radio for updates on Man United's 3-0 win at West Brom, a typical walk in the park; but I remembered how unfulfilling it had been sat in my bedroom cursing if 5Live didn't pick Man United for their commentary game. Instead I was at the game watching my team, experiencing the highs and, in this case, the lows. Who wouldn't have swapped everything for this? I might seem mad to an outsider, but few things in life made as much sense to me.

Approaching the big day

Getting married in America, I'd resigned myself to the fact that only my immediate family and best man Martin would be there from England to see it. I'd probably have to rely on Rachel's male friends to act as Groomsmen – a role more important in American weddings. We were going to have a reception back in Skipton where my English friends and family could attend, but the big day itself would be almost entirely viewed by Americans. Then two of my friends, Danny and Placy, announced that they were both coming over as they didn't want to miss me getting married. I was hugely touched that they would spend hundreds of pounds flying over to see it, and even more amazed when several other friends followed. Vicky, who'd been to America a couple of times before, was up for coming over and seeing a bit more of the States at the same time. Then Tom and Sarah decided to, then Roy and Ellis followed. With Martin coming too, I was left with the exciting problem of trying to find room for them all to stay.

In the weeks leading up to the big event, it was impossible to avoid the topic of the wedding during conversations. My friends were flying over in twos and threes and everyone would be on American soil before me and my family arrived. Some were going a week ahead and would be staying in Atlanta; Vicky was going to New York before flying down. Soon it was time for Danny and Placy, the two who first said they were going and inspired others to follow suit, to set off to the Airport. See you in America next week.

As the days closed in to when we would be setting off, sorting my life out became more and more anxious. I still wanted to live in Leeds, so I now had to do something about it by going through and viewing available rented properties. All of the ones in our price range were in the rougher areas, miles out of town and that was one of a few things holding me back. I was still working in Skipton and, while I could quit and probably find a similar job in Leeds with little trouble, this was a big step. As I wandered around unfamiliar streets at night looking up properties I had seen photos of on the internet, I felt a long way away from anyone I knew. Could I really agree to rent a house here and now which we would move into in the New Year? What if neither of us could find work? This wasn't the dream of living in Leeds I had pictured.

So I spoke to Rachel and we agreed moving like this was a bad idea. Attention quickly turned to moving to Skipton instead and I began searching properties available. It was the day before we were due to fly to America and I was still visiting houses and arranging appointments. Meanwhile my dad had driven to pick up Kevin from Uni at Newcastle and was on his way through Skipton. The first couple I viewed seemed unpromising and, doing this on my own, I felt fearful of making such a big decision myself for fear of getting it very wrong. Just after 5pm I had a final appointment of the day and last chance to sort something out before getting married. My dad arrived in time to be there too and we toured the place, a spacious flat on the edge of town. It was nice, it was roomy and it was reasonably priced. I said I'd speak to Rachel that night, she told me let's go for it and that she trusted my judgement. The following morning, as we waited in the departure lounge at Manchester airport, I called the letting agency and told them we would take it. Talk about cutting it fine.

We experienced the once in a lifetime fortune of being bumped up to first class on the plane – not a bad thing to happen for my parents to experience on their first ever flight. As we soared into the clouds and I enjoyed a glass of champagne my head was spinning with thoughts and concerns about the future. Rachel had now completed her teaching degree and already contacted and applied to work for a teaching agency in Yorkshire, who would help her find work. Will she get jobs? Will she adapt to living in England? Will I get a better job in the field I'd like? I should have felt like a failure really, I'd had 18 months to find a job before we got married, but hadn't made it past the interview stage. Yet for the first time since graduating I could put it to the back of my mind for a couple of weeks. I wasn't going to give up, I hadn't reached where I wanted in the time I'd hoped, but I felt I could still do it. I was nervous about the future, but also excited. The long and painful two years of separation from Rachel were about to be over, we'd made it. It didn't seem as though that was possible, such was how miserable I felt and how slow time moved during those first few months. Yet we'd gone through two years of constantly feeling a little bit empty and waiting for better times and now we'd reached the pot of gold at the end of the rainbow. If we could make it through a time like this surely we could do anything, including both finding the jobs we'd like.

Soon we were in America and met my friends, with Rachel's family up in three cars ready to take this large and strange-looking group of English people to their home. The basement where I had slept during my visits would now be full of eight lads; luckily we had our own bathroom. Sarah and Vicky would be staying at Rachel's friend Lauren's, but were very much part of all the activities we were doing. That night we went to a Hooters' bar to celebrate Placy's birthday, the following day was the wedding rehearsal and rehearsal dinner. The day after I, at 23 years of age, was getting married.

My wedding day was the same day City played Huddersfield away. In the morning Rachel's dad took the English party to a shooting range where we all had a go at shooting guns – a scary but enjoyable experience for us all. Banter over who was the worst at shooting ensued. I also checked my phone on the internet to hear the glorious news that City had beaten Huddersfield 1-0. It felt like a good omen for the rest of the day.

The wedding itself was fantastic, held in a posh stately home which Rachel's family had hired out. The nerves hit me and hour before we were due to set off and I struggled to keep it together. Martin was a tower of strength and he grabbed us a couple of cold beers to enjoy as we waited. It calmed me down no end and prompted excitement thinking of what was about to happen. Probably one of the best beers I've ever had.

Once at the posh house, myself and my groomsmen were required to wait in a room downstairs for an hour, which proved to be exhilarating. There was excitement and anticipation running through all of us at what was ahead. Our circle of friends – which didn't include Martin and Kevin prior to this trip, but who had both been made to feel very welcome – were preparing for the first one of us get married. We went into group huddles and cheered loudly. We had no beers to keep us calm, we were high on life.

Rachel looked amazing in her wedding dress. I'd occasionally been scared about this moment, when thinking ahead to the big day, that she'd say no instead when asked to say 'I do', but being there in the room with all her friends and family and looking happy and beautiful, there was no doubt in my mind. The ceremony was over in a blur and outside we were congratulated by everyone. Some of my friends, particularly male, were in tears. I was staggered at the affect the wedding had on them, and utterly touched.

The following day we came back to her parents' house and heard stories of my friends' behaviour at a later party they went to. Soon after, a realisation that the adventure was over and that it was time to pack up seemed to hit us all. Three car loads of us were soon on the road to Atlanta. For everyone but me and Rachel, they were going to spend a few days seeing the sights of Georgia's capital. Me and Rachel were flying to New York for the honeymoon. Not a bad choice, though one driven by the future. We needed to complete Rachel's visa application in order for her to live in the UK, with the office for completing this in the Big Apple. Christmas was spent back in Macon with both sets of family and on Boxing Day we flew over to England for the second reception a few days later. It was great to go through the whole thing a second time, this time with my friends and family. Rachel also enjoyed the opportunity to wear her wedding dress again, not many brides get to wear theirs twice.

Rachel's family stayed over New Year and we showed them the sights of Yorkshire. It was nice to have both sets of family together and good for Rachel to adapt to England with the familiarity of her family around. Soon they were flying back though and we were moving into our new flat in Skipton. The party was over and, for the people right at the hub including my friends who went to America, it was a time they relished and still talk about years later. For now though it was time to straighten the sofa of our new place, hang our clothes up in closets and get some shopping in. Eventually the last people who helped us to move in left and we closed the door on the outside world for the first time in weeks.

We were together at last. Life was just beginning.

Torquay and Huddersfield (home) – feeding the ducks

With all that had gone in December, it was always going to be a Bradford City season of two halves for me. If the first was relatively normal, other than the greater appreciation of still having a club to support and adapting to League One surroundings, the second was unfamiliar and uncomfortable.

Getting married and setting up a new home isn't cheap. With only my pitiful wage and wedding money to live off, it soon became apparent how tough starting out was going to be. We hoped that Rachel would quickly start getting regular supply teaching work with an eye to getting a full time job starting next September, but this wasn't as simple as we'd hoped. Rachel had to be on standby in the mornings waiting for phone calls in case a teacher called in sick somewhere, but the phone never rang. I would wake up and get ready for work, nervously hoping the phone would go off. By the time I had to leave and the phone had remained silent, it was obvious that another day was going to pass without Rachel getting teaching work and bringing in money.

For Rachel it was particularly tough, she had nothing to do at first but stay at home and watch daytime TV. Then walk into town to meet me on my lunch break, maybe wander around some shops, before returning home and waiting for me to get back at 5.30. She would explore Skipton and took to bringing bread along to feed the ducks when walking along the canal path to meet me, which she enjoyed. But life was tough; she didn't really know anyone and had nothing to do. It was going to take time to adapt.

With only my wage coming in, there were sacrifices to make and this included going to watch City. It wasn't the first time in my life I'd not been able to watch City games, while at Uni I had three years away of course, but this was different. At Uni I was 100 miles away which left it impractical to be there, but now I was only 20 miles down the road from Valley Parade and missing out on what was happening. I'd listen to games on the radio and feel very disjointed. Life at City was going on without me, but right in front of my face. It was disconcerting and wrong. I felt like a disloyal supporter, a

215

phoney. I knew that there was no other option, I couldn't risk our livelihood just to go to a game against Tranmere, particularly as there's two of us so the expense is double. I had to wait and hope our financial situation would improve quickly.

We still saw the occasional game. I took Rachel to see us play Torquay shortly after the wedding. It felt like a home banker, with City still around the play off places. Torquay were near the bottom and would be relegated come May. But it was a strange game. City started off poorly, but we quickly found ourselves 2-0 up through new signing Andy Cooke and Dean Windass. Just as we had a platform to go on and win, we then quickly conceded two poor goals. Despite plenty of huff and puff, City weren't able to win the game in the second half. There were groans and boos everywhere around Valley Parade. A poor game, woeful performance and dismal atmosphere; it was hardly the most enticing re-introduction to City for Rachel.

Results were bittersweet. If I missed what sounded like a dull draw or poor defeat then was it that bad? I'd saved some money and wouldn't be in as foul of a mood as I would if making my way home from it. But what if I missed something fantastic that people will talk about for years? Every Saturday afternoon when City were at home I'd experience the sudden urge to run out of the door and catch the train to VP. It might be 2pm now, but if I catch the next train and ran when I got to Forster Square station I would only miss the first 10 minutes. I never acted on this impulse, finding a degree of solace in the radio and an acceptance that life had to be like this for a time. It could be a lot worse, I'd hate for Rachel to still be in America just so I could afford to go to the football.

At least there was one moment of joy to savour. Huddersfield came to Valley Parade at the start of March and I had simply had to go to the first home derby meeting for six years. So we stretched things as much as possible – Rachel still not getting calls – and bought two tickets. Stephen and David, who were still going to matches without me, were on holiday, so it was just the two of us. Rachel had less of an appreciation for the occasion of course, so I tried to talk up its significance. We had seats on the very front row of the top tier of the Kop. Just before half time, Andy Cooke tapped us into the lead right in front of us, and we both cheered wildly. But I wasn't thinking enough about Rachel adapting to it and – ungentlemanly – made her queue up to buy her own cup of tea at half time while I stayed in the seats. The second half kicked off and she still wasn't back. I kept watching the game while continually glancing over my shoulder to see if she was on her way. I could go off and look for her, but she could be anywhere.

The minutes ticked on and still no sign, so I got up to search. Then Rachel appeared with a cup of tea but tears streaming down her face. She isn't the tallest and was still shy, so had suffered from people pushing her out of the way and queue-jumping. She was upset at how long it had taken and to experience people being so unfriendly. As she sat down in tears I apologised and felt awful, my own selfishness of fearing I might miss some of the game had stopped me going. At that exact moment Windass scored our second goal. Everyone in the Kop stood up to cheer, except me and Rachel who sat there still feeling upset. Eventually she was okay again and I was desperate for a third so we could have that moment of cheering which we had missed, but that was the end of the scoring. Still the jovial atmosphere and sight of fans in the lower tier standing up to taunt 'easy, easy' every time Huddersfield messed up kept us laughing.

Things were still tough for us, but we were happy to be together at least and that was carrying us through this uncertain period. Life wasn't as bad as 4-1 home defeat to the MK Dons (gratefully missed in February), more like that 2-2 draw with Torquay. But we still retained hope it wouldn't be long before it would be a 2-0 win over Town.

Doncaster (away) – fair-weather fan

It was one my biggest fears and it was being realised. There I was, stood up in the away seating at Doncaster's tatty ground waiting for the game to begin. It was a Thursday night before Easter and, with my friend Simon and his American fiancée Rachel now living in Doncaster, I'd decided we should go to City's away match in South Yorkshire with an excuse to go and see our friends first. This was only my third City game since getting married and it was going to show. As I stood there before kick of, surveying the scene of the run-down ground, a young Asian lad took his seat by me and we soon fell into conversation. He was clearly City-mad and full of enthusiasm, he saw me as a good chance to share views of recent performances.

What did you think of Saturday's defeat, do you think it's time to drop Atherton?" he asked me. I had to reply that I missed Saturday's defeat to Hartlepool. "I'm pleased we've signed Marc Bridge-Wilkinson permanently, he's looked good hasn't he?" I was able to clumsily talk about his impressive debut against Huddersfield but nothing more. "How many away games have you been to this season, what did you think of Peterborough's ground?" Erm, this is my first away game of the season. "Where abouts is your season ticket at Valley Parade?" I don't have a season ticket; I can rarely go and watch City at the moment. The conversation was fizzling out and, while I tried to bring up topics of City interest, my lack of recent first-hand knowledge of City was painfully obvious. He was a nice guy, but I couldn't help but feel paranoid thoughts of how he considered me a fair-weather supporter who wasn't really that bothered. Soon he was talking to the person sat on the other side of him, someone who did have a qualified view of Atherton's recent form.

It hit home how out of touch I was becoming with City's affairs and I felt gloomy. Of course I was happy with life now that Rachel was here with me, but no longer being able to afford to go and watch City was difficult to take. Even going to this game had stretched us and I knew that, as the game kicked off, it would be the last I would see this season. Rachel was finally starting to get some supply work, much to our collective relief. Money would soon be coming in and, a couple of weeks later, she would get the opportunity to supply in one school for the rest of the school year.

The money she received for supply work was really good, she could make almost a much in a week as I did in a month. We needed the money, our finances were draining fast. I was also still looking for writing jobs and had an unsuccessful interview for a fashion magazine based near Huddersfield. Luck might be slowly turning in our favour, but we now needed to look at buying a second hand car so Rachel could make the supply dates she had, often up to 30 miles away from

Skipton. Bills still needed paying and there were other things in life we wanted to do, like go out with friends. City was still on the agenda for me, but I was now willing the season to be over so that I could stop feeling miserable every time they played and I was not there. I knew this evening's game at Doncaster was one I had to make the most of, so to get off to such a bad start through an innocent conversation with a fellow supporter was not what I needed.

At least the game kicked off and I could my embarrassment to the back of my mind. Within six minutes we had taken the lead through Bridge-Wilkinson. Doncaster were a tough physical side and equalised mid way through the first half through a Mark Bower own goal. The rest of the game was frustrating as City were unable to work up a decent spell of pressure and Doncaster looked the more likely to score. My own disappointment was compounded by Rachel's reaction to it all. She was not enjoying watching City struggle in such dismal surroundings and was soon fed up. City weren't playing great and it wasn't the sort of night that would win her around. I was desperate for the joy of a late winning goal to lift her, but it looked unlikely. We trudged back to the car feeling collective disappointment.

I spent the journey home composing my BfB match report in my mind, whilst also feeling gloomy about the near future. There were six games to go, but I wouldn't be seeing any of it. This was my final game of the season but there was no lap of honour from the players at the end to mark it. City were safe in mid-table, so I knew I wasn't going to be missing anything, but still this was frustrating and unfulfilling. For Rachel, going to watch City was no where near her first choice of things to do and I knew I had my work cut out winning her round. I didn't want to go and watch City without her, this part of my life meant too much to me for her to not be in it with me. But dull draws at horrible places like Doncaster's Belle Vue stadium weren't going to help, or stop her asking the question she uttered on the car ride home, not for the first time, "Why can't we support Chelsea?" It was an uncomfortable evening; I didn't ever want to get into this position again.

Better days

It all began fairly inauspiciously. My friend, who worked in another department, sent me an email about it. I didn't believe it was anything interesting and was reluctant even to bother checking what he told me. But as I scanned down what I was reading on the screen, ready to fire back an email explaining why it was no use, something pulled me in and I read and re-read the text again. Could it be that the perfect opportunity was right on my doorstep?

Through my searching for a writing job, I'd become used to receiving advice and ideas on what I should be doing from concerned friends and family which weren't always particularly helpful or realistic. But this was different. Jonathan had sent me an email raising my attention to a job vacancy on the work intranet site, which was at the parent company, a building society, looking for an internal communications consultant. I had no idea what this was but, as I read through the job description and took in what sort of tasks the position entailed, I realised this could be a position suitable for me that I should at least be applying for. It involved writing communications, such as intranet stories and articles for the staff magazine. So I emailed it to my manager, a nice guy who knew I was looking for a writing position, and he helped me out by providing an application form and writing me a good reference.

I was first asked to attend an informal chat with the other person I'd be working alongside, a friendly enough girl called Rachel, She was meeting all applicants and putting forward the people she thought most suitable for an interview. I'd done enough to secure one and went through a rigorous hour-and-half session with the would-be-manager Louise, followed by having to complete a series of tests. I felt I'd done alright. All I could do was wait and pray. Lots.

A week later Louise called to ask to meet for a chat later that day, I knew that I was to find out either way and spent the six hours in-between with my mind a bag of nerves and unable to concentrate. Eventually it was time to meet and I was sat down and told the words I'd spent almost two years longing to hear, "I'd like to offer you this position."

I didn't need time to think about it, I was taking it. I couldn't believe that, at long last, I'd secured a job in the type of field I'd wanted. On the face of it, it may not appear that way and it wasn't the local football journalist position I'd been craving. Yet it was a fantastic opportunity to finally get my foot on the ladder and begin doing something relevant to my five years studying media and Journalism. I was elated, I was stunned. I felt excited for the future, but I also felt largely relived.

A long month passed as I served my notice, but soon it was time to start my new job with my nice pay rise. There was a lot to take in and I knew that my standards, such as grammar, would need to improve. But soon I was interviewing members of staff for stories and writing up articles on business strategy for everyone to read. I was experiencing new challenges and ways of doing things. I was given plenty of responsibility and became part of a small, young enthusiastic team. I was being paid to sit at a desk and write. This was bliss.

It came too late in the season to enable me to start affording City games, my first week coincided with the final game of the season at Oldham, but it certainly offered hope for next season. With Rachel doing long term supply and bringing in a large pay packet, if only for a couple of months, suddenly things looked a whole lot brighter. We hoped that her supply could be made permanent when another teacher at the school left a few months later, although ultimately that wasn't to happen. Still it was nice to be able to afford the odd night out and, with my friend Simon marrying his American Rachel in the middle of June, the stag and hen dos held in Newcastle in the middle of May were a little celebration of our own. It'd been tough, but better times appeared to be here.

It had been quite a season for me and City. In our own ways, we'd got through some dark days and had some truly memorable moments to reflect on as things improved. Life could still be better than this for us both, but the hard work we'd put in was finally paying off. With my season cut short, much to my frustration, I was already desperately looking forward to the next one.

Chapter Eleven

2005 - 06
A cycle of false hope

How often do you spend the summer dreaming that the upcoming season will end in glory for your team? And how often are those dreams squashed before that summer is even officially over? For the 2005-06 season I was giddily optimistic that City would earn promotion, even at one stage genuinely believing we could go up as Champions. By the end of August City had won two and lost three, we would finish 11th.

My optimism stemmed from many different factors; not least the impressive manner City had ended the previous campaign with stylish wins over promotion-chasing Brentford (4-1) and Bournemouth (4-2). City finished 11th, but given the first half of the season had been partially over-shadowed by the club, still stuck in administration, there was reason to believe the worst was over and the only direction would be upwards. We were in a division I and most City fans considered the club too big to be in, and the impressive manner Colin Todd had managed the team offered belief he was the man to lift us back to the top two divisions.

Sadly it wasn't to be, and although during the first three months of the season an average start saw our expectation levels downgraded to mere play off challengers, that also quickly disappeared over the winter and at one point fears of relegation occurred. The club at least had a very strong end to the season which lifted the mood and provided optimism to take into that summer, but two-thirds of the campaign had been very forgettable.

Many lower league clubs have countless seasons like this. When you realistically believe you should be challenging to get out of the division, getting stuck in mid-table can feel very tedious. Inevitably there are some promising performances and wins along the way that generate good-feeling, but then there are daft defeats or dismal draws to frustrate and depress. When the team raises its game it can be a match for anyone, but the problem often lies in the fact that – collectively – the team isn't good enough to raise its game every week.

So long before the next summer arrives, you're playing out the final games with nothing significant to fight for. Faint play off hopes extinguished by a home defeat to a relegation-threatened team in February, that recent victory over a promotion challenger bittersweet because you can't help but feel annoyed at why the players couldn't have performed like that when the pressure was on them. The end of the season can't really come soon enough, and you go into the summer looking ahead to the next campaign when surely it will all come together.

Time to dream again...

Southend United (home) – punctured hopes

I had two major goals for the 2005/06 season – to start going to as many City games as possible again and to try and get Rachel more into it.

The first of those aims was hugely dependent on money but, with Rachel having just finished a long term supply position and money in our account, I thought we'd at least be able to start the season well and then hope more supply work would quickly come in during the new school year. The second goal I was less confident about, but knew I was desperate to see achieved. I loved having Rachel in my life with me and desperately wanted her to love going to watch City with me too. As a couple we'd do pretty much everything together. She was still adapting to England and, while making friends, it took time to feel settled. City was a big part of my life and I didn't want to lose that, but I knew that without Rachel's interest it would be hard to win arguments about going to watch games or go off by myself and spend money. I wanted her to enjoy the same things as me and understand the love I had for Bradford City, so that we could eventually share it.

A good start towards this that summer was a special open day the club held at Valley Parade. It was a chance for supporters to meet with players and enjoy a tour of the stadium. There was also a chance to get autographs from half of the first team squad present, which proved a good opportunity for Rachel to learn more about our players. Until this point she only really knew who Dean Windass and Paul Henderson – our impressive keeper who had since moved on to Leicester – were; so it was great for her to meet players like David Wetherall, Tom Kearney and Danny Cadamarteri. It was an enjoyable afternoon centred primarily at families, but also a great opportunity to increase Rachel's education of the Bantams

This open day was held a couple of weeks before the season was due to start. Having missed so much of the second half of the previous one, I was itching to get going. I was convinced that the new recruits Todd had brought in during the summer – which included Dutch winger Bobby Petta and returning striker Cadamarteri – would sufficiently strengthen the team and make us good enough for a play off spot. It was going to be an exciting time to take Rachel to watch City and I couldn't wait to get her hooked. Eventually the season kicked off up at Hartlepool again and a 2-0 victory for City at a team who had been beaten in last season's play off final only heightened my optimism. Windass and Petta got the goals and I looked forward to us attending the first home on the Tuesday night, against newly promoted Southend United, believing we'd witness a good City win to build on our strong start.

Typical City. We lost 2-0.

Blackpool (away) – the glamour of League One

It was a sunny August Bank Holiday Monday and there we were, walking along the beach at Blackpool. Rachel was collecting rocks, as she loved to do whenever we visited the seaside. With a bag-full successfully acquired after half an hour, we walked back towards the promenade and I dreamily told her, "You see, you don't get glamour like this supporting Chelsea."

I felt as though I had a point. After all, Chelsea's adventures never take them to seaside towns on bank holiday weekends (at least not until 2011!). I'm sure their fans would relish a trip to Blackpool for an away game one weekend. Then again, Chelsea fans rarely have to witness their team lose woefully to a poor side in a half built stadium very often, especially when that poor side with the half built stadium have been playing with only ten men for over an hour.

That's what unfortunately happened that Bank Holiday Monday. We left the beach to find Stephen and David, who had gone to the Pleasure Beach fairground to go on some rides, as it was time to make the short walk to Bloomfield Road. But there was bad news for David. He and Stephen had gone on the Pepsi Max roller-coaster and David kept his bag inside the car which took them round, rather than leave it in the luggage compartment. As the ride had whizzed up and down hills and around some tight corners, his bag fell out of the car and was somewhere underneath the mile-long track. The bag carried many important items, not least his match ticket for the game. We stayed with him while he made enquiries to get the bag retrieved by staff, but it was soon time for us to get going and we had to leave him behind, hoping he could get the ticket in time for the kick off. David wouldn't get it back until the second half was well underway so missed the game. You could say he was lucky.

I was keen to take Rachel to another away game to sample the different type of match atmosphere and Blackpool on a bank holiday was sure to attract a decent City following. Yet the basic roofless temporary away stand we sat in alongside the pitch failed to get the atmosphere going and it wasn't an especially enjoyable game. We started quite well and Blackpool, without a win up to this moment, were reduced to 10 men after a silly foul on Ben Muirhead. We had plenty of possession but rarely created chances. With five minutes to go dozy defending allowed Blackpool the opportunity to score, which was gleefully taken. We walked back to the Pleasure

Beach feeling very unhappy with the 1-0 defeat and Rachel no more convinced of our sanity in being here.

It had been a mixed start to the season, both in terms of City's form and in getting Rachel into watching City. Losing 2-0 to Southend in the opening home game had been an unexpected blow that was difficult to stomach. I'd decided at the end of last season that we should try a new viewpoint at Valley Parade so we bought tickets for the game in the Midland Road stand rather than the Kop. Although I enjoyed being at the back of the Kop singing with others, I had grown tired of being so far away from the pitch and the players resembling dots. Sure you could see everything, but not up close. I felt it would help Rachel to get into watching City more if she could see the players faces closer up and feel nearer to the action, I thought back to my first few years supporting City and always being close to the front. You felt more a part of things.

The view in the Midland Road stand was excellent and Stephen and David were both happy as well. Sure we weren't singing as much as the people around us were, but sitting by the half way line we had a good view of both ends of the pitch. Sadly on this evening it was too good a view of the Southend goals and the City huff and puff which achieved little. The atmosphere was terrible with fans on the backs of players quickly. Nothing new of course, but still frustrating.

Luckily the next home game, on the Saturday, was much better. The MK Dons were in town and we performed really well. We were aided by a dismissal of a Dons centre back after he tripped Andy Cooke, just as he was going to fire City in front. Windass scored the resultant penalty and added a second shortly after half time. The performance was really promising and we should have scored plenty more. Muirhead played particularly well on the wing and I left chuffed Rachel had been able to witness such a decent performance. We can make the play offs, I confidently predicted.

The next two league games, however, saw a draw and defeat and took much of the gloss away. So let's hope we can beat Blackpool or our season is going to feel negative. That late winner put paid to that. Collecting rocks on the beach had appealed to Rachel about our trip to the seaside, but the all-important football failed to convince that she should have bothered leaving the beach.

Huddersfield Town (home) – derby woes

There was only going to be one thing I was doing for my 24th birthday. As soon as Sky had announced they were moving the date of our derby match with Huddersfield, for live coverage, onto the Monday night which was my birthday – my plans were sorted. All my friends could come along as well, watch an exciting local derby and sample what will no doubt be a great atmosphere. In the end seven responded positively to my invitation and I bought tickets for us all in the Kop (Huddersfield fans were given the Midland Road stand for the game). With Town making a decent start to the season and been close to the top, while we were just short of the play offs, it promised to be exciting night with a good chance of the right result. What a great thing to do to celebrate my birthday.

Or should that be what a stupid, painful thing to do?

In the end it was the latter as Huddersfield, who were enjoying a much better start to the season as us, beat us 2-1. We'd arrived at the ground just as the game was about to begin to be greeted by a superb atmosphere from both ends; the game was end to end, but it was Huddersfield who struck first when a Mark Hudson free kick curled home, with our keeper Russell Howarth, who was playing because Donovan Ricketts had been out injured for a month, should have saved. Still we were on a six match unbeaten run since that Bank Holiday Blackpool defeat and equalised just before half time through a superb free kick from Bobby Petta. I chatted to my friends about the game at half time but it wasn't nice to hear – they all rated Town's performance and believed we were going to lose. Sadly they were proved right as Town controlled the second half and hit the winner ten minutes from time. Dean Windass was missing through suspension and it showed.

As the game drifted towards full time I looked at Rachel sat by me and felt instantly bad by how miserable she looked. She was not enjoying the defeat anymore than I was and it felt clear to me she was feeling the pain of a derby defeat as well. In some perverse way this should have felt like a good moment in her progress of supporting City. Had we lost to

227

Huddersfield last March she probably wouldn't have been bothered, but now here she was desperately hoping City could win and now feeling as sad as the rest of us City fans when they didn't. Yet there was no pleasure to be gained from seeing it mean something to her, only sadness and a sense of guilt. What was I inflicting on her?

The last few years watching City had been generally miserable and, while I was hoping this could be a glorious season, it wasn't looking promising. Even if City did go and suddenly blitz the league and have us dancing in the stands come May, great moments don't last for ever. Sooner or later she'd be witnessing a horrible moment and feeling the type of pain most sane, reasonable people don't have to go through during their weekends. It was too late for me; I cared too much to get away from it. But there was still time for Rachel to escape, should I do the honourable thing and ban her from ever attending a City match with me again? She'd surely thank me in the long run.

It was a great shame this was Rachel's first City match since the Blackpool debacle too. With no supply work coming through in September, we were quickly back to feeling the pinch and struggling with life. The weekend after the Blackpool defeat saw Chesterfield visit Valley Parade on a Friday night, but I could only cheer the 2-0 victory from home. Match tickets were £18 but this was of course now double for us. I had already learned one of the downsides to being married and having a joint account was paying double for things like cinema trips, nightclub entries, match tickets, even going for a drink at the pub. What seems reasonable to pay on your own is now twice as much and was restricting what we could do. It wasn't just going to watch City games, but doing things with friends too. At the end of the summer Rachel had managed to secure a Sunday job working for a department store in Skipton, so we were grateful for that money coming in. Still there were bills to pay and I was back to picking and choosing City games to attend.

Though fortunately nothing like as bad as the previous season. The following home game, Yeovil, saw me there watching the game on my own. Rachel's American friend Meghan had decided to move to England for six months and was going to the cinema with Rachel for the afternoon. Paying for myself only didn't seem so bad and, with Stephen and David on holiday again, I sat by myself in the Midland Road stand. It was a largely frustrating game with newly promoted Yeovil taking the lead and us having to rely on a second half equaliser from Ben Muirhead to take a point. The performance was laboured and slow. My pre season optimism was looking badly placed.

This result was followed by a win at Swindon, with veteran striker Steve Claridge coming off the bench to score two goals. A 1-1 draw at home to Colchester was followed on the radio at home and the 2-2 draw with Doncaster the following Saturday stretched the unbeaten run to six games, though sadly four of them were draws. Then came Huddersfield to cast some doom and gloom on the season and spoil my birthday.

At least City picked up the following two games with a 1-0 win at Port Vale - Claridge scoring again and Ricketts making a welcome return to shore up the clean sheet – then another 1-0 win at home to Gillingham. Andy Cooke belatedly scored his first goal of the season with five minutes to go to win that one. I was there to witness it with Stephen and David, Rachel was again doing something with Meghan. The performance was largely average and we were fortunate to sneak it, but were now up to sixth in the league – a play off spot. There was still optimism that we could go up this season, though Rachel was probably glad she had swapped an afternoon that had such a strong potential for misery for a nice safe relaxing one with her mate.

Nottingham Forest (away) – the end?

There were 10 minutes to go at the City Ground of a dull match with City trailing 1-0 to Forest. The ball was passed around to our right back Darren Holloway, a player liable to make defensive errors and be caught in possession. With time to clear, he kept hold of the ball and moved more inside, waiting to make a suitable pass. Time was against him though and a Forest player rushed to close him down, succeeded in winning the ball and facing a clear run, one-on-one with Donovan Ricketts, on our goal. As he charged towards the area Holloway ran back and produced a woeful last ditch challenge that only succeeding in tripping the player over. The referee instantly blew for a free kick on the edge of the area and sent off the hapless defender.

At this point, sat behind the goal Forest were attacking, Rachel turned to me in disgust before revealing, "I don't want to come and watch Bradford City anymore."

It was a horrible moment. Not the red card I mean, but Rachel's statement. Having spent 80 minutes feeling frustrated by a dreary game in which both sides were playing poorly, to now hear it had been so bad Rachel didn't want to come anymore was upsetting. I was desperate to get Rachel into liking City and had taken her to games where I hoped she'd be won over. I thought that the chance to watch City play away in a large stadium like Forest's would be ideal for Rachel and expected a decent game which we had a fair chance of winning. Instead the game had been awful with David Johnson's 24th minute goal for Forest the only bit of noteworthy action from either side.

This was easily City's worst game of the season and now Rachel was telling me she wanted it to be her last.

I was upset. All my plans had appeared to backfire and what made it particularly hard to take was how much it was beyond my control. So far this season Rachel had seen City play Southend, MK Dons and Huddersfield at Valley Parade and Blackpool away – only the MK Dons game didn't end in defeat. City were hardly playing sparkling exciting football and the entertainment level was lacking. I felt let down by my club. They had the chance to impress and, if not win every game, at least show determination and effort to convince Rachel they deserved her support. Here they were on the big occasion at the City Ground, looking scared to touch the ball and not particular desperate to save the game. No wonder Rachel considered enough to be enough.

But still to hear her say she didn't want to come again felt hurtful. During the last 10 minutes I was desperate for City to somehow turn it around and get an equaliser that might change her mind. Remarkably we did start playing better with 10 men and created some good chances. It was hard to enjoy it though as it felt there was so much at stake, I'm not sure I'd even have been able to celebrate had we struck at the end, instead only muster relief. The final whistle was soon blown with defeat confirmed, but it felt like relegation to me. I wanted Rachel by my side watching City, but this now looked over. Thanks, City, for playing so ineptly.

As we drove home to Skipton that night I brought up with Rachel the words she uttered and she said it was heat of the moment stuff which she hadn't exactly meant. I hoped she was right, but one thing I did know was that she needed a break from watching them for a little while, if I was to have any chance of winning her over in the end.

Rachel wasn't the only one leaving the City Ground that day disillusioned. A week earlier, as City beat Gillingham with that late Andy Cooke goal, Dave hadn't looked very happy at the end and was convinced Cooke's goal was papering over cracks. The entertainment level so far this season was poor and the City side were struggling to fire on all cylinders. It was a world away from the exciting games we used to watch when we first went to see City in Division One – and certainly a long way from the glamour of the Premiership. Dave watched the Forest game with us in near silence and looked particularly miserable. Life still wasn't going great for him, his job searching had been fruitless and he had to set his sights ever lower. He got a job working in the local off-licence; not a bad role but not what he had been aiming for when he got his IT degree at Bradford University just under 10 years ago. He was generally unhappy with life and, as watching City was little fun, was becoming fed up of going. City were at home to Tranmere in the cup the following week, he decided he wasn't going to come with us.

When me, Stephen and Alan had first gone to watch City as a group in the 1997/98 season, David was the experienced fan who had started going before us. Alan had quickly given up on City when the going got a little tough back in the Premiership, and it was left to the other three of us to still go. Now Dave was breaking away too. It wouldn't be his last game (though he's only been five times since), but his relationship with City would never be the same. He was fed up of the style of football and didn't particularly like Colin Todd. If City were suddenly promoted back to the Championship he would probably come back, but he never really adapted to life in League One and would continually be complaining when we had fixtures against small teams like Southend. With Rachel fed up to and far from won over, there was just me and Steve left. Were we the ones who were mad?

Barnsley (home) – facing legal action

Although I wasn't getting to as many games as I'd ideally like, I still closely followed City affairs and wrote often for the BoyfromBrazil website. Sometimes I felt as though I was writing a bit too often and that the editor, Michael, might be getting fed up. I wrote a piece defending Todd when the pressure was starting to build. Not that it was my fault, but Michael was receiving stick from some readers of the site because no one was writing articles slating the manager.

Michael always said he accepts articles from anyone, but no one was submitting pieces demanding he left. Michael seemed quite balanced about if Todd should stay or go, but the other main writers, including me, were behind him at this point. It might have looked a bit unbalanced and, in some ways, the criticism showed just how popular the site was among City fans – that they could be annoyed at it for not agreeing with them. I guess life would have been easier for Michael if I had decided Todd wasn't up to the job, though I was indirectly about to cause him even more problems.

When City drew 1-1 at Southend, we were over at my friend Simon's in Doncaster as he cooked us a Christmas meal. There was a decent size gathering and, not wanting to be anti-social, I was reduced to checking how City were doing by looking at my phone when I visited the bathroom. A 1-1 draw away at the leaders, despite us leading through a Steven Schumacher goal for a while, seemed decent. Later that evening with the drinks in full flow we had a look at the football results on his Sky system and I discovered Donovan Ricketts had been sent off in the first half and Dean Windass had gone in goal. It wasn't until the next day that I finally discovered why Ricketts had been dismissed – for giving an uncharacteristic gesture towards opposition fans in reaction to alleged racist abuse.

I was incensed. Not only to hear Ricketts had apparently been abused, but the media reaction to it. Where was the mention of this on The Championship and on Sky when I had been watching? Why had they ignored what sounded like a very serious issue and just highlighted the fun story of a non-keeper going in goal? I wrote and sent an article to be included on BfB asking such questions and was relieved to hear that Michael at least felt the same way. Meanwhile City appealed the red card decision ahead of the Barnsley FA Cup replay a few days later and, while nothing was certain, surely common sense would prevail and Ricketts would see his three match ban receded.

The appeal was heard the afternoon of the cup match and, at the end of my afternoon at work, I logged onto the City website to discover, incredibly, the appeal had failed. The FA ignored City's claims and ignored a serious issue. Whether or not Ricketts was right to react, or even received racist abuse in the first place, this was no way to handle it. On BfB Michael wrote an opinion piece strongly criticising the situation, called 'FA let the racists win'.

I was still angry as we arrived at Valley Parade for the game. There was a very low crowd, not helped as it was just before Christmas. At least the game was entertaining, which was a relief for me with Rachel attending her first game since Forest away. City took the lead through Andy Cooke but, soon after half time, went 2-1 behind. We then scored twice in five minutes, through Mark Bower and David Wetherall to surely win the tie. At this point I should probably have made us leave the ground and made sure Rachel never heard the final result, yet instead we stayed to suffer a feeble collapse. Barnsley equalised just before the end and, in extra time, City's defence and reserve keeper Russell Howarth gifted two more goals to seal our exit, 3-5. With extra time to suffer and going back on the train, it took a long time to get home and I still had a match report to write up.

The following day was my last at work before we went to America for Christmas. We took the overnight bus from Leeds to London to fly from Gatwick, so stopped at my parents just before, as they were giving us a lift to the bus station. I went onto check my emails and found one from an unknown person responding to my recent BfB article about Ricketts' sending off. It was sent by angry Southend fan, blasting me for apparently getting my facts wrong and saying that no Southend fans started any racist chants. He was witness to it all, he claimed, and Ricketts had made the whole thing up.

I forwarded the email to Michael and received a quick reply stating he has also received a nasty email from the same fan, who is now looking into taking legal action to get the website shut down. I couldn't believe it. Luckily the article that had really offended him was the one written by Michael and not me, but indirectly I might have played a part in the site I love getting shut down. I quickly sent a reply to the Southend fan defending why I had written what I did and pointing out we were both going to stick up for our own. Meanwhile Michael wrote a message on the site explaining the situation and the possibility that BfB might be shut down.

Through the long journey to Georgia I couldn't help but remain edgy and desperate to get to Rachel's parents home to check the internet, but it was a long trip down on the bus to London and then to fly to Atlanta and even when we get to the house I could hardly run downstairs and check the internet on their computer straightway. Eventually, it was time to go to bed and I was able to go online and check. I loaded up BfB in the web server and held my breath as I waited to see what comes up. It was a glorious sight – with the homepage carrying on with the latest news, as normal.

I checked my emails and there was one again from the Southend fan, who'd calmed down and took on board my views. The threat of legal action had been dropped, too. It was a scary episode that reminded me the power of the internet. I might be writing articles for City fans to read, but anyone around the world can go and view what is written and it's important the facts are right. Luckily I hadn't written anything libellous, but the reaction of one opposition fan suggested I wasn't far away. It was a reminder to tighten up and be careful, as I didn't want to be responsible for the brilliant site disappearing.

Not that I would be writing much for a bit. As the Christmas games were underway I was over in the other side of the world feeling more than a little left out. In some ways perhaps it's easier to be in America missing games than 20 miles down the road; at least now no one could be judging me for not going. But as results continued to go bad and City slumped down the league I felt helpless as Todd came in for more abuse from fans.

Just before the end of the year we flew back to England. The trip away was very enjoyable and it was great to be with Rachel's family over Christmas, but I began to feel even more down about City. It didn't help the season wasn't going to plan and a play off push was looking beyond us, but it had now been a year since I stopped being able to afford every home game and I'd not enjoyed adapting to it. Good and bad, I'd prefer to be there – ideally with Rachel by my side - experiencing it. Though the reality was that, to get City higher up our priorities of things to do, they needed to start winning games and playing better. The second half of the season was shaping up to be a big one for Todd. It was also an important one for me in persuading Rachel watching City was a worthy part of life, before they drift away.

Brentford, Swansea City and Bristol City (home) – new year, more visits

It's usually not the case, but I was in no doubt what I wanted for Christmas this year when my parents asked – money, to go and watch City games with. It might not sound much and wasn't easy to wrap for them, but with Rachel still struggling to find teaching work and my wages swallowed up by the important costs of living, going to football matches was still a luxury item. I was desperate for us to go to some games but this wasn't looking likely anytime soon, so to open an envelope with some money inside when we returned to England was a great moment. This isn't going on the electricity bill; but on City's next two home games.

The first of these was against Brentford, who were top of the league going into the game. I had mixed feelings of whether taking Rachel to a game we would most likely lose was a good idea, but my desperation to get to a game rather than wait took over. This was my first Valley Parade league match since the 1-0 win over Gillingham in October, an awful run that I felt more than a little ashamed of. So while it wasn't nice to see City 2-0 down inside 25 minutes part of me still felt happy because at least I was there to see and moan about the poor defending. A dismal 20 minutes followed before, just as the game moved into first half stoppage time, City pulled a goal back through a Marc Bridge-Wilkinson free kick. There was real hope for the second half and City started well hitting the woodwork, before poor defending at a corner saw Brentford go 3-1 up. Now it was game over, surely? City huffed and puffed but, with 10 minutes to go, it looked over.

Yet some decent substitutions saw fresh impetus with Steve Claridge making a difference and we began to attack with more intent. From a corner, David Wetherall headed one back and the last five minutes looked very interesting. With a minute to go City were piling on the pressure in the box and Claridge was tripped by the keeper which resulted in the referee blowing for a penalty. A spot kick in front of the Kop in the last minute, it doesn't get much more tense and exciting. We were all on our feet as Bridge-Wilkinson, assigned penalty duties as Windass had been subbed, calmly fired home. Get in! We celebrated wildly as the ball flew into the top corner to cap an excellent comeback. Thank goodness Rachel was here to see it; she was overjoyed by the drama. I thought back at the games she had seen previously and, while the Huddersfield win last year was great, this was probably the most exciting game she'd been to. With a superb ending, she said she'd enjoyed her day and I felt City were back on track again towards winning her heart.

Two weeks later we were back for the Swansea home game, who by this stage had now become leaders. They were a much better footballing side than Brentford; bossing the first half but with only one goal to show for it. Wingers Ben Muirhead and Bobby Petta were both shying away from responsibility. Petta in particular wasn't giving his all and criminally ducked out of a 50/50 challenge. Todd, receiving plenty of abuse, made two surprising changes. Taking off both wingers but replacing them with another central midfielder and a centre back as City went 3-5-2. It had a huge impact and suddenly we were the dominant side.

The midfielder who came on, youngster Tom Penford, was particularly superb and set up the equaliser, scored by Windass. There were 10 minutes on the clock and it was all City. Could we steal a glorious late winner? Sadly not, but in stoppage time the Swansea keeper Willy Guret made two astonishing saves to keep out Claridge efforts. It had been a great second half to watch and, while it didn't have the thrilling end the Brentford game had seen, I was happy that Rachel had finally seen two decent games with which to build her liking of City on. Much better than the rubbish she'd had to endure earlier in the season.

Todd's new formation worked so well it prompted renewed hopes of a play off push, although it was quickly abandoned when City started slowly at Yeovil the following week. At least City won the game 1-0 with a Windass free kick to climb to within seven points of the play offs. Unfortunately it was to be the last win in six games as the pressure continued to build on Todd – not helped by losing Windass for five games through suspension after an incident in the club car park where a referee had claimed - a claim denied by the player - that Windass had sworn at him. The only bright spot over this period was the introduction of young winger Joe Colbeck to the team; he came on as sub against Bristol City and made an immediate impact.

We were both there to see Colbeck's debut – Rachel had started to get more regular supply work, meaning finances weren't looking so tight. I wasn't to know it then, but I wouldn't miss another home match for the rest of the season – and only seven home games over the subsequent five seasons.

"What's it for?"

It was the Easter holidays for Rachel, who had recently started a maternity cover teaching position for the rest of the school year. She was being paid good money and it was a welcome relief given how difficult it had been to live off only my salary and her Sunday job wages. Suddenly we can start looking towards the future a bit more and make some plans. This included attending all of City's remaining home games.

I have the day off today as well and we're visiting the Valley Parade ticket office. Nothing to unusual about that, as we were buying tickets for City's final two home games against Port Vale and Nottingham Forest, but then we were also buying two extra tickets that came at a much higher cost – season tickets. The day of the Oldham thrashing City had released details of next season's ticket prices and I began to wonder if we could afford to buy a pair and if Rachel would go for it. After all, going match by match we're paying £20 each and the season ticket price of £276 per person is a lot cheaper than the £460 we'd each have to pay out to pay to go to each game. I was tired of having to miss matches and, with some good money coming in over the next three months; couldn't we spare the equivalent of just over one week of her wage to ensure we don't have to pay for any tickets next season?

I'd been fortunate that the last two City games we'd seen had seen them win well in front of Rachel. Firstly was a thrilling 4-2 win over Scunthorpe where we had been 2-1 down at half time and the pressure was firmly building on Todd. This had been the first game back for Dean Windass since his five match suspension – and his birthday as well. He had already scored our opening goal and, soon in the second, got the equaliser. Barely a minute later Marc Bridge-Wilkinson tapped home to put us in front and the celebrations in the stands were brilliant. Windass completed his hat trick with some great control and a lovely low finish to complete the scoring in the most entertaining game Rachel had been to so far.

Two weeks later we saw City defeat Doncaster 2-1, with both City goals coming from the unusual source of Lewis Emmanuel. It was another decent game and Rachel was suddenly enjoying coming along.

It was a good time to be watching City. In March we were thrashed 4-1 at home to Oldham which seemed to spell the end for Todd, only to win thrillingly over Blackpool three days later when two youngsters – Joe Colbeck and Joe Brown – combined in stoppage time to score a winner. Rachel had plans that night, so I'd watched the uplifting moment on my own. Including that win, City would only lose one of their nine remaining games and climb to mid table respectability. More enjoyably, a number of youngsters began to become regular fixtures in the team, including Colbeck and Brown, young defensive midfielder Craig Bentham and full back Jon Swift. Another intriguing factor was news of a potential investor in talks with City about taking partial control of the club and injecting some much-needed funds.

Rachel agreed to get season tickets, though I think she also felt we could and should be using our money better than this. So on this day off we went along to buy them. We arrived to discover that the club didn't accept card payments on season tickets, so had to anxiously run into town to visit our bank, who would only allow customers to withdraw so much a day from ATMs. We spoke to the woman on the desk and explained we needed to withdraw over £500 urgently. She was sympathetic and got us a form to fill. "What's it for?" she politely asked, making conversation. "Erm, season tickets for Bradford City", I sheepishly replied. "Is that it? I thought you'd be spending it on something exciting like a holiday or new car!", so too, probably, did my wife at seeing this large pile of cash.

As we handed the money over back at the ticket office, I felt slightly guilty and that we could be putting this money to better use and may live to regret it. But then City was still such an important part of my life and missing so many games during the last 18 months had been difficult to cope with. I didn't want to carry on such an existence of only going when we had money to enable us to. During a period where we are gathering and still will be receiving plenty of wages, now was the time to do it. I felt very proud to be returning to become a season ticket holder, after not having once since the 1999-2000 season before I left for University. I hoped Rachel would grow to be really pleased if she continued to enjoy going. Roll on next season.

Stephen was also buying one with us and part of the reason we could do so was how well he and Rachel got on. I never doubted for a second Rachel would be comfortable with how Stephen is, but seeing the reaction of so many other people towards him over the years had shown me the less pleasant side of human kindness. Rachel was always good and patient with him and Stephen really took to her. It might seem like an odd arrangement for the three of us to go together, but it was working well. From August we'd be sitting together in the same seats, towards the back of the Midland Road stand, to enjoy what a new season had to offer.

The penultimate home game saw a comfortable 1-0 for City over Port Vale. With both teams in mid-table it was a meaningless match, though one in which we played well and should have won by more. The final match was a 1-1 draw with Nottingham Forest, where Martin and his friend Andy sat in the away end hoping for a win that would have put them in the play offs. During the week before it had also been revealed that the mystery investor was City commercial manager Peter Etherington, who came on board earlier in the season. His son, Matthew Etherington, was playing for West Ham but had enjoyed loan spell with us a few years ago. Suddenly Todd could look forward to signing players of a better calibre. It was an exciting feeling looking ahead to what the summer and next season might have in store.

All of which we'll be watching. At last me, Rachel and Stephen had season tickets again and could look forward to watching every City home game. No more sitting at home listening to the radio when City are only playing 20 miles up the road, no more feeling bad because we couldn't afford to go along and no more frustration at paying £36 a time. Whatever was ahead, good or bad, we will have regular seats to witness it.

Chapter Twelve

2006 - 07
Journey to rock bottom

It wasn't that we were hugely optimistic about our chances of promotion this season – certainly I had learned my lesson from a year ago – but the worse case scenario appeared to be another campaign of mid-table mediocrity.

We hoped to be dark horses for promotion, sneaking into the top six and seeing what might happen. If failing that, we'd like to at least come close and believe progress is being made. Yet a very strong start to the season sparked greater optimism and, at the start of October, City were in 4th position having not lost for five matches. We were playing some of the best football seen in years, with an attack-minded line up taking the game to the opposition and achieving some impressive results. Sadly it was a false dawn, and then some.

At the end of September City defeated Tranmere 2-0 at Valley Parade, meaning they had still only lost once at home – that Oldham thrashing in March – since the turn of the year. Yet over the next 12 months only one visiting team would be defeated by City, and we fell to 3rd bottom – relegation.

There are many reasons that combined to lead to this, not least the ongoing financial difficulties. But still this was a stunning level of ineptitude, with a series of decisions taken proving disastrous. City were heading to the bottom division for the first time in quarter of a century, still not quite sure how they had managed it.

So many people think lower league clubs are rubbish, and this season at least they were right. Whatever we think of the Premier League elitism and how unfair life has become for the have nots, it has to be acknowledged that every member of the Premier League is there because they have been run reasonably well on and off the pitch. Three clubs go down each year and this is often down to incompetence, but it's hard for even supporters of these clubs to appreciate just how bad you have to be to go from promotion challengers after a quarter of the season to relegated in April.

Finances dictated City had to let go some of their best players mid-season, while the level of frustration at Todd eventually led to a managerial change. But while many supporters had argued City's failure was all down to the manager, Todd's removal prompted a shocking nosedive that ended with a summer preparing for League Two football.

By supporting any football team you sign up to endure failure, it's just the lower down you go the more often it seems to happen.

Sitting on a time bomb

The 2006-07 should have included better times. Towards the end of the previous season, City had improved considerably and much-needed investment from Peter Etherington should have allowed manager Colin Todd to bring in some decent signings.

So we waited for new players to come in...and we waited some more. Another Jamaican, winger Jermaine Johnson, was brought in, along with released Manchester United striker Eddie Johnson. Matt Clarke, a centre back from Darlington. But then news of signings became non-existent. Meanwhile friendlies were taking place and City were worryingly losing often. A 2-1 defeat to League Two Shrewsbury seemed bad, but then consecutive 4-1 thrashings at League Two outfits Boston and Darlington really set alarm bells racing. The squad in place was looking low on numbers and weak in depth. Why were there no more new signings? We were told the investment deal with Peter Etherington was still being finalised so Todd had to wait for the green light to bring players in, this didn't stop the City boss once again coming in for huge criticism from some fans.

Through my time supporting City I'd often heard rumours of what was happening behind the scenes, but always second hand from somewhere else. I'd occasionally fantasised about knowing a player or club official so that I could hear the goings on of Valley Parade before everyone else. How nice it would be to know secrets no one else gets to hear. In July I was to suddenly receive privileged access to such goings on, but instead of excited it left me nervous, worried and scared.

It all came through my friend Tom, who was good mates with a then-member of the commercial department at City. He'd told me a couple of times about what his friend had said about life at City, but there was never anything particularly juicy about them. Then one morning at work Tom emailed me to tell me some news I didn't dare believe: Etherington had left the club and the investment deal had collapsed. He also provided me with reasons why this had fallen through and swore me to the need for secrecy, for fear his friend would get in trouble. Tom knew that I wrote for BfB and particularly asked me not to write something for it, because the club check the site.

I refused to believe him and challenged him back, but I soon realised that he had to be telling the truth. My friend was a Leeds fan with a limited interest of what goes on at Valley Parade, it wasn't the sort of story he could make up and there was no reason for his friend to lie. I kept checking the official City website for any announcements but there was no word. City were performing dismally in pre-season and new signings were needed, now I knew why there was such an odd delay. I emailed Michael, the editor of the BfB website, asking him not to publish it just yet. His reply confirmed the whole thing was true; he'd heard the same story from one of his sources and was debating what to do.

It was a strange feeling to know some distressing news would soon be made pubic and it left me fearing the worst for City yet again. It was widely known that the club had made a loss of over £1 million during the last season. This investment was supposed to cover those losses and allow the club to push forward with ambition; now the season tickets we had bought could prove to be useless, as the club's future must be in doubt again.

After two days of feeling nervous the news finally broke publicly. I listened to Radio Leeds for the latest and read an interview with Julian Rhodes in the paper explaining what it all meant. For the majority of City fans they were now debating things I had been considering a couple of days ahead of them. Where does this leave us? Are we going bust? Can we afford any players? Are we going to get relegated again? Just when we thought we could look forward to a brighter future, things were going wrong again. Fortunately Rhodes was upbeat and revealed the club would carry on, with an increased wage budget for players as well – in the subsequent days new faces finally arrived. Etherington leaving came as a blow, but Rhodes was still talking to another couple of investors and, for now, City would carry on as they were.

Bristol City (home) – meeting the moaners

So there we were, Tuesday night and the first home game, against Bristol City. For Rachel, Steve and me it was an opportunity to sit in our new, permanent seats. We'd picked them out on a chart when it came to ordering them and had a quick look at them before the end of the last campaign, but now we were sitting in them properly for the first time. They were five rows from the back of the Midland Road stand, level with the half way line and just underneath the TV gantry. It was a perfect view and, as I sat back and looked forward with relish to the nine months ahead watching City's season from it, I couldn't help but wonder why such excellent seats were not taken by long-standing season ticket holders.

It took until two minutes into the game to find out. A few minutes before it started four fans took their seats directly behind us and began talking loudly about nothing in particular. Bristol City immediately took the lead, not a great start to the home campaign and already beyond the patience of our new 'friends' behind us. "Fuck off Todd you stupid cunt!" the one behind me abruptly yelled. As City battled to get back into the game we were treated to a soundtrack of moans, complaints and grumbles about City going nowhere and why it's disgraceful Todd hasn't been sacked yet. Considering it's only the second game of the season and we finished the last one in such excellent form, I was shocked. Todd had been under pressure in March, but the good end to the season had won many around. Now one of the pre-season favourites for promotion had made a bright start against us, already it was time to turn on the team.

They would continue for the whole season. As we made our way home after the match – in which City came from behind to win 2-1 thanks to two goals in 20 seconds from Dean Windass and new signing David Graham – the talk was more about the four moaners sat behind us, who had spent the whole match loudly talking rubbish and failing to appreciate anything good City did. Todd was the consistent target of their anger and having to listen to them loudly swear non-stop about him was unpleasant. It felt like we had some of the best seats in the house, but now we knew why no one else wanted them.

Each week, for the next nine months, we endured their pearls of wisdom. We soon learned they were 25 year season ticket holders and would be sitting in these same seats for the next 17 years. They joked about how much they have to suffer and what fools they were for buying the tickets, but seemed to quite enjoy pointing out City's failings. They were at their quietest when City were winning and there was less to complain about, or when City would go 2-0 behind with some 30 minutes to play, as happened on a few occasions during the campaign, which would prompt them to simply walk out. How I wished City could have staged a grand recovery in any of those games, leaving them feeling sick when they found out during their subsequent moaning session in the pub. Sadly it was never to be.

The following Saturday their moaning was even louder as City made a dreadful start against Gillingham, going two goals behind inside 15 minutes. They were animated in their anger and screamed in the direction of Todd. It was almost comical to see Gillingham attack and hear them scream "for fucks sake do something Todd!" What could the City manager do at this point? Run onto the pitch and help his under pressure defence clear the ball?

City were poor but, just before half time, Mark Bower pulled a goal back to give us hope. In the second half summer signing Eddie Johnson was brought on for the disappointing Graham and made an immediate impact in helping City get on top. We soon a penalty when another new signing, Lee Holmes was tripped. Windass scored the spot kick and, with 10 minutes to go, scored again with a brilliant half volley on the edge of the area. A remarkable turnaround was completed when, in stoppage time, the impressive Jermaine Johnson sprinted the full length of the pitch on the counter attack and finished well. What a turnaround! What a game! Where were the moaning idiots behind us now? They had left before the fourth goal – presumably so they didn't have to applaud the team off and give the manager the credit he deserved.

Two home matches gone, two brilliant games and two brilliant results; City then went to Crewe and impressively won 3-0, before drawing 1-1 at home to Rotherham in a slightly disappointing performance. Two defeats on the road followed, at Brentford (2-1) and Swansea (1-0), but still it was a better-than-expected start to the season. Todd's critics were either being won round or staying quieter.

Except the four moaners behind us, of course.

Next was Carlisle at Valley Parade on a Tuesday night. City took the lead through Windass but the impressive visitors snatched a slightly fortuitous equaliser in the second. As the game went from end to end, the mutterings of anger at Todd, which we were now frustratingly becoming used to directly behind us, continued. Yet clearly we weren't the only ones within their earshot and an argument suddenly erupted with another fan behind them. This bloke had snapped and began berating one of the four who was particularly vocal in his hatred of Todd, pointing out how well the team was doing and how Todd isn't getting the funds needed to take City forward. Remarkably the three other moaners took this guy's side and joined in with shouting down their friend and agreeing he should appreciate the job Todd was doing. For a few weeks after we almost enjoyed total peace and quiet.

The good form continued, on the following Saturday Port Vale were defeated 2-0 at Valley Parade, then a 3-3 draw at Doncaster and another home 2-0 win, against Tranmere. We were 4th in the league and, while I dared not agree when friends mentioned it, looked serious promotion contenders. The team Todd had put together in a hurry was looking good. The two new wingers, Holmes and Jermaine Johnson, were putting in some outstanding performances. Johnson in particular was superb to watch and his pace and trickery scared the life out of the opposition. In the centre Steve Schumacher had discovered his best form and was outstanding alongside Marc Bridge-Wilkinson. The defence continued to impress with summer signing Nathan Doyle slotting in particularly well at right back. Up front neither Graham nor Eddie Johnson were convincing, but Windass was in typical hot form and the team was playing well as a unit. Against Tranmere Jermaine Johnson started off on fire but had to go off injured 20 minutes in. Young Joe Colbeck – who impressed towards the end of last season – came on and managed to fill some pretty big shoes with a decent performance.

As Bower and Schumacher struck the second half goals to win the game I couldn't help but dream about what the rest of the season had in store for us. We weren't far off the automatic promotion spots and, while star man Jermaine Johnson would be out for a few weeks now, there was every reason to be optimistic about our chances of mounting a credible play off push. Todd had started the season still under pressure, but was winning people round. As someone who had kept faith with him during those difficult days last March, I felt particularly proud. It was a good time to have a season ticket and we had enjoyed the first two months of the season.

Scunthorpe United (home) x 2 – break from writing

On Monday 23 October I logged onto BfB to discover the news I'd been half expecting for a while, Michael, the editor, was taking a break and the site was stopping for the foreseeable future. I felt a mixture of emotions, mainly sadness, but couldn't pretend to be shocked.

Since starting to write for the site three years earlier, BfB had become a big part of my life. Initially it was a way to write opinion pieces to sharpen my writing skills and hopefully impress potential employers, as I searched hard for a job; but I played an increasing role by also writing match reports of nearly every game I'd been to since the 2-1 reverse to West Ham in February 2004. The site was clearly popular among City fans, but the fact that the main writers of it, including myself, had all supported Todd when other fans were loudly calling for his head was seen in some people's eyes as the site losing credibility.

247

Michael had always encouraged articles from any City fan with any viewpoint but – rather than bother to write anything themselves – those fans disillusioned with Todd were angry that they couldn't read similar viewpoints. Some fans were apparently claiming, by angry emails, that Michael was ignoring these views. I still had never met Michael so didn't know him well enough to know, but the criticism appeared to hurt. And while it could be seen as a back-handed compliment that fans followed BfB enough to be upset their viewpoint wasn't represented, for Michael it was seen as too much and not what he even intended BfB to be about.

Over the summer and during the start of the season, it was becoming increasingly obvious Michael's enthusiasm was waning. Clearly the amount of effort he put into regularly updating the site must have placed a big impact on his spare time, and the updates to the site became increasingly sporadic. Whereas before every piece of City news would be written up, there was now only be updates twice a week at best. As I would send him articles and match reports to publish, he would often fail to reply to my email with the usual exchange of views on recent games and news, instead just posting my stuff live.

During the final week the site was updated three times, once to add a match report of a 0-0 draw at Northampton which had followed a season-changing loss to Huddersfield Town, the other two to add my match reports of the double meeting – league and Johnstone's Paint Trophy – with Scunthorpe at Valley Parade. My report of the 1-0 league defeat, to Billy Sharp's late goal, was added the Sunday evening and by Monday evening a post from Michael explaining the site was taking a break had been added. A quick look around the various City internet forums showed there was genuine sadness at the loss.

A view I shared. It wasn't always easy and took a lot of time, but I'd really enjoyed the chance to write regularly about City. Like the majority of fans I had strong views, so being able to express them in this was rewarding. From time to time I would receive some good feedback from others who had enjoyed what I'd written and I was aware that the name Jason McKeown was known among some fans. At match days I was as anonymous as the rest and pleased to be, but I was able to write up my opinions – some controversial – and know others were taking the time to read them. It was a great site to be associated with – clearly the best among other City fans sites around. It would be the first place to go for City news, even ahead of the club's official site.

To have it taken away felt sad and I was keen to still be able to write up my views on City, so I decided to get in touch with the City Gent fanzine and see if I could write for them instead. The editor, Mike Harrison, welcomed me writing in and I set about drafting my first of what would become a regular column, which I would eventually call Midland Road Mutterings. In some ways this was a good way to be writing instead.

The following week saw a shocking 4-1 reverse at Blackpool which prompted fans to once again angrily call for Todd's head. We had begun the month in 4th and quietly confident of a promotion challenge, suddenly we were sinking fast. It was all the more depressing for me in that the financial pinch was firmly being felt. We were struggling for money and bills were still flying in, including a particularly depressing large electricity bill, and our car was about to go in for its MOT which looked set to prove expensive. We would soon find out it needed so much repairing there was no point in going any further, and we needed to buy a new car. I wasn't sure how we'd cope. The good news, though, was Rachel had a supply teaching job lined up from February to July which we could look forward to.

Next up were Brighton at home and suddenly the team were under pressure from fans. The moaners behind us were now firmly back in vocal force, slamming everything Todd did – even the way he leaned on the dug out. Within 10 minutes Brighton were in front and they added a second just after half time. Another depressing defeat looked ominous and I could only hope, rather than believe, we could come back to 2-2. Remarkably we did, first with Dean Windass netting from the spot and then, with 10 minutes to go, through an excellent strike from Steven Schumacher. I had been desperate for an equaliser and celebrating wildly when it came. At the very least a face saving point and who knows, with ten minutes to go lets go and win it.

As the board went up to say how much injury time there was, City broke forward through Jermaine Johnson and I was praying for a third goal to send us all into ecstasy. Johnson then weakly lost the ball and seconds later a Brighton player was crossing the ball into our box and their striker fired home the winner. In the split second the goal went in I told myself I'm okay and that I'm not too upset at what I've just seen, but the reality is the pain was only just setting in and was now building up. Is there time for an equaliser? Yes, but it won't happen. One disjointed attack went wrong and the referee blew his whistle, to cue booing everywhere.

The week that followed remained painful and the criticism of Todd continued. We'd been up there challenging, we'd looked a good team. This is a blip, surely? The next game looked a bit more like it as we thrashed Crewe 4-0 at home in the FA Cup, it was probably the best performance of the season as City had some 30 attempts on goal against a very poor visiting side. As I walked out of the ground feeling much happier, I had no idea this would be the last time I would see City win this season.

Bournemouth (home) – selfishness

Despite the awful run of form, having a season ticket again felt good and I was glad we were able to witness first hand what was going wrong, even if it was starting to make unpleasant viewing. Bradford City were really important to me and the fact I'd stopped going clubbing or attending gigs with my friends in order to afford it again was a statement of priority. Yet I worried my devotion was too much and impacted negatively on others. This felt especially the case as I watched City struggle at home to Bournemouth, while half a mile away two of my best friends played pool in a pub.

It had seemed like a straightforward plan. The last Thursday of November is Thanksgiving, and with Rachel keen to cook food and entertain friends, we'd held a get-together on the same Saturday City were at home to Bournemouth. I was keen not to miss a game, so I arranged with Rachel that friends wouldn't arrive until 6pm so I could still go to the game while she cooked (I would be no use in the kitchen and she was glad to get me out the way!). Simon and Rachel were coming over from Doncaster though, and didn't want to arrive so late. With Rachel's season ticket not being used I took the chance to invite Simon along so I could entertain him at the game. As a Man United fan who doesn't see much live football, he was happy to come along.

Then Martin, who I hadn't expected to want to attend Thanksgiving, decided he was coming to visit. Living in Nottingham, arriving for 6pm was also not an option but I had no season ticket for him. But then an announcement that ticket prices were to be reduced for this game made me feel as though it was meant to be. Martin could come along and sit with us, only paying a fiver to do so. The plan had come together.

We went over to Bradford in time to sample a few pubs and only set off to the ground 20 minutes before kick off. With Stephen also with us, I led everyone to the Midland Road stand where I expected Martin to be able to pay on the gate. I was stunned to be told by a steward that you had to go in the Kop to take advantage of the cheap offer and we would have to go and queue at the ticket office to get everyone sat together. I angrily blasted the steward at the lack of proper communication from City and he was sympathetic; there was nothing he could do though, so we dashed round to the Kop. The queues were enormous and it was obvious we'd not just miss kick off, but a good chunk of the first half. Seeing the hopelessness of the situation, Martin and Simon volunteered not to go to the game and find a pub instead, they encouraged me and Stephen to carry on as normal and they'd meet us after the game.

I felt guilty, upset at City and confused. I couldn't leave them in a City they don't know when I'm supposed to be entertaining them, could I?

By kick off me and Stephen were sat in our usual seats, with Martin and Simon wandering back into town following my directions. This wasn't right; I was not able to enjoy the game, feeling guilty at how daft my devotion to City is in that I couldn't give it up as a bad job, join them in the pub and spend time with friends I was increasingly seeing less of. I was barely following the action in front of me, but was conscious City had started well. Then, 10 minutes into the must-win game, Dean Windass produced a horrific two footed lunge on a Bournemouth defender and the referee sent him off. For a few minutes my mind focused back to the football. Why the hell did he just do that? The Bournemouth player stayed down hurt and I feared he may have had his leg broken, thankfully it wasn't so bad. Yet the actions of our top scorer had now left City with ten men and eighty minutes still to play.

Back to the guilt. I called Martin to check they'd both found a pub okay. They were in the Bradford Arms on Manningham Lane and were doing fine, watching scores on TV and playing pool. I'd made up my mind that we were going to leave at half time and find them, I couldn't be such a selfish person and, after Windass' stupidity, why bother staying for the inevitable defeat? Martin was a good friend and told me not to bother; convincing me they were both fine and happy to stay in the pub where they were having a good time. "We'll meet you after the game, stay and enjoy it." So I did. Stay that is. It wasn't a game to enjoy.

What would other people do in such a situation? It may have been an important game, but so will the next one. I hated to miss matches, but in just over an hour this game will be over so why worry about it? I might miss something fantastic, something so good people will be talking about it for years to come, but I wouldn't bet on it. Why did I feel I had to be here when I had friends who had come to visit me? Why have I even lasted this long at the game?

But stay I did, to watch the struggling visitors dominate the game with Donovan Ricketts thankfully in superb form. To Todd's credit, he had tried to stay positive by moving Jermaine Johnson up front to partner David Graham, rather than just hold out for a point. It was difficult though and as the game crept towards the end some players, such as Johnson, looked shattered. Todd had to take him off, which prompted a chant of "you don't know what you're doing!" from fans. Another Bournemouth attack came and went, suddenly "Todd out!" began reverberating from the Kop, soon it seemed the whole ground was joining in. I refused to do so, as did Stephen, but the moaners behind me were wild with excitement, "This is what I've been saying for months, finally everyone agrees with me." The Todd out chants continued after each break in play and the final whistle saw more boos ring out.

There was, at least, no Todd out chants at the next game, even if the scoreline (0-0) was the same. It was a Friday night FA Cup match against Millwall and although we hit the woodwork three times it was a poor display. Windass was now suspended for three games and on the end of a major backlash from supporters that would see a minority issue death threats; even Chairman Julian Rhodes publicly spoke of his anger.

How badly City needed a win in the League, which thankfully happened in the next game at Leyton Orient (2-1). Eddie Johnson and Marc Bridge-Wilkinson got the goals on a Tuesday evening, which I listened to on the radio. It wasn't quite the turning point as two consecutive defeats to Millwall followed – 2-0 in the League and 1-0 in the cup replay. Windass was back for the cup replay but couldn't find the net, but at least did in the next game as City defeated Chesterfield 1-0 at home. I missed the match, my only home game of the season, as we were over at Simon and Rachel's for Christmas dinner. Had I known this victory would be City's last at Valley Parade until August 2007, I might not have been such a happy guest at being forced to miss the game.

Still it was payback, in some ways, for being selfish when they had visited the weekend of the Bournemouth game.

Doncaster and Cheltenham (home) – Christmas of little cheer

It was a sign of growing older perhaps, but Christmas felt particularly ordinary this year. We were staying in England this time and spent Christmas Day at my parents, which was nice but the fact we had to drive home that night meant I couldn't have a drink. Two days later I was back at work, covering over the slow period between Christmas and New Year where only skeleton staff is required. It wasn't great being there as the atmosphere was quiet and workloads weren't particularly hectic, dragging out the day.

Still it could have been worse; I could have been Colin Todd over Christmas. On Boxing Day City suffered a 1-0 defeat at home to in-form promotion hopefuls Doncaster Rovers, and Todd returned to his car to discover some supporters had attempted to trash it. Four days later and, after drawing 2-2 at home to relegation candidates Cheltenham, in difficult circumstances, he faced some tough questions from the local radio after the game while suffering the indignity of City supporters still in the ground chanting 'Todd out' loudly – picked up by the microphone and broadcast all around West Yorkshire.

It was certainly a difficult time and the two Christmas games were not enjoyable ones to attend. Rachel's friend Meghan had decided to come over to the UK and visit us and we'd gone to the airport Boxing Day morning to pick her up. Rachel didn't come to the Doncaster game so she could entertain Meghan; and the spare season ticket when to Stephen's brother's friend, who was staying with the family over Christmas. He was a quiet, unassuming lad, partly interested in football but a fan of Manchester United. He didn't say much as Doncaster went into an early lead which they never looked like losing, or at the resultant negative atmosphere in the home end. As it all went on I couldn't help but think what our 'guest' made of it all.

Around 20 years old, living in Saltaire and interested enough to come along; this should be an afternoon where he might be enthused by the experience and want to come again, like I was after my first time. Yet the football was awful and the atmosphere wretched. At the final whistle I felt the need to apologise repeatedly to him, "We're not usually this bad, honest."

For the Cheltenham game Rachel was back watching, as my brother Kevin entertained Meghan for the afternoon. We took an early lead but the performance was still very poor, which led to the crazy situation of some fans booing off the team at half time, even though we were winning. Things went horribly wrong in the second half as David Wetherall tripped their player in the box, a penalty made worse by a red card for the City skipper. Cheltenham scored from the spot and five minutes later took the lead, now the atmosphere was bad. At least Jermaine Johnson was able to grab us an equaliser, but a draw against a side near the bottom was not going to lighten the dark mood, regardless of their numerical advantage. Listening to Todd try to get his points across to that 'Todd out' backdrop was depressing.

The atmosphere at the club had become uglier and there was no doubt the majority of fans wanted Todd sacked, but I still couldn't find myself joining in. Yes results and performances were poor, but the reality of the lack of resources and thin and bare squad was obvious. Could anyone come in and do a better job in the circumstances? I had my doubts. Yet it now felt as though the pressure on Todd was so much it was impossible for him to win them back over. There were still many fans, like myself, supporting Todd, and in its own way this made the situation worse because there was a divide among supporters. The only way things could get better would be if results improved, and as performances still largely seemed better than results I retained some hope this could happen. On New Years Day City lost 1-0 at Carlisle and Julian Rhodes spoke publicly that Todd's position was not safe. The response was a 1-0 win at Port Vale, with Steven Schumacher getting the goal. I was really pleased for Todd and hoped it could be the catalyst to get City back on track.

The following week promotion challengers Swansea visited Valley Parade, which at least meant the expectation levels were lower than they had been. We started well and Windass gave us the lead, but two mistakes by Ricketts allowed Swansea to go 2-1 up. We battled back but our efforts looked in vain, until in the final minute a melee in the box left Windass lying on the floor and the referee stopping Swansea on the counter attack. His decision was to award City a penalty and send off the Swansea player who had elbowed him. It was stoppage time and probably the last kick of the game, so the pressure was intense. Windass duly buried the spot kick.

Everyone seemed to celebrate wildly and for a few seconds at least it felt as if we'd all forgotten the troubles and conflicts and just remembered what a glorious, unpredictable game football can be. We could all go home satisfied at what we'd seen and at least be grateful we weren't spared another week of feeling miserable at work.

Crewe (home) – the wheels come off

It was a crazy few weeks, from the moment Dean Windass struck that stoppage time penalty against Swansea on 13th January until City entertained Crewe on February 18th, with

David Wetherall receiving an emotional round of applause while he take his seat in the dugout – as caretaker manager. Big changes were occurring to the club and not all of them positive; it was still a difficult time, but could we put some of those troubles behind us and unite in support of Wetherall? We needed to get some positivity going. Suddenly the relegation trap door was creaking open under our feet.

The barmy period began inauspiciously enough, with news of a new signing. Todd's success with the Jamaicans of Donovan Ricketts, defender Damion Stewart (on loan the previous year) and Jermaine Johnson led to the signing of a fourth; Omar Daley from American side Charleston Battery. Todd billed him as quicker than Johnson, and his arrival appeared to be in preparation for Jermaine leaving. Rumours were rife that a clutch of clubs were eying up Johnson, with Derby County publicly having a £250k bid rejected. The Telegraph & Argus told of a huge gathering of scouts at each City game in January, all spying the in-form winger who was now playing up front for us. It was rumoured most were Championship clubs and, with the January transfer window in full flow, we were suddenly counting down the days until it closed hoping no one would make City an offer that couldn't be refused.

But there was a high profile exit – Windass went out on loan. It came as a huge surprise, though it was fair to say his popularity had dipped among City fans after his stupid sending off against Bournemouth. At the Swansea game I'd spent time convincing my friend Tom – who had come along – that he should be in the team, as other City fans had told him he was a liability who should be dropped. And when he opened the scoring with a decent finish I was able to prove my point. "We don't have anyone else at the club who can put away chances like that," I stated. How sadly right I would prove to be.

Days after this draw he was off to Hull City on loan. The explanation from the club was that it was getting a loan fee for allowing Deano to join his home town club for the rest of the season and that, with City looking unlikely to go up or down, we'd be okay without him. The other hope was that the fee would strengthen our efforts to keep hold of Johnson, with the club in a better position to turn down bids.

But that didn't prove the case. The run up to transfer deadline day was a nervous time and I couldn't help but check the internet constantly for any news of a transfer. Everything appeared to be quiet and I went to work on Thursday, the final day, feeling glad that there were only a few hours to hold out before the window shuts. A quick check on the Bradford City website when I got to my desk included the dreaded news though; City had accepted a bid from Sheffield Wednesday, it was now up to Jermaine if he went.

I felt bitterly disappointed at seeing one of the season's bright lights exit. He'd been around for such a short time that I didn't feel I'd ever fully appreciated him. His pace and trickery could be phenomenal but he did frustrate me, and clearly several team mates, with his selfishness in front of goal. Still when he picked up the ball you couldn't help but feel excited and more often than not he did something that made you applaud. Now Sheffield Wednesday would benefit from his talents and City had worryingly lost their two best players.

Make that three. At the end of a busy day at work I logged on to the City site to find out the latest and see who Todd has been able to bring in on loan as replacements for Deano and Johnson. There was another heartbreaking story as it was revealed we'd lost the services of on-loan full back Nathan Doyle, who looked a superb talent, after his parent club Derby decided to sell him to Hull. A few days later it would emerge Windass had recommended Doyle to the Hull manager Phil Brown – thanks a lot Deano. At least there was some news of new signings on the site; left back Kelly Youga had been signed on loan from Charlton, before Todd was to find out he'd lost his right back, and strikers Billy Paynter and Bruce Dyer were also loaned from Southend and Doncaster respectively. In the space of a couple of weeks Todd had lost his three best players and had to scratch around for replacements on loan. Even his biggest critics must have felt for him but if they did they did not let that stop their ire.

Thank goodness there was the normality of a game to enjoy on Saturday, with play-off challengers Notts Forest in town. My friend Martin and his friend Andy again came to visit for the weekend and watched the game close to where we usually sit in the Midland Road stand, as we were all moved to the

257

other stands to make way for the larger than usual away following. With such a dramatic turnover of players it was difficult to predict how we'd cope against a side challenging for promotion, but inside ten minutes we were in front through Dyer. No sooner had we began to feel optimistic of a credible win we fell 2-1 behind, as Forest stepped it up a gear. For the rest of the half they bossed the game and looked the best side we'd faced all season.

But they couldn't sustain that in the second and we began to get back in the game. After Martin had decided to call me at half time to take the mick at the scoreline, I was even more desperate for us to get something from the game. Chances came and were wasted and it looked like Forest might steal another goal. But then, as the game moved into injury time, the impressive Paynter got on the end of a knock down and tapped the ball into the net to equalise. Cue bedlam from the City fans around me, I could barely contain myself. We needed this, we deserved this, and boy I was going to celebrate wildly and take the mick out of Martin when I saw him. I also felt pleased for Todd who'd had a worse week than anyone.

Yet after the next game he was gone. We lost 1-0 at Gillingham, not helped by having Youga sent off early on. It was another disappointing defeat and we were now 16th, only four points above the drop zone. But still it came as a real surprise to find out on Monday that Todd had been sacked. Julian Rhodes argued that form was not good enough and a change was needed, but it felt like a gamble with City beginning to slip from mid-table mediocrity to lying just above the bottom four.

As caretaker manager Wetherall walked down to the dug out for that first time – to a unified standing ovation from everyone chanting his name – it felt good to be a City fan again. We'd stopped talking about the future really; the club was struggling on and bobbing along doing little in League One. A change was called for by the majority and a change was made. We could now all get excited at what the future held and believe better times might be around the corner.

There was to be no quick fix sadly, City lost 1-0 to a last minute goal.

Huddersfield (away) – nose diving

I was angry, hurt and ashamed - worse still I felt stupid. Why had I gone to all of this effort, not just in getting to be here today, but spending time worrying, feeling bursts of optimism and seemingly non-stop during the week before? The least I could have expected was some acknowledgment and reciprocation of the trouble I'd gone to, something to show they cared and perhaps could even be inspired. But nothing back, why on earth do I bother?

It's a sunny March afternoon and we're walking back towards Huddersfield train station, thankfully not being followed like we had been some eight years earlier on our last visit. I felt worried, pessimistic and upset, more than anything though I felt livid; we'd just been to watch Bradford City surrender tamely at the hands of our local rivals in one of the worst performances I've ever seen. That the final score was only 2-0 to Town reflected their ordinariness, rather than any form of resistance from those in Claret and Amber. During the 90 minutes we'd had one, pathetic attempt on goal from Steven Schumacher that was so bad it almost cleared the ground. Town had struck their first inside two minutes and added the clinching second midway through the second half. With the exception of David Wetherall, Ben Parker and Billy Paynter – the latter of whom was the only player to properly acknowledge the huge travelling support at the final whistle – the team had been a disgrace.

I can appreciate derby rivalries mean less to players than us supporters, yet we were fighting a desperate relegation battle and badly needed to win. After the Crewe defeat in Wetherall's first game in charge, we'd played Brentford at home – below us in the bottom four – and only drawn 1-1 despite dominating the match and creating numerous chances. Schumacher had grabbed our equaliser with three minutes to go, from the spot, and the overall performance had at least raised hopes we could avoid the drop. Then we were thrashed 4-1 at Rotherham to drop into the bottom four, and suddenly the next game, Huddersfield, was massive.

I'd decided we should attend the Huddersfield game a few weeks earlier. Rachel had finally started her maternity cover teaching position and good money was coming in, so we could afford the tickets to Huddersfield's stadium, now renamed The Galpharm. We made our way their on the train and were rounded up, with other supporters by the police, and put into special buses to the ground. It felt quite exciting and added to the togetherness of us City fans. We were going into enemy territory and 3,500 of us would be filling a full stand and loudly backing our players.

Yet the players didn't turn up, going 1-0 behind so early quietened us supporters, and we never looked like coming back. The game was dull, with nothing happening at either end. Yet still we needed to raise our efforts and had to come out fighting in the second half, surely? It was painful to watch as, attacking towards us, moves broke down and any corners and free kicks were wasted. Town got a simple second and that was it. On the way back to the train station I texted a few friends to say we were going down. On this evidence we had no chance.

But then three days later came an incredible result – we beat second place Bristol City and 3-2 on their own turf. I listened on the radio, hoping we could somehow grab a draw. We predictably went 1-0 down early on, but Paynter equalised just before half time with a brilliant long range volley. In the second half new signing Moses Ashikodi and Joe Colbeck both scored and, although Bristol City pulled a goal back in injury time, we held on. Earlier that morning Chairman Julian Rhodes had announced Wetherall would stay caretaker manager for the rest of the season, rather than looking to make a permanent appointment.

After the Rotherham game I'd calculated City needed to win four, draw two and lose five to avoid the drop. Now one win was achieved and a second looked set to quickly follow as we went 1-0 up to fellow strugglers Northampton at Valley Parade the following Saturday. Paynter – fast becoming a hero for his unquestionable commitment to the cause – scored the goal. But just as we might have been able to believe that this horrible nightmare of an unwelcome relegation battle might be quickly over, Northampton equalised following a defensive mistake and snatched a winner deep into injury time. Yet another painful week of feeling miserable was to follow. In fact I had to be careful as my manager Louise at work had begun picking up on me feeling so depressed in the wake of a

City defeat and – having no interest in football – was struggling to understand. I had to put on a brave face, but the anguish was growing.

And it carried on. Play-off bound Blackpool were up next, at home, and in flying form near the top of the division. They scored early on and another defeat looked inevitable. Yet in the second half we began to pick up and Omar Daley struck a screamer from distance to make it 1-1. What a moment! I celebrated wildly with Rachel and Stephen, could this turn our season round? Blackpool looked on the ropes and we continued to attack with menace, creating some great chances and flying down the wings in particular. But then former City player Claus Jorgenson went in for a 50-50 challenge with Schumacher and the referee blew up for a foul. Both players had gone in hard, but it looked like the free kick should go our way. I yelled in frustration as the referee signalled it was Blackpool's free kick, and then held my head in my hands in disbelief as a red card was issued to Schumacher.

Did that really happen? We're at a critical point of the season and looking like we can snatch a vital win, now the referee had sent out player off for nothing. The despair grew when, two minutes later, Blackpool scored. We injected some heavy pressure for the remainder of the game in an effort to force an equaliser, but Blackpool were able to break away and score a third. The next time this referee was in charge of a game involving Schumacher, he apologised for getting the decision so badly wrong. If only he'd realised at the time.

Suddenly that achievable-looking prediction of needing to win four, draw two and lose five to do enough to stay up was looking beyond us. We'd not won a home game for over three months and finding the net was a real problem.

On the same afternoon of our next game, a 2-0 loss at Scunthorpe, Dean Windass was notching a hat trick for Hull City. It was easy to pinpoint why things had gone so wrong.

Leyton Orient (home) – heading to the wire

It's an old cliché, but so very true – it's the hope that kills you. Through the last few weeks of City seemingly not needing to do a lot in order to survive, it had been easy to look at the final few fixtures and mentally total up enough points for City to preserve their League One status. Home games against relegation rivals – three points for the taking surely, Derby games at clubs having a tough time of things – the chance to steal a march. Tough away trips to promotion contenders – if we can just hold out for a draw...Sadly the hopes were being extinguished that little bit more with seemingly every match that went by. It was now Easter weekend and, after the unsurprising 2-0 defeat to leaders Scunthorpe, it was do or die time. Fortunately, or perhaps unfortunately, new hope began to spring.

First up was a trip to Bournemouth, also battling against the drop. A few weeks ago this fixture had looked very winnable, but the South coast club had found some form, particularly at home, and were seemingly sprinting clear of danger. As it was bank holiday weekend me and Rachel went to Scarborough for the day and, while the weather was nice, and we had an enjoyable time, I couldn't help but nervously keep checking the time as 3pm approached. By the time the game kicked off some 313 miles south of us, we were down at the beach. Rachel was carrying out a favoured hobby of collecting pebbles on the beach, while I kept checking my phone every five minutes for score updates. Nothing much happened, other than other results affecting relegation rivals kept looking good and then bad. Then there was the moment I dreaded as I loaded up my phone again for the scored, Bournemouth 1 Bradford City 0, with the goal coming after 61 minutes. Having started the day desperate for a win, I would now gratefully take a point.

What was checking the phone every five minutes became every four, then every three and then every two. Rachel had collected enough rocks so we made our way back to the car to set off home ahead of the traffic. I instantly put the radio on for football scores, hoping for some miracle there would be last minute equaliser. No sooner had we got on the main road out of town when the commentator revealed there had been a late goal at Dean Court: recent loan signing Spencer Weir-Daley had scored on his debut, three minutes into injury time, to equalise for us! I wanted to beep the horn loudly in celebration; at least we'd salvaged something.

The dream of an Easter four-point haul was still on, despite the fact that Monday's visitors to Valley Parade, Oldham, were in the play off spots. A nerve jangling game ensued with the stakes really high. Oldham didn't really look like a team challenging for the promotion, however, and City took the game to the Lancashire side wasting some great chances. On 65 minutes came the moment to saviour as Moses Ashikodi ran onto a through ball before flicking it over the defender and lashing it into the top corner. What a moment! It felt as though Valley Parade erupted as everyone wildly celebrated such a stunning and important goal. There was just 20+ minutes to hold out for a win that could lift us out of the bottom four.

Unfortunately a moment of madness by Joe Colbeck eight minutes later was to cost us. With the ball knocked towards him inaccurately, it went out of play for a throw in and to, waste some time, he booted the ball hard down the pitch. Not the cleverest ploy, particularly when you've already been booked. The referee had no option but to issue you a second yellow card and send the young winger off. Anger rising inside of me, I rose to my feet to shout at him. There was what now looked to be a painfully long 15 minutes to hold on.

The inevitable equaliser came with three minutes to go and, frustratingly, looked easily preventable with City's defence falling asleep. Fortunately Oldham didn't snatch a winner in the remaining minutes, but draws weren't going to be good enough and there were now just four games left for City to save themselves

Remarkably the pendulum swung City's way the following Saturday as they recorded a desperately-needed victory at mid-table Brighton. With results also going our way it meant City were two points behind their nearest rival, Leyton Orient, outside the relegation zone. The next opponents to Valley Parade were Orient and it was now in our own hands to pull off the great escape. The fact we then had Chesterfield away after that, who were in the relegation zone just like us and looking more doomed, offered even further hope of League One football again next season. We had already bought tickets to Chesterfield, sensing it might be an occasion to savour. We would now be seeing all of City's remaining season and if they would stay up or go down, which felt exciting.

The Leyton Orient home game was huge, but proved an even bigger anti-climax. We dominated first half, but were guilty of missing a hatful of easy chances with Omar Daley and Weir-Daley the main culprits. The atmosphere was really good as we all got behind the team clapping and chanting, but the nerves were evident. In the second half Kelly Youga, who'd performed well in recent weeks, had to go off the field for treatment and suddenly Orient scored. It was poor defending and Donovan Ricketts should also have saved the shot. The worst fears were being realised, it was almost impossible for City to stay up if it stayed like this.

What quickly followed was civil war in the stands, as those fans that'd either stayed silent or were just fickle suddenly began loudly slagging off the players. Next to me Rachel was in tears as the realisation of what the goal meant became apparent - my personal sorrow was replaced by guilt at having inflicted such pain on her, by converting her into a City fan. A big argument began between one supporter who'd been chanting passionately screamed that the moaners should get behind their team. They countered that the team were rubbish and didn't deserve support. I was watching this bust-up unfold behind me while Orient broke forward and grabbed a second through a defensive mistake from Richard Edghill, making it two goals in two minutes. The moaners took sickening pride at the goal going in shouting "ha see I told you we're shit!" The fan who'd stood up to them and for his team had tears streaming down his face. He simply got up and left.

The team had no more fight in them and, although there were 25 minutes to play, the game was up. We were now five points behind Orient with two games to go.

So we travelled to Chesterfield with nothing but that dangerous hope. We could beat Chesterfield and our last home game, against Millwall, and it might not be enough, though some of our rivals had some hard games to play. Could this be a miracle win or miserable defeat that would mathematically relegate us? A draw wouldn't be enough and for Chesterfield even a win probably wasn't going to be enough to save them. A huge City following descended on Saltergate and we were in good voice, but after a bright start Schumacher, whose form had shockingly dipped in the final few weeks, managed to make a complete botch-up of an easy looking pass and

Chesterfield broke forward. A weak low shot was fired at City's goal, which Ricketts somehow let squirm in under his body and over the line. He was another player whose form had vanished at such a crucial time.

Just over ten minutes later it was 2-0 as Chesterfield peppered our goal with shots and the defence couldn't scramble the ball away. We were desperate for a big second half and had to hope Wetherall could find the inspirational words to lift the players beyond such feeble efforts. We did manage to put some pressure on in the early stages of the second 45, but one attacking move broke down and Chesterfield charged forward. The ball was crossed low into the area and Mark Bower slid the ball into his own net. It somehow seemed a fitting way for relegation to be confirmed, given that it was entirely preventable and we had no one to blame other than ourselves. With results elsewhere not going City or Chesterfield's way, it was clear both teams were going to be relegated at the final whistle. Some of our players cried at the end, which was nice in a way. The tunnel was right below where we were sat and we all gave Schumacher some frightful abuse as he walked off in tears.

I looked around at the players on the pitch towards the end of the game and pondered how things had gone so wrong. At the end of September we'd defeated Tranmere 2-0 to go 4th, and were looking upwards at a possible place in the Championship. Even though form dipped and pressure grew, the anger was about failing to mount a promotion bid and only being in mid-table. If only we were in mid-table now. We'd only won five games in the league since that win over Tranmere, which told its own story. Next season City were going to be kicking off in the bottom division for the first time in 25 years. I looked at my own time supporting City and reflected I'd soon have seen them play in all four divisions. It had been some decade.

As the game had moved into stoppage time a chant of "City till I die" began and everyone seemed to join in. It felt hugely uplifting; I'd sung it so often in the past with feeling and passion, but now those words represented a future of better times and the relief that we could soon put this sorry season to bed. No matter who's on the pitch (and thank god most of these players won't be wearing Claret and Amber much longer), who's in charge in the dug out and who's running the club next season and the seasons after that, us supporters will be there through good times and the many bad. For how much pain we felt in the sunshine of Saltergate, we'd be back in August dreaming of better times.

Once again we'd have hope, and we all know what that does.

The future

Barely a month after the dismal afternoon in Chesterfield, me and Rachel were among some 200+ supporters attending a fans forum at Valley Parade. It's partly to welcome a new manager, but more than just that. For that of a relegated club, the atmosphere and buzz has not felt this exciting since promotion to the Premiership.

So what's happened to turn around the gloom? The season had ended with a meaningless 2-2 draw at home to Millwall, but the focus of everyone was on other matters. News had broken during the week that potential new investment might be coming into the club, possibly even to buy the Rhodes family out. Within a couple of weeks we would learn that Mark Lawn, a person who I knew a little about as my friend Tom had worked under him in his locally-based Driver Hire company, was the investor.

The managerial situation was also weighing heavily and the final weekend of the Premier League season carried surprising significance. It was no secret Stuart McCall, assistant manager of Sheffield United, was the first choice to take over; but the City legend – who had left the club in 2002 – had kept quiet and ducked any questions over his future. Earlier in the season Stuart had made public his ambition to become a 'number 1' next season and, with Blades Neil Warnock threatening to leave over a contract dispute, it seemed possible Stuart could have an offer from Sheffield United in addition to City.

In order for the possible Blades vacancy to be a Premier League one, Sheffield United had to at least earn a draw on the final day of the season at home to fellow strugglers Wigan. I watched the game on TV over at Stephen's, my allegiance firmly with Wigan because of their manager Paul Jewell. I also believed Stuart's chances of getting the Blades job would be lower if they went down. As it turned out Sheffield United lost and were relegated, a few days later Warnock was sacked.

Stuart remained tight-lipped over his future, but then the Blades chairman announced he wouldn't be considered for the vacant job. Surely he was coming home now? Watching the developments was torture, I spent many a time debating with City-supporting colleagues at work over whether each new development was good or bad and checked the internet constantly for news. I was as much a regular reader of the Sheffield Star website as I was the Bradford Telegraph and Argus. Finally the news we'd all dreamed but scarcely believe might happen was announced – Stuart was to be our new manager.

After another six months where, if it could go wrong, it went so wrong for City, it was exhilarating to hear such great news. Stuart was a hero to practically every City fan and now he was coming back to start his managerial career at the place he'd began his playing career. Suddenly next season was something to look forward to.

A fans forum was put on to give us supporters the chance to hear from Lawn and Stuart. Me and Rachel went along and it gave her the opportunity to see and hear Stuart for the first time. He had left well before we met and his name was just another legend I'd sometimes drone on about, like Beagrie, Lawrence and Moore. Stuart's jokey persona and warm personality meant Rachel was quickly won over. It was fantastic to be present at the packed executive suite listening to the questions, everyone feeling excited and talking of the future with a smile. The event was broadcast live on BBC Radio Leeds and, as we disappeared into the night, it felt like the beginnings of a special time.

A special time for me and Rachel too. March-July was beginning to mean only one thing as we struggled to get going in life – job searching time for Rachel ahead of the next school year. Like the previous two years I would go to the library on my lunch break once a week to look up and print off possible vacancies for Rachel to apply for, which she would do on in the evenings or weekends after carrying our long-term supply work during the week. She was at a really good school this year and enjoying the people she was working with, but sadly the new-mum she was maternity covering for was definitely coming back.

Again the applications were sent out and polite rejections returned. There was a boost though when finally she was asked to attend a job interview, which sadly she would just miss out on getting.

Then another school, this time in Bradford, invited her in for an interview. It was the day before the FA Cup Final when we heard and the interview was Monday afternoon, so she had to get time off at short notice. The interview seemed to go well and, and, a few days later, I got the text message at work I'd been desperate to receive for three years. It was from Rachel, she had got the job!

It was a huge weight lifted off out shoulders. The last few years had been hard as Rachel tried desperately to get a job, and it often looked as though it was going to impossible as she was constantly overlooked. I rang her mobile straight away to congratulate her; it was an emotional conversation. Finally it seemed as though we had made it, and with Rachel set to earn much more than I did, our money struggles could finally be put to one side. Suddenly the future looked bright and we were spared another summer worrying when the next pay packet was coming and if she'd ever get to where she wanted to be.

One of the most exciting things for me – other than the money and security Rachel's job offered – was she got a laptop to use. I would be able to use it for my writing and we could even get the internet at home again, I was now spreading my writing as the BfB website was revived just before the end of the season. Michael, the editor, had changed things around and, instead of being a site for news updates, it was to be a blog format with freedom for me to write and upload my own articles myself. I was still enjoying writing my regular column for the City Gent, so agreed with both editors I could write for both. If felt like the best of both worlds as, with the City Gent column, I could write a more rounded considered view on things and, with BfB, I could cover more current affairs.

Suddenly life was looking fantastic and we could sit back and enjoy the ride. The 2007-08 season would hopefully feature hopes of promotion and the return of my hero to manager us. More importantly for us, it would definitely feature Rachel working full time and a more solid future. Who cared about relegation now?

Chapter Thirteen

2011
Lower leagues, the best place in the world to be

So that's my story. Compared to the amount of change which had taken place between 1997 (16 years old) to 2007 (26), life suddenly became relatively quiet and normal for the next few years.

Both Rachel and me work full time, each very happy with our job. Rachel's reception teaching position in Bradford has worked out superbly. She enjoys the challenges of educating the children, has formed many strong friendships with other members of staff that stretches to socialising in their spare time. For the 2010/11 school year she was asked to take over a Year One class, presenting new opportunities to increase her skill range.

I too was enjoying my internal communications role, continually learning and considerably improving my writing skills. Working in a building society when the credit crunch struck wasn't the easiest place to be, but it presented me with some fantastic writing opportunities. As the various worldwide financial events occurred, I was responsible for writing up what they meant and communicating it to front line branch staff across the country. In 2008 I was made a senior consultant and in 2010, as I had got to the point where I felt I'd achieved all I could, I moved jobs to become a Copywriter for one of the building society's subsidiary companies, which specialises in offering financial advice. It's proving to be a fantastic step up and is providing me with some brilliant new opportunities to widen my writing skills.

Elsewhere I continued to write my City Gent column – and with BfB back up and running have contributed a huge amount of articles and match reports to the site over the past four years. I write for a living, and spend a great deal of my spare time writing about my football team. Bliss.

In October 2007, with Rachel now receiving a regular wage, we moved to another house in Skipton. We've enjoyed many great nights out, undertaken plenty of trips to the USA to visit her family, argued about money on occasions.

Life is normal for us – and that includes going to watch City. A lot. Getting season tickets each year is never in question now, and I have been able to return to attending away games on a regular basis. Not since the promotion season of 1998-99 and first year in the Premier League have I attended away fixtures so often. Rachel wasn't sure about going to them at first, but soon learned to enjoy how different the experience was. Stephen was very keen to go to more away games, and always comes along.

Including all the cup matches, over the four League Two seasons between 2007-2011 City played 202 times – I saw 147 of them. That may not be the greatest record compared to fans that go home and away without fail, but after the three-year break for Uni and the difficulty affording to go when we first got married, I feel as though I've caught up on what I missed.

We all grow up, and the supporter I am today has learned along the way from the experiences since first discovering Valley Parade in 1997. City play a huge part in my life, but they don't define it. When we lose I'm devastated and miserable for the rest of the weekend, but I've also learned to put such feelings to one side when it's time for work on Monday rather than force others to endure it. There is more perspective; it may not be 'only a game', but going to watch football is supposed to be enjoyable. Although these last four years haven't seen success for City – we're still stuck in League Two – I've been determined to still make the most of it.

And the joys of the lower leagues have helped. While City have nestled about in the bottom division since 2007, the

Premier League became ever bigger and crude. In 2008 the 'Game 39' proposal was first raised – where the Premier League would be extended by one extra round of games which would be played in different locations around the world – simply to make money. Then there have been the on-going foreign takeovers where some of the country's biggest clubs have happily sold off some of their traditions to people who almost always are buying for the motivation of achieving a strong, profitable return on their investment. Fans still happily delude themselves that these guys are going to throw a load of money from their own pocket so the manager can make new signings, when very often it's shown they are merely lending money they expect to receive back – plus a handsome profit. Man City is perhaps the exception, with billionaire owners almost playing fantasy football in the way they have spent so much money. Despite the Bantams still having their own financial issues, I can't say I'm jealous.

Ticket prices have continued to rise; players' wages have become astronomical and well out of synch with a country struggling through a recession. The Premier League has become increasing uncompetitive with a big four eventually extended to big six by Man City and Spurs, but who are still a world away from the rest – which merely make up the numbers. Chelsea were Champions in 2010 after thrashing teams for seven on three separate occasions. They sealed the title by narrowly beating Wigan 8-0.

Over these four years I concluded to myself once and for all that I wouldn't like to see City ever return to the elite in its current state. Why would we want to spend year after year merely hoping we can achieve 17th place, having no chance of ever challenging for Europe let alone the title? Why would we want to spend £60 going to watch our players get thrashed by a Chelsea reserve side? The reality of City in the Premier League was fantastic at the time, but we've all moved on.

I honestly love City playing in the Football League. Sure I don't want us to stay in League Two, and I'd prefer we don't spend too long in League One either. The Championship, the level we were at when I first started watching City, is where I'd like us to return to. In the meantime, League Two has been tremendous fun and I have enjoyed the experiences of travelling to the likes of Rochdale, Barnet, Wycombe, Accrington and Darlington to support my team.

Back in June 2010, a curious news item caught my attention. Manchester United had announced that they had failed to sell their full allocation of season tickets for the 2010-11 season to their members, and so 4,000 were now on open sale for anyone to buy. 14 years on from that October afternoon where my parents had enquired at the Old Trafford ticket office about whether they could buy tickets for one game – only to be told of huge waiting lists and high demand which meant I barely stood a chance of ever going – I could now have had my choice of seats if I wanted.

The reason for the lack of uptake in Manchester United season tickets was due to their dubious owners, the American Glazer family. In 2005 they borrowed a vast sum of money to buy the club, and quickly shifted the debt onto United. They then ramped up the cost of season tickets to keep up with those debt repayments. Fans have been split on the Glazers, with a significant number abandoning United and setting up their own club, FC United of Manchester, so they could recapture what they'd lost through years of an increasing corporate-focus at Old Trafford.

Those United fans who stuck with the club initially seemed to tolerate the Glazers; but during the 2009-10 season, further protests against their ownership gathered momentum. For now they continue to use the club to service debts it had no reason to take on – while allegedly taking some £20million out of United's vast profits for themselves in "management and administration fees". Fans are fed up, and increasingly priced out of attending; so there is suddenly room for those people – like me – who were previously advised to go to the back of a very long queue.

But had fate not conspired to see me go to Valley Parade that November afternoon in 1997, to fall head over heels in love with my local team, what kind of a football fan would I be now? I imagine I'd have also become used to accepting watching my football team on Sky, always going to the pub for United games and eventually been able to afford to have a dish installed at home. I might have gone to some matches too, after all if I had have been prepared to play the waiting game in 1996 and become a member, in time match tickets would have been available for me to buy. Perhaps I'd go to a few games a season, glad of the experience. Perhaps in the summer of 2010 I'd have believed I could finally become a season ticket holder, although the steep prices (prices range from £513 to £931 for the unsold 2010/11 season tickets) would have made that almost impossible to attain.

Or perhaps I'd have just drifted away from football altogether. I didn't *just* switch allegiance to City in 1997 because of how wonderful Valley Parade appeared to me, but partly because I was already feeling deeply unfulfilled about life as a United fan. Had I continued following the Red Devils, the glass ceiling which meant I couldn't go and watch them would largely have stayed in place. And it's possible my interest would have cooled off and I'd have found another hobby to really get my teeth into. Sure I'd still support them and watch games on TV, but it would never have been as big a part of my life as City have become.

The big question is would I be happier? After all, my time following City has featured little but doom and gloom, not to mention bucket loads of stress. From the joy of promotion and staying up in the Premiership at the beginning, it's been all downhill since with three relegations, two spells in administration and numerous seasons of mid-table obscurity. And let's just compare that to what United have achieved over the same period – seven Premier League titles, two European Cups, two FA Cups, two League Cups, four Community Shields, one FIFA Club World Cup and one Intercontinental Cup. Oh and no trips to Morecambe in League Two, lucky beggars.

Yet I am happy, and I have largely been happy all the time I've been venturing down to Valley Parade to watch my team. Not once have I looked at United's subsequent success through green eyes of envy or with regret. Winning is not everything, and I've found something much more deep and meaningful.

That's not just Bradford City, but the lower leagues of English football. Where the heart and soul of the game is so prevalent, where the joy and passion comes before money, where the values are something everyone can agree on and believe in. Lower league football supporting is not without success, but it's not the reason why we are here.

And there is nothing more grand or important about supporters of a Premier League team compared to followers of a lower league club. Sure there's a lot more of you, and you have a great history to recall and all, but the joy and pain of cheering your team on is not any less meaningful lower down the ladder. The main difference is, we matter more to our clubs and so are less likely to be screwed over by them.

So you can keep your £931 Manchester United season ticket thanks very much. I couldn't be happier with my £150 Bradford City one.